An Old Merchant's House

An Old Merchant's House

Life at Home in New York City 1835-1865

Mary L. Knapp

Girandole Books, New York
The Merchant's House Museum, New York

Published by Girandole Books and the Merchant's House Museum
590 West End Avenue, New York, New York 10024

Designed by Steven M. Alper

Printed in the United States of America

Cataloging-in-Publication Data

Knapp, Mary, 1931–.
   An old merchant's house : life at home in New York City 1835-1865 / Mary L. Knapp.
   p. cm.
   Includes bibliographical references and index.
                    ISBN 978-0-578-04856-7
              1. New York (N.Y.)—History—1835–1865.
           2. New York (N.Y.)—Social life and customs—19th century.
        3. Merchants—New York (State)—New York—19th century.
             4. Historic buildings—New York (State)—New York.
           5. Row houses—New York (State)—New York.   I. Title.
F128.44 K38 2012
974.7/103—dc23   2012933391

Grateful acknowledgment is made to FURTHERMORE: a program of of the
J.M. Kaplan Fund for their generous support of this project.

For Herb

The poetry of history lies in the quasi-miraculous fact that once on this familiar spot of ground walked other men and women as actual as we are today, thinking their own thoughts, swayed by their own passions, but now all gone, one generation vanishing after another, gone as utterly as we ourselves shall shortly be gone like ghosts at cock-crow.

G.M. Trevelyan

Table of Contents

Preamble

On East Fourth Street in New York City, there is a hidden treasure. Built in 1832 and known today as the Merchant's House Museum, this antebellum home is remarkably still furnished with the belongings of the Seabury Tredwell family, who moved there in 1835 when Andrew Jackson was president and most of the island of Manhattan was still countryside and forest. Once there were hundreds of such city houses belonging to New York's most prominent citizens: politicians, bankers, attorneys, auctioneers, insurers, shipbuilders, and merchants engaged in maritime commerce. Today only one of those houses remains intact to tell us the story of how privileged New Yorkers lived in the extraordinary era before the Civil War when New York City had become the preeminent port and the "commercial emporium" of the nation.

The Tredwell family lived in the house for almost one hundred years, until 1933, when the last surviving family member, Gertrude Tredwell, died just a few days short of her ninety-third birthday. Shortly after her death, George Chapman, her cousin once removed, decided to preserve the Tredwell home as a museum. In doing so, he intended to pay tribute to the "old merchants," those whom Joseph Scoville memorialized in his multivolume work, The Old Merchants of New York City.[1] Like Scoville, Chapman regretted the passing of the old mercantile aristocracy with its emphasis on high morals, good blood, and genteel manners. In honor of these men of dignity and enterprise, he named the museum "The Old Merchant's House."[2]

---

1   Joseph Scoville [Walter Barrett], *The Old Merchants of New York City*, 5 vols. (New York: J.W. Lovell, 1889).

2   In 1996 the Board of Directors of the Museum changed the name of the Old Merchant's House to the Merchant's House Museum. Those in charge felt that the new name would more clearly reflect the nature of the institution.

The merchants whom Chapman so admired were exemplified by Seabury Tredwell, who owned a large New York City hardware firm. His stock in trade was anything made of metal, which he imported from England: frying pans, brass kettles, spittoons and cutlery; hoes, shovels, guns, and anvils; window latches, nails, and door hinges, as well as heavy building material like the ton of cast steel he received from Liverpool in the spring of 1823.

Because Chapman was more interested in honoring an entire class than he was the Tredwell family, he did not take care to preserve Tredwell letters or diaries. Only five letters and a few miscellaneous documents written in a Tredwell hand remain. However, many diaries, memoirs, and letters of the Tredwells' neighbors are available, and they all have something important to tell those who would understand the personal history of the city's privileged class in the three decades before the Civil War. One of the most interesting diaries is that of John Skidmore, a relative of Seabury Tredwell, who lived just four doors to the east. In 1858, when he was twenty-eight years old, he kept a pocket diary in which he recorded his daily activities. That diary, and other preserved documents belonging to the Tredwells' contemporaries, are resources on which this story greatly depends. But perhaps the evidence that speaks loudest is the house itself. Standing in those rooms, surrounded by the Tredwells' possessions, feeling the space they inhabited, we come as close as we ever will to understanding what life was like then. The walls really do talk.

1. DIARY OF JOHN SKIDMORE, APRIL 4–9, 1858.

Collection of The New York Historical Society, negative number 84297.

John Skidmore, a relative and neighbor of Seabury Tredwell, kept a diary of his daily activities in 1858 when he was twenty-eight years old. The diary, shown actual size, was written with a steel-nibbed dip pen.

Prologue

Seabury Tredwell was a member of the first generation to come of age after the American Revolution. Born in 1780, he was eight years old when George Washington took the oath of office at New York City's Federal Hall. His father, Benjamin Tredwell, was a physician farmer in what is now East Williston, Long Island. His great-great-great grandfather on his father's side had come to America around 1635 from the village of Swacliffe in Oxfordshire, England. His

2. SILHOUETTES OF ELIZABETH SEABURY TREDWELL (1743-1818) AND BENJAMIN TREDWELL (1735-1830), PARENTS OF SEABURY TREDWELL.
Courtesy of the Merchant's House Museum.

Before the invention of photography, the silhouette, cut out of paper, was a common method of capturing a likeness.

mother, Elizabeth Seabury Tredwell, traced her ancestry back to John Alden and Priscilla Mullins, the Mayflower passengers whom Longfellow immortalized in the poem, "The Courtship of Miles Standish." ("Speak for yourself, John.") Both Elizabeth and Benjamin came from devout Anglican families; Elizabeth's father was a Congregational minister who converted to the Church of England and became an Episcopalian priest in 1730. Her half brother, Samuel Seabury, would become the first bishop of the Protestant Episcopal Church in America.

3. SEABURY TREDWELL'S LONG ISLAND BOYHOOD HOME.
Courtesy of the Merchant's House Museum.
Seabury's father, Dr. Benjamin Tredwell, moved his family from North Hempstead to what is now East Williston, New York in 1784 when Seabury was four years old. The house was still in the possession of the Tredwell family when it was sold and torn down in 1951 to make way for commercial development.

Growing up on the Long Island farm, Seabury learned to shoot a rifle, to count his money in shillings and pounds, and to care for and ride the fast horses that were the passion of the Tredwell men. Like many other New Yorkers, Seabury's parents remained loyal to the Crown during the Revolution. But there were patriots among the large Tredwell clan—Seabury's older brother Samuel for one. George Washington appointed Samuel Collector of the Port of Edenton, North Carolina, in 1793. So while many loyalists found it necessary to flee to Canada after the war, Benjamin, thanks to the influence of his son Samuel and others, was able to stay put on his Long Island farm, continue his medical practice, and make the best of what was, for him, a disappointing outcome of the American Revolution.

VIEW OF THE BAY AND HARBOUR OF NEW-YORK, FROM THE BATTERY.

Drawn and Engraved for the New York Mirror, 1830.

4. *VIEW OF THE HARBOUR OF NEW YORK FROM THE BATTERY, 1830.*
Engraved from a drawing by C. Burton. Collection of The New-York Historical Society, negative number 83549d.
During the years of Seabury Tredwell's career as a hardware merchant, New York was a city of merchants and mariners. It was the "golden age of sail," when sailing packets transported cargo and passengers across the Atlantic. On a fine day, the Battery at the tip of Manhattan Island attracted fashionable New York promenaders.

In 1798 Seabury, at the age of eighteen, set out for New York City where two of his brothers were already established—Adam, as a fur merchant, and John, as a dealer in china and glass. Fifteen years had passed since the end of the Revolution and the seven-year British occupation of the city. The rotted piers had been rebuilt, as had many of the buildings that had been destroyed by two devastating fires. The population, which had diminished to only 10,000 during the War, now numbered 60,000. New York had surpassed Philadelphia in both exports and imports, and the docks were a hive of activity. Travellers from abroad invariably commented on "the forest of masts" that screened the city from the bay. It was a metaphor so apt it seems to have occurred to all of them.

It was a good time for a young man to be starting out.

The city proper extended north on Broadway only to the present day Worth Street where the New York Hospital was located. Its grounds sloped gently down to the south, joining those of Columbia College. Beyond Worth, rutted roads wound through the countryside past an occasional farm or country home. The graceful contours of spires and steeples and rounded cupolas defined the skyline, but no building was tall enough to interrupt one's view of the overarching sky. And everywhere there was a sense of the sea.

Wealthy citizens lived in large brick or stone houses on lower Broadway near the Battery and on State and Wall Streets. Less prosperous folks lived in narrow two-or three-story Federal style houses with brick facades, pitched roofs, and dormer windows, or in modest frame dwellings. Some buildings were designed as a combination residence and shop or countinghouse with a separate entrance and staircase for the merchant's family, who lived upstairs. The poor lived crowded together in ramshackle cottages; the destitute, in the new almshouse on Chambers Street. Here and there were some old seventeenth-century Dutch buildings with their quaint stepped gables. Gardens and vacant lots were scattered among the buildings.

By the end of the eighteenth century, the city had five newspapers, three banks, five markets, one theater, one hotel, thirty-four churches serving fifteen religious denominations, and numerous taverns that provided accommodations for travelers and venues for assemblies, suppers, and balls. There were literary clubs, a subscription library with 5,000 volumes, and several musical societies. Soon there would be a philharmonic society offering two concerts a year.

But New York City at the turn of the century was dirty, dangerous, and brutal. Free-running hogs rooted in garbage-filled gutters. Dead animals were often left to rot in the street before they were picked up. Human waste was carted to the rivers by night and dumped there where the tide swept most, but not all of it, out to sea. After dark, the feeble yellow light of an oil streetlamp flickered here and there. The streets were patrolled by night watchmen, but they were not very numerous, and thieves who lurked in the dark were a constant danger.

Bulls and bears were baited by dogs in an arena that held over 1,500 people. The gallows and the whipping post in the Commons or "Fields" (the area that would become City Hall Park) testified to the harshness of sanctioned punishment for crime, and poor children roamed the streets begging for food and money. Slavery in New York State would not come to an end until 1827.[1]

Water pumps were located every few blocks in the middle of the street, but the groundwater had been contaminated for years. Those who could afford it had water delivered by carters who drew it from the Tea Water Pump near the Collect, a freshwater pond located northeast of the Fields. However, by the time Seabury arrived in the city, the Collect itself was becoming polluted by the noxious products of tanneries and other industries on its shores. In 1815, it would be filled in, but it would be decades before New Yorkers enjoyed a clean public water supply.

Given these unsanitary conditions, it is not surprising that the city was regularly visited by epidemic diseases. When yellow fever swept into town in August of 1798, many New Yorkers fled to Greenwich Village, then far removed from the city. We don't know which month Seabury arrived in the city, but if he was already there in August, we can be fairly certain that he went back to the safety of the Long Island farm with his brothers. When the yellow fever epidemic subsided in November, 2,000 people had died. Many were buried in the newly opened Potters' Field in what is now Washington Square Park.

Seabury spent his first few years in the city working as a clerk, probably in the countinghouse of a relative or family friend. He is first listed as a merchant in his own right in the City Directory of 1804-05. His hardware business was at 260 Pearl Street, between Fulton and John Streets. Over the course of his career it would be located at four different Pearl Street addresses in buildings that he leased.[2]

---

1   An act providing for gradual abolition was passed in 1799 declaring children born after July 4 of that year free, but these children were required to serve their mother's master as indentured servants until the age of twenty-five for women, twenty-eight for men. The act did not affect slaves born before July 4, 1799; in other words, no slave was freed immediately by the slave act of 1799. In 1817, the legislature passed a law providing that both male and female slaves not affected by the 1799 act would become free on July 4, 1827 but would be required to serve as indentured servants until the age of twenty-one. This meant that some African Americans would not be free until 1848.

2   From 1803-08, Seabury's business was located at 260 Pearl; from 1809-16, at 233 Pearl; from 1817-25, at 245 Pearl; and from 1826-35, at 228 Pearl.

5. 245 Pearl, New York City, 1825.

Museum of the City of New York, Print Archives.

In 1825, when this engraving was made, the hardware firm of Tredwell and Kissam had just vacated the building at 245 Pearl, which was then taken over by David Felt, stationer. The building next door housed George and John Tredwell's china business. Goods were hoisted to the upper stories of these buildings; the ground floor was devoted to the clerical activities of the counting house..

John Bernard, an English actor who traveled widely in the United States from 1797 to 1811, described the typical merchant's day:

> They breakfasted at eight or half past, and by nine were in their counting-houses, laying out the business of the day; at ten they were on their wharves with aprons around their waists, rolling hogsheads of rum and molasses; at twelve at market, flying about as dirty and as diligent as porters; at two, back again to the rolling, heaving, hallooing, and scribbling. At four they went home to dress for dinner; at seven, to the

play; at eleven, to supper with a crew of lusty Bachanals who would smoke cigars, gulp down brandy, and sing, roar, and shout … till three in the morning. At eight up again to scribble, run, and roll hogsheads.[3]

When in 1812 the United States declared war against Great Britain, British naval vessels blockaded the port, trade collapsed, and the merchants braced themselves for hard times. By then, Seabury and his younger brother George, who had joined John in the china business, were living in the Widow Williams's boardinghouse at 282 Pearl Street. Single men typically lived in such establishments, which varied greatly in the quality of their accommodations and in the number of persons who lived there. Sometimes they catered to gentlemen boarders; sometimes the clientele was mixed and might even include families with children. At the Widow Williams's there were only four boarders—all single men. The ground floor was rented to the firm of Newbold and Leggett.

In December of 1814, a peace treaty was signed at Ghent. The news didn't reach New York until February of 1815, but when it did, jubilant New Yorkers celebrated throughout the snowy night with torchlight parades. With the coming of peace, trade resumed, and confidence returned to the city. British manufacturers chose New York in preference to other U.S. ports for "dumping" the manufactured goods that had accumulated during the war years. This brought down prices but increased volume. The hardware business flourished, and Seabury took on his nephew, Joseph Kissam, as a partner. Thereafter the business was known as Tredwell and Kissam.

Around this time, another event took place that would prove to have great personal consequence for Seabury. Sometime in 1814, the Widow Williams gave up the management of the boarding house where Seabury and his brother were living, and Mary Parker took over. Nothing is known about what happened to Mrs. Parker's husband, but we do know that both he and she had roots in Rumson, New Jersey. For some reason she and her four children were now on their own. Like many other women in this situation, she arranged to take over a boarding house.

The inauguration in 1817 of the Black Ball Line of packet ships, which left on schedule once a month regardless of whether or not they had a full cargo and no matter what the weather, introduced regularity into transatlantic trade. Hardware bound for Tredwell and Kissam was frequently to be found in the holds of these

---

3 John Bernard, *Retrospections of America, 1797-1811*, quoted in Bayrd Still, *Mirror for Gotham* (New York: New York University Press, 1956), 68-69.

sturdy ships, and Seabury's business continued to prosper. Soon he took on another partner, Joseph's brother, Samuel Kissam.

By 1820 Seabury was forty years old, "a single man in possession of a good fortune and evidently in want of a wife." Mrs. Parker's daughter Eliza, who was a girl of seventeen when her mother took over the boardinghouse, was now a young woman of twenty-three, and as sometimes happened in the boardinghouses of the day, the proximity of the landlady's daughter to the marriageable merchant led to an engagement.[4] On June 13, 1820, Seabury Tredwell and Eliza Parker were married in St. George's Episcopal Church then located on Beekman Street. The couple's first home was at 34 Cedar Street, where a baby daughter, whom they named Elizabeth Seabury, was born in 1821. In the spring of 1823, when the Tredwells were expecting their second child, Seabury purchased a house at 12 Dey Street for $6000. The new house was a short walk from Seabury's place of business on Pearl Street. City Hall Park, where twelve years earlier the new City Hall had been built, was four blocks to the north, and St. Paul's Episcopal Church was just around the corner. Both City Hall and St. Paul's are still standing today, serving their original functions.

The Erie Canal opened for business on October 16, 1825. New Yorkers, aware of the impact this would have on the commercial growth of the city, marked the occasion with exuberant public ceremony. With a waterway available from Albany to Buffalo, New York merchants could now send their imported goods up the Hudson River to Albany, through the Canal to Lake Erie, and from there to markets in the Midwest at a fraction of what it had formerly cost them by road. Midwestern farmers and builders needed what Tredwell and Kissam had to sell, and the business continued to grow. In 1831 Seabury took on a third partner, James Iredell Tredwell, the son of his brother Samuel.

A year later, Asiatic cholera struck New York City. Yellow fever epidemics had periodically threatened New Yorkers since Seabury's arrival in the city, but this was the first time that the terrifying cholera had crossed the Atlantic. Residents vacated the city en masse to escape the scourge that killed so swiftly—sometimes within hours. By now, the Tredwell family included six children. The logical place for them to wait out the epidemic that summer was with Seabury's family in Long Island. At that time, Seabury may have reasoned that his family

---

4 The most notable example of a merchant who married the landlady's daughter is John Jacob Astor, who married Sarah Todd, the daughter of his landlady, Sarah Cox Todd, in 1785. They continued to live in the boardinghouse until their first child was born three years later.

needed a sanctuary of their own, or he may already have been looking forward to an early retirement as a gentleman farmer. Whatever the motivation, in September he bought 700 acres of land in Rumson, New Jersey, for $13,000. The property was situated on Rumson Neck, a peninsula between the Shrewsbury and Navesink Rivers where they empty into the Atlantic Ocean. The following April he bought 150 more acres, bringing the entire holding to 850 acres that included forest, shoreline, a large working farm, a colonial farm house and tenant farmer's house, and an oyster pond.[5]

Meanwhile, commerce at the New York seaport continued to expand, and more and more downtown streets gave way to commercial interests. The noise and upset that accompanied the tearing down and building up that was taking place there prompted Seabury, along with many others, to look northward for more amenable surroundings. By the 1830s the area from Broadway to Bowery, between Bleecker Street and Astor Place (then called Art Street) was attracting the city's most prominent and wealthy citizens. It was to this stylish suburb that Seabury Tredwell decided to move his family.

In November 1835 he sold his Dey Street property to his partner and nephew, Joseph Kissam, for $10,000 and bought a house on Fourth Street between Bowery and Lafayette Place for $18,000. The house was three years old, having been built along with an identical rowhouse next door in 1832. The builder, Joseph Brewster, sold one of the houses immediately; he and his wife lived in the other.

Brewster was a hatter who also speculated in real estate and like Seabury was a Mayflower descendant. He was also a zealous Presbyterian reformer and a leader of the nascent temperance movement.

Just a month after Seabury bought the Fourth Street house, New York City was rocked by the disastrous Great Fire of 1835, which destroyed fifty-two acres of the commercial heart of the city, incinerating some 700 buildings. Seabury's place of business, however, as well as the Dey Street home were located well out of the path of the fire.

The Tredwells' new home was in a transitional architectural style, combining characteristics of the Late Federal style, with those of the Greek Revival, which

---

5   Seabury Tredwell was the first New Yorker to buy property in what came to be known as "the borough beautiful" where over the years many affluent New Yorkers would build magnificent summer homes. Both the farmhouse and the tenant farmer's house were destroyed by fire on June 15, 2006, in a blaze authorities deemed to be of "suspicious origin."

by the 1830s had achieved great popularity in New York City. Although the house was taller than the Federal homes downtown, from the outside, it looked a lot like them. The facade of red brick was laid in Flemish Bond, the long end of the brick alternating with the short end, and dormer windows pierced the steeply pitched slate roof. The windows were double-hung, six-over-six, with dark green exterior shutters. But flanking the doorway were Greek Ionic columns, and the interior ornament was pure Greek Revival.

6. THE TREDWELL COUNTRY HOME IN RUMSON, NEW JERSEY.
Courtesy of the Merchant's House Museum.
The Tredwells abandoned the city in the hot summer months, taking up residence in a colonial farmhouse on the Jersey shore.

On moving day, the Tredwells and their household goods made the trip uptown by carriage and wagon. Now there were seven children: Elizabeth, fourteen; Horace, twelve; Mary Adelaide, ten; Samuel Lenox, eight; Phebe, six; Julia, two; and Sarah, an infant in arms. Five years later, the Tredwells' eighth child, a girl whom they named Gertrude, would be born in the new house.

Seabury Tredwell had been in the hardware business for thirty-two years during one of the most favorable eras in American history for growing a business. He owned a large country estate and a city home located in the fashionable New York City neighborhood "above Bleecker." In a little over three decades, he had accumulated a fortune large enough to enable him, at the comparatively young age of fifty-five, to retire from the hurly-burly of maritime trade and turn over his business to his younger partners.

With domestic markets in the Midwest open, the coastal trade flourishing, and imports at an all-time high, the economic future of New York City seemed bright indeed. Seabury Tredwell, having done his share to lay the foundation for what was coming, intended to sit back and enjoy the show.

Men's and Women's Roles

For thirty years, until his death in 1865, Seabury Tredwell divided his time between his city home on Fourth Street and his country home in New Jersey where he shot snipe and quail, rode his horses, and oversaw the management of his farm and oyster pond. Officially retired from the hardware business, he nevertheless maintained business contacts in the city, acting in an advisory capacity to his nephews and as an independent investor, favoring investments like railroad bonds, bank bonds, and shares in the city's gas companies. He bought and sold building lots in Manhattan and Brooklyn and leased property he owned, including houses, commercial property in Brooklyn, and a farm in Wisconsin. He also lent money to individuals for the purchase of real estate on which he held the mortgages.

Meanwhile, Eliza Tredwell was busy with her own affairs, which had nothing to do with hardware, high finance, hunting, or horses. The men and women of the Tredwells' social class had different, clearly defined roles, and although they shared an active social life, their worlds, for the most part, spun in different orbits.

In a landmark study of the ideal woman in the four decades before the Civil War, Barbara Welter concluded that her four essential virtues were domesticity, submissiveness, purity, and above all, piety.[1] The complex of characteristics defined by Welter constituted the "cult of domesticity," which was accepted by both men and women as a natural and satisfying state of affairs. An essayist writing in 1844 summed up woman's position and responsibility:

---

1 Barbara Welter, "The Cult of True Womanhood: 1820–1860," in *Dimity Collections* (Athens: Ohio University Press, 1976), 21.

Home is the empire, the throne of woman. Here she reigns in the legitimate power of all her united charms. She is the luminary which enlightens, and the talisman which endears it. It is she who makes "home, sweet home."[2]

This is not to say that men were totally uninvolved in the domestic arena. During the years preceding the Civil War, it was customary in some families for men to do the marketing. One of the first things the impeccable Philip Hone did on moving into his new house on Broadway opposite Washington Place was to visit Tompkins market where he found that "good meat and vegetables are to be

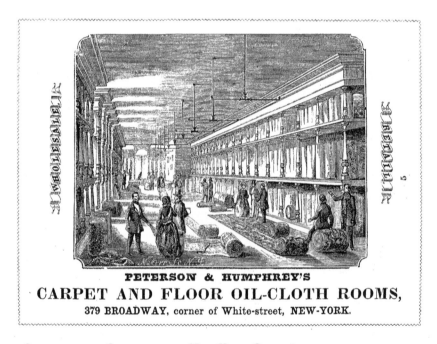

PETERSON & HUMPHREY'S
CARPET AND FLOOR OIL-CLOTH ROOMS,
379 BROADWAY, corner of White-street, NEW-YORK.

7. SHOPPING FOR CARPETING IN NEW YORK CITY, 1853.
Advertisement for Peterson and Humphrey's Carpet and Floor Oil-Cloth Rooms, 379 Broadway, New York, from Citizens and Strangers—and Business Directory for the City of New York and Its Vicinity, 1853. Collection of The New-York Historical Society, negative number 83560d.
Seabury and Eliza Tredwell were among the couples shopping for carpeting in the 1850s. Before the introduction of broadloom carpet, carpeting came in narrow rolls, and strips were sewn together to fit the dimensions of the room.

---

2   J.N. Danforth, ed., *The Token of Friendship, or Home, The Centre of the Affection,* quoted in Meade Minnigerode, *The Fabulous Forties: 1840–1850* (Garden City: Garden City Publishing Co., 1924), 75.

had."[3] The practice gradually declined, but Frederick Van Wyck, who lived on West Twelfth Street, remembered that as late as the early 1860s, selecting the groceries was his father's job:

> Father left our house at nine o'clock each morning ... [and] walked to Washington Square where our butcher and green grocer were. They handed him a chair, and sitting there, he inspected everything we were to consume, whether it was meat, poultry, or vegetables. As you can imagine, with a family of sixteen—outside of company, which we were rarely without—it meant quite a larder to be filled.[4]

Men also collaborated with their wives on "parlor making," when it came to the expenditure of large sums for new carpeting or furniture, for instance.

In January of 1858, John Skidmore, who lived with his parents and four brothers just four doors from the Tredwells, accompanied his best friend, John Jay White, to a scrubwoman's home to arrange for her to clean the house Skidmore had purchased in anticipation of his marriage to Louisa Wetmore. He had filled the house with the latest in furnishings, including a new pianoforte.[5] However, from the moment the couple returned from their honeymoon, the house was Louisa's domain. Here she was expected to create a serene haven for her husband to return to after a day spent in the hectic world of commerce. It was her job to see to the day-to-day running of the home and to create a showplace for parties, balls, and musical entertainments.

She hired the servants, told them what to do, and supervised their doing of it, keeping domestic crises from her husband's notice insofar as possible. She guarded the keys to the many cabinets and drawers in the house, made sure the larder was well supplied, the silverware and the sugar secure, and the linens in order. She planned the meals and was responsible for household expenditures, which she paid from her household allowance, although as noted, she did not necessarily do the actual marketing.

---

3   Philip Hone diary, May 25, 1836, Manuscript Division (New York: New-York Historical Society).

4   Frederick Van Wyck, *Recollections of an Old New Yorker* (New York: Liveright, 1932), 122.

5   John Skidmore diary, January 17, 1858, Manuscript Division (New York: New-York Historical Society). The Skidmore house at 39 East Fourth Street is privately owned but landmarked by the City of New York. It was built in 1845 and was the home of Samuel Tredwell Skidmore, who was Seabury Tredwell's first cousin once removed. (Skidmore's grandfather and Seabury's father were brothers.)

A woman's chief responsibility, however, was the raising of her children. Motherhood was her crowning achievement, her fulfillment as a woman, and was even considered an indirect source of political power. Since the Revolution, woman's role as her children's teacher had assumed a vital importance. As a molder of the character of future citizens of the new republic, the American mother was seen ultimately to influence government and society in a profound way. She was the one who was to start her children on the path toward developing powers of the intellect and the habits of character they would need as members of a democratic society. [6]

8. THE FAMILY AT HOME, 1834.
Courtesy of Old Sturbridge Village, Sturbridge, MA, negative number 249Ab2f.

9. LIGHT OF HOME.
Engraving from Godey's Lady's Book, January 1860. Collection of The New-York Historical Society, negative number 83561d.

The nineteenth-century woman was often portrayed surrounded by her children, serenely content with her role as "Light of the Home," "Angel in the House," or "Madonna in the Nursery."

Well before children entered school, their mother taught them to read and cipher. Even more important than these accomplishments, however, were the

---

6 Historian Linda Kerber coined the term "republican motherhood" to describe the idea, held since the Revolution, that motherhood gave women a powerful political role in the new republic. *Women of the Republic: Intellect and Ideology in Revolutionary America* (Chapel Hill, N.C.: University of North Carolina Press, 1980).

qualities of character that children learned from their mother. They needed to be taught to be independent, yet at the same time strictly obedient to parental authority and thoroughly self controlled. Honesty, justice, perseverance—these were among the most important qualities to be inculcated in the young. In addition, the Christian mother had the truly awesome obligation of preparing her children for immortality. Considering how many children she was likely to have, it was all a very tall order, one she took very seriously.

A woman was expected to be conciliatory towards her husband and long-suffering if necessary, avoiding controversy in her marriage, submitting to her husband's wishes even if she disagreed. Most marriages fell somewhat short of this goal, some drastically so, and a few women publicly and ardently renounced the idea. The feminist Margaret Fuller was living just around the corner from the Tredwells in 1845 when she wrote *Woman in the Nineteenth Century*, a book in which she asserted the right of women to be equal to men in every way: intellectually, politically, and economically. Her ideas were a radical departure from accepted thinking, but by the 1840s, the idea of equal rights for women had begun percolating. In 1848 New York State passed the Married Women's Property Act, which allowed women to inherit and own property in their own right, and in the same year, the first women's rights convention would be held in Seneca Falls, New York.

Seabury Tredwell was clearly in accord with these developments, for in his will, made just three months before his death in 1865, he made the by-then-unnecessary provision that his legatees "married or hereafter becoming, married women" were to take their shares "free from any control, debts or interference of their husbands."

Women were thought to be religious by nature, and because of their special receptiveness to the Divine, they were counted on to bring their husbands and their children nearer to God. It was only in the spiritual realm that women were considered equal (indeed superior) to men. However, we should not be misled into thinking that men did not harbor deep religious feelings. Among the residents of the Bond Street area, faith in God went without saying. Sitting side by side in a church pew on Sunday, the Tredwells and their neighbors came together without regard to gender.

There could be no better illustration of the ideal woman than Julia Lay, the wife of a bookkeeper in a bank and the mother of Oliver Lay, who would become a successful New York portrait artist. The Lays were the parents of seven children, two of whom died in childhood and one whom they adopted as an infant after both his mother and father, Julia's brother and sister-in-law, died. Julia kept a diary for thirty-eight years, recording her life as a wife and mother. On February 6, 1858, she wrote:

> Saturday evening, the pleasantest evening in the week for me—the anticipation of a blessed Sabbath when the weary ones can rest, and we can listen to the voices of our beloved pastors. The house is all clean, baking done, meat cooked, the dear little feet washed and chubby hands and precious forms all sponged off, clean and sweet. Fresh flannels and clean sheets, then the warm cotton flannel nightgown cover up the well shaped limbs. Our prayers are said, the good night kiss given, and the younger ones all snugly tucked in their soft comfortable beds and I sit down not with the needle but with folded hands to think over our great blessings and of our Heavenly Father who so mercifully sustains us day and night. Happy Saturday night. [7]

Women unaccompanied by gentlemen were free to travel around town in omnibus, private carriage, or on foot. They went to the shops, to the homes of their friends, and to certain restaurants and public places such as art galleries, libraries, and ice cream parlors. Some public spaces were reserved for women only. There were separate ladies' parlors on steamboats and railroad cars, separate dining rooms in hotels, and separate spaces set aside in banks and post offices and libraries. Such segregation spared women to some extent from the impertinent gaze of strange men as well from witnessing the disgusting male habit of spitting tobacco juice. It also afforded women the privacy necessary when traveling long distances. [8]

One of the favorite haunts of women was Taylor's Restaurant. Women without escorts, taking a break from shopping, congregated at Taylor's, located at Broadway and Franklin Street. It was, according to Putnam's Magazine, "the largest and most elegant restaurant in the world." [9] The main dining room was a marvel of over-the-top décor: a twenty-two-foot gilt and frescoed ceiling, a mirrored wall, a stained glass window, and fountains playing among a bower of flowers. Elisa-

---

7 Julia Lay diary, February 6, 1858, Manuscripts and Archives Division (New York: New York Public Library, Astor, Lenox and Tilden Foundations).

8 Mary P. Ryan, *Women in Public: Between Banners and Ballots, 1825–1880* (Baltimore: Johns Hopkins University Press, 1990), 69. See also Linda K. Kerber, "Separate Spheres, Female Worlds, Women's Place: The Rhetoric of Women's History," *Journal of American History* 75 (June 1988): 9–39.

9 *Putnam's Magazine* 1, no. 4 (April 1853): 363.

10. Interior View of the Ladies Saloon of the Steamer Atlantic, 1846.
Courtesy of The Mariner's Museum, Newport News, Virginia.

Separate spaces were set aside for women in many public places such as steamships, rail passenger cars, libraries, banks, and restaurants, In such spaces, women were relieved from the tension that came from being in close quarters with strange men.

beth Koren, a Norwegian immigrant, who arrived on these shores in November of 1853, made her way with her husband directly from the ship to Taylor's where they had their first meal on American soil.

> First we went up Broadway and into Taylor's Restaurant. How splendid it is! It is extremely large, with a balcony over half of it. The other half is an open floor. Above are two hundred gaslights, some chandeliers, some glass candelabra; below, sixty or eighty lights. The floor is set with tables, and along the walls at each table are lovely semicircular sofas covered with crimson velvet. In the center is a large fountain, partly of marble, partly of glass, in which goldfish are swimming. We had a hot meal and ices, marveling at the more than ample American servings.[10]

10 Elisabeth Koren, *The Diary of Elisabeth Koren, 1853–55*, trans. and ed. David T. Nelson (Northfield, Minn.: Norwegian-American Historical Association, 1955), 62.

This dining room accommodated both men and women, though during the day the clientele was largely women shoppers, who partook of oysters, omelettes, sandwiches, coffee, hot chocolate, and ice cream. Downstairs, there was another dining room reserved exclusively for gentlemen where the menu was more robust.

11. Merchants' Room, Exchange.
Engraving by J. Archer. Emmet Collection, Miriam and Ira D. Wallach Division of Art, Prints and Photographs, The New York Public Library, Astor, Lenox and Tilden Foundations.
The original Merchants' Exchange was built in 1827 on Wall Street. At some time during the day, Seabury Tredwell could no doubt be found in the sun-drenched rotunda. This building was destroyed in the Great Fire of 1835 but was quickly replaced by another even grander building.

The husband's mission in life was to make money—the more the better—in order to provide a home worthy of the family's status. During the day, in the course of doing business, men could be found all over the city: at their store or office, or at someone else's store or office; at dockside supervising the unloading of merchandise, and at the Merchants' Exchange, where they left and received letters for overseas suppliers and could be fairly sure of encountering other merchants with whom they had business dealings. They also frequented restaurants like Delmonicos, hotel dining rooms, the many subterranean oyster cellars, or gentlemen's clubs where they combined the business of dealmaking with the pleasures of social exchange.

In fact, men engaged in a number of social activities in the company of men only. Fanny Trollope, an Englishwoman who observed Americans with a critical eye during her temporary residence in this country, was particularly struck by the habit of American men to have dinner parties that excluded females, a custom which she found "a great defect in society."[11] Julia Ward Howe, however, accepted the custom with good grace. At a public dinner honoring Charles Dickens when he visited New York in 1842, she remembered that

> We ladies were not bidden to the feast, but were allowed to occupy a small anteroom whose open door commanded a view of the tables. When the speaking was about to begin, a message came, suggesting that we should take possession of some vacant seats at the great table. This we were glad to do.[12]

When John Ward decided to celebrate his twentieth birthday in November 1858, he chose to do so with his men friends only:

> I got my library ready for the company, arranged two card tables, etc. We dined in the parlor about 7.... I took the head with my back to the mirror. It was chiefly a game supper. I carved hard and talked little ... Rowland proposed my health. I was too shy to make a speech. After dinner we played cards in my library and much smoking was done. Just after dinner I sang my law school songs at the piano. Some stayed all night.[13]

Many of the exclusive gentlemen's clubs of the time were organized to appeal to those who had a specialized interest. Some were devoted to dining; some, to literary, scientific, or cultural pursuits, and some to the sporting life. By 1860 there were seven men's clubs in New York City devoted to the national pastime of harness racing, a particular interest of the Tredwell brothers.

Seabury's brother, John Tredwell ("Uncle Johnny"), was a well-known breeder of fine horses. In 1823 a bay horse named Abdallah was foaled on John Tredwell's

---

11 Fanny Trollope, *Domestic Manners of the Americans* (1832; reprint, London: Penguin Books, 1997), 262.

12 Julia Ward Howe, *Reminiscences, 1819–1899* (Boston: Houghton Mifflin Company, 1899), 25.

13 John Ward diary, November 30, 1858, Manuscript Division (New York: New-York Historical Society). At the time, John Ward was a single man, who lived with his widowed mother at Thompson and Bleecker Streets, just a few blocks from the Tredwells.

Long Island farm. Abdallah's name would go down in the annals of harness racing as the sire of Hambletonian, the most famous trotter in the history of the sport, whose descendants include nearly all the great harness racing champions.

Trotters were introduced to this country in colonial times, and by the time Seabury moved to Fourth Street, the sport had gained immense popularity. Horsemen engaged in exhilarating impromptu races along one of two stretches of soft dirt roads. The Bloomingdale Road Speedway stretched from Twenty-Third Street and Broadway to 126th Street, while the Third Avenue Speedway commenced at Twenty-Eighth Street and proceeded for five miles to Harlem. The center portion of Third Avenue was macadamized, but there were broad soft earth shoulders on both sides of the wide avenue where the races took place, the best of the trotters running a mile in somewhat over two minutes.[14]

Writing in his memoir, Abram C. Dayton recalled seeing "Mr. Tredwell" and Abdallah engaged in a spirited race with another notable horse and driver on the Third Avenue Speedway. We are able to confirm that "Mr. Tredwell" was indeed Seabury, because unlike his brother John, Seabury wore his hair in an old fashioned queue or pigtail long after that hairstyle was in fashion, an eccentricity Dayton makes note of.

> In memory, on a given day we see . . . William T. Porter, "The Tall Son of York," shouting vigorously to Confidence in his endeavor to head Abdallah, the famous stallion, handled in those days by Mr. Tredwell, a veteran with the ribbons, who in spurts showed a gait which made the old-fashioned queue, which the old gentleman persistently wore until his death, stand out straight behind.[15]

Seabury must have been a strong and determined horseman, for Abdallah was a cantankerous horse, used primarily under saddle, and not kindly disposed to wagons or carts.

The thrill of the race was by no means the only attraction to the sport. All along the stretch of the speedways were numerous roadhouses like The Four Mile

---

14 Gurney C. Gue, "The Speedways of New York Old and New," *The Horse Review*, December 12, 1899, 1262.

15 Abram C. Dayton, *Last Days of Knickerbocker Life* (New York: G.P. Putnam's Sons, 1897), 329–30. Originally written in 1871 as a series of sketches about life in New York City, Dayton's work was published in a small edition in 1880, limited mainly to circulation among his friends. An illustrated edition was brought out by his son in 1897.

House, a white frame building with a neat garden and whitewashed fences and sheds. At these roadhouses, men ate and drank (pale brandy being the favorite drink for men during the 1840s and 1850s), challenged each other to a race, placed bets on their favorites, and engaged in vigorous horse trading.[16]

16 Gue, 1262–64.

2

Setting the Stage: The Neighborhood

The Bond Street area where Seabury moved his family in September of 1835 had been attracting the city's wealthiest and most influential citizens since the 1820s. Broadway, a block and a half west of the Tredwells' new home, was still a residential street. And just two blocks to the south, Bond Street, lined with rowhouses of red brick and white marble, stretched for a thousand uninterrupted feet between Bowery and Broadway.

New York City was a very different place in 1835 than it had been when Seabury arrived in 1798. Exports then amounted to $13,300,000. By 1835 they had risen to $30,000,000, and the population had grown from approximately 60,000 to over 270,000. In 1827 a letter writer to the *New York Mirror* had dubbed New York "the greatest commercial emporium of the world"[1]—a phrase that would be used over and over to describe the city as it continued to grow.

By 1835 the city had pushed as far north as Astor Place on Broadway and now boasted 10 theaters, 40 large hotels, 19 banks, 135 churches, and 26 daily newspapers. Omnibuses carried passengers up and down Broadway where traffic jams were legendary. On the Bowery, horse-drawn cars that ran on tracks presaged the trolley. The streets and some homes below Grand were lit by gas. Steamships plied the rivers, and transatlantic steam travel was but a few years in the future.

However, hogs still ran wild in the streets, which were filthier than ever, and even though the contaminated Collect had been filled in years earlier, the city was still without an adequate water supply. In April of 1835, voters finally were presented with a plan to construct the forty-one-mile-long Croton Aqueduct, which would eventually bring an abundance of clean water to the city.

---

1   *New York Mirror and Ladies Gazette,* January 6, 1827.

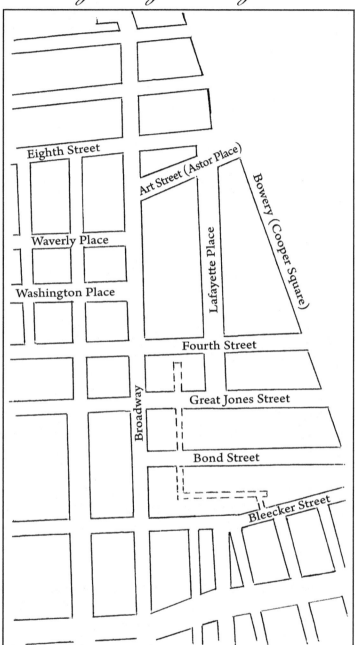

12. THE BOND STREET AREA, BROADWAY TO BOWERY, ASTOR PLACE TO BLEECKER STREET, 1835.

Author's Collection.

The dotted line approximates a horse alley that permitted horses and carriages to be brought from stables on Great Jones to the front doors of the homes on Bond Street.

In 1826, when it had become evident that the Bond Street area was becoming a destination for affluent homebuyers, John Jacob Astor cut a long broad thoroughfare from Astor Place to Great Jones Street through property he owned extending from Broadway to Bowery. At the time, the property was leased to a Frenchman named Delacroix, who had transformed it into a romantic pleasure garden called Vauxhall Garden. From May to September, couples strolled along gravel paths among shrubs and flowers and classical statuary. In the middle of the garden there was an equestrian statue of George Washington. Wooden booths, where patrons could enjoy ice cream and lemonade were arranged around the edges. At night, thousands of oil lamps glimmered in the trees. Featured attractions included high wire performances, firework displays, equestrian acts, a band, and theatrical performances.

The new street, which cut the garden in two, was named Lafayette Place in honor of the Marquis de Lafayette, who had played an important part in the American Revolution, and who had made a recent triumphal visit to the United States. Lafayette Place provided a lucrative opportunity for the astute Astor to profit from the demand for real estate in the area. He sold lots on both sides of the street, and it wasn't long before fine homes began to appear there, including the brick mansion owned by his son, William Backhouse Astor, and the large home the elder Astor built for his daughter on the southwest corner of Lafayette Place and Astor Place. The western half of Vauxhall Garden was quickly replaced by commercial buildings fronting on Broadway, but the eastern portion of the pleasure garden from Lafayette Place to Bowery continued to operate until 1851, when encroaching commercial and residential development brought it to an end.

In 1833, the financier Samuel Ward (whose daughter Julia would grow up to write "The Battle Hymn of the Republic") finished building his famous "Corner House" on the northeast corner of Bond Street and Broadway. Its most distinctive feature was a windowless private art gallery located at the rear of the building, extending along Broadway.

But the neighborhood's most impressive residential structure was a group of nine connected townhouses on Lafayette Place. Unified behind a row of twenty-eight sparkling white marble Corinthian columns, La Grange Terrace, as it was then called, was reminiscent of the sweeping crescents of Bath or London. Curious New Yorkers drove up from the City proper in their carriages to gawk as the structure took shape. Each twenty-six-room house was twenty-seven feet wide and came complete with central heating, hot and cold running water, and an indoor toilet. It was heralded as "unequaled for grandeur and effect."[2]

13. La Grange Terrace — Lafayette Place.
Collection of the New-York Historical Society, negative number 4840.
The magnificent row of nine sparkling white marble homes, originally named for the country home of the Marquis de Lafayette, later came to be known as Colonnade Row. Before Lafayette Place was widened, a terrace separated the homes from the street.

There were already two Episcopalian churches nearby: St. Mark's in the Bowery at Tenth Street and Second Avenue, which had been built on the site of Peter Stuyvesant's farm in 1799, and St. Thomas's at Houston Street and Broadway, established in 1823. However, to accommodate the many Episcopalian newcomers to the neighborhood, a new Episcopalian parish was organized in 1835, and St. Bartholomew's Church was built at Lafayette Place and Great Jones Street. Consecrated on October 28, 1835, it was a modest stone structure in the style of a Roman temple with stuccoed columns, but it attracted many of the city's wealthiest

---

2   Martha Lamb, "A Neglected Corner of the Metropolis: Historic Homes in Lafayette Place," *Magazine of American History* 16, no. 1 (July 1886): 1. Later, La Grange Terrace would become known as Colonnade Row. The five southernmost houses were demolished in 1901 to make room for a Wanamaker warehouse. Today, the four remaining homes remain, landmarked by the City of New York, but sadly deteriorated.

parishioners. The Tredwells had been married at St. George's Episcopal Church downtown where they worshipped when they lived on Dey Street. Now, as if on demand, they had been provided a new church home just a block away from their new house. Their two older daughters, Elizabeth and Mary Adelaide, would be married there—the former to a nephew of one of the church's founders.

Other churches followed their congregations uptown to the neighborhood. Soon after the consecration of St. Bartholomew's, ground was broken at the corner of Lafayette Place and Fourth Street for the Middle Dutch Church, a Protestant denomination of Calvinist persuasion, which moved from its former location on Nassau Street. The Middle Dutch Church was an imposing structure in the style of a Greek Revival temple. Eight granite columns, twenty-five feet tall and weighing twenty-five tons each, were ranged across the front with four more in the recessed portico. The sanctuary held 1,500 worshippers, with space for 500 more in the gallery above. The church opened for worship in 1839, as did the new Unitarian Church of the Messiah, which had been built on Broadway opposite Waverly Place.

Next to relocate was The Murray Street Presbyterian Church, which was literally moved from its location downtown. Workmen dismantled the building and transported it stone by stone to Eighth Street and Lafayette Place where they reconstructed it in 1842. When the Eighth Street Church, as it had come to be known, moved still further uptown several years later, the Presbyterians left their building behind, and in 1852, it was converted to St. Ann's Roman Catholic Church.[3]

Meanwhile, Grace Episcopal Church had decided to move uptown to Broadway and Tenth Street. A young twenty-three-year-old architect, James Renwick Jr., designed the new building, and there, where the avenue bends to the west, a magnificent church edifice opened for worship in 1846. It was (and still is) a perfect wedding cake of elegant Gothic design. Grace Church became the most fashionable church of all, attracting a large congregation of society's elite, who paid as much as $1,400 for a pew when they were first offered for sale. Pew owners also paid an annual fee of eight percent of the pew's value.[4]

---

3 In 1871 St. Ann's Church was deconsecrated, the steeple removed, and the building converted to commercial use. Beginning in 1879, it became home to various theaters, and in 1902, it was demolished to make way for the subway.

4 Philip Hone diary, February 5, 1846. At this time pew rentals provided the financial support for the churches. Customarily, one member of the family rented a pew for the entire family. John Skidmore rented a pew at St. Thomas, and Phebe Tredwell rented one at St. Bart's for the Tredwell family. The Tredwells also owned pews at St. George's Episcopal Church and at Trinity Church downtown.

14. St. Bartholomew's Episcopalian Church, Lafayette Place and Great Jones Street. *Author's Collection.*

15. Grace Episcopalian Church, Broadway and Tenth Street.
Courtesy of Cornell University Library, Making of America Digital Collection.

16. St. Mark's Episcopalian Church, Second Avenue and Tenth Street.
Eno Collection, Miriam and Ira D. Wallach Division of Art, Prints and Photographs, The New York Public Library, Astor, Lenox and Tilden Foundations.

17. Presbyterian Church, later St. Ann's Roman Catholic Church, Lafayette Place and Eighth Street. *Collection of the New-York Historical Society, negative number 75660.*

18. Middle Dutch Reformed Church, Lafayette Place and Fourth Street.
Picture Collection, The New York Public Library, Astor, Lenox and Tilden Foundations.

19. Church of the Messiah, Unitarian Church, Broadway and Waverly Street.
Courtesy of Cornell University Library, Making of America Digital Collection.

On Sundays elegantly dressed parishioners swarmed to these churches, not just for morning worship but for afternoon Sunday School and evening services as well.

As further evidence of the aristocratic character of the neighborhood, the Astor Place Opera House, devoted to the performance of Italian opera, was completed in 1847 at the northern end of Lafayette Place. The residents of the Bond Street area surely felt satisfied then that they were living in an enclave that was unexcelled for genteel piety and sophisticated culture. However, just two years later, in May of 1849, the Opera House became the focus of a bloody riot that rocked the city and marked the beginning of the neighborhood's decline. As improbable as it may seem, a long-standing rivalry between two actors served as the impetus for the riot. The Opera House epitomized the elitism of the upper class and provoked deep resentment among the city's working class. Patrons typically wore kid gloves and silk waistcoats to the performances. When it was announced that the British actor William Macready was to perform the role of Macbeth at the Opera House at the same time that the American actor Edwin Forrest was to perform the same role at a theater just blocks away, the supporters of Forrest reacted with anger. Forrest's fans considered Macready to be the embodiment of an effete aristocratic tradition. Forrest, on the other hand, represented to them the egalitarian ideals of American democracy. Encouraged by the press and others, Forrest supporters showed up at the Opera House on May 7 to heckle Macready and pelt him with eggs and vegetables. When they began throwing chairs, Macready left the stage and vowed to leave the city, but community leaders, outraged at the behavior and alarmed to think that the rowdies could impose their will in this fashion, promised Macready protection and convinced him to perform again on the night of May 10.

On that night in May, representatives of New York City's privileged class clashed with enraged Bowery toughs and disgruntled Irish immigrants with disastrous results. Many of Forrest's supporters had secured tickets and were spread around the house. When they started a disturbance, the police, who had been alerted and were stationed inside, arrested them and appeared to restore order. But when the crowd that had gathered outside the theater discovered what had happened, they attempted to storm the barricaded building, hurling stones and bricks at the police and the theater. Windows were broken, the fine crystal chandelier was smashed, and the Opera House patrons were thrown into a panic. The police proved ineffective in repelling the crowd, and finally two divisions of the Seventh Regiment, which were standing by, were called in. The troops fired three times: the first volley was directed above the heads of the crowd; the second, at their legs. Still the crowd kept coming, apparently believing that the soldiers were firing warning blanks. The third volley was fired directly into the crowd. Twenty-two persons lost their lives, and over a hundred others were wounded. Thousands had gathered outside the theater, though it is estimated that only about 250 actually participated in attacking the police and the militia.[5]

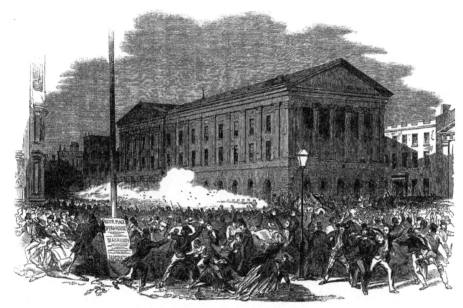

20. RIOT AT THE ASTOR PLACE OPERA HOUSE, NEW YORK.
Woodcut from the Illustrated London News, *June 2, 1849. New York State Historical Association, Cooperstown.*
The Astor Place Opera House was located at the juncture of Broadway and the Bowery, streets which had long represented a deep cultural divide among New Yorkers. In 1849 Irish immigrants joined with American working class toughs in violently expressing their resentment of the elitism represented by the Opera House and the British actor performing there, an elitism that they saw as antithetical to republican American values.

The Opera House soon became known as the "Massacre Place Opera House," and, by association, the reputation of the whole neighborhood was tarnished. The following year, the building was sold to the Mercantile Library Association, which remodeled the interior, renamed it Clinton Hall, and opened it to the public on April 19, 1854. The library had a first-floor lecture room seating 1,000 and

---

5   Richard Moody, *The Astor Place Riot* (Bloomington: Indiana University Press, 1958). For events leading up to the riot, see Leo Hershkowitz, "Anatomy of a Riot: Astor Place Opera House, 1849," *New York History* 87 (Summer 2006), 277–310.

a second-floor reading room. A larger, elliptically shaped room, surrounded by Corinthian columns and surmounted by a dome, occupied the third and fourth

21. THE NEW YORK MERCANTILE LIBRARY, ASTOR PLACE AND LAFAYETTE PLACE.
Engraving from Scribner's Monthly, February 1871. Courtesy of Cornell University Library, Making of America Digital Collection.
By the time the Mercantile Library moved from its location downtown to Astor Place in 1854, it had far surpassed its original mission of providing a wholesome leisure time pursuit for merchants' clerks. Patrons paid an annual fee for the privilege of borrowing books and using the reading room where reference material and newspapers and periodicals from all over the world were available for perusal.

floors and housed the library's 43,000 volumes. Patrons paid an annual subscription fee for the privilege of checking out books.[6]

---

6 The Mercantile Library was originally established downtown in 1820 to benefit young men employed as merchants' clerks. It moved from the Astor Place site to 17 East Forty-Seventh Street in 1933 where it continued to operate as a subscription library focusing on fiction. Today, the name of the library has been

The Mercantile Library was actually the second library to be located in the neighborhood. When John Jacob Astor died in 1848, he left a legacy of $400,000 to build a public library for New York City. The site chosen was on Lafayette Place, across the street from La Grange Terrace, immediately north of the home

22. THE ASTOR LIBRARY, ORIGINAL STRUCTURE, 1853.
Picture Collection, The New York Public Library, Astor, Lenox and Tilden Foundations.
The original library building was completed in 1853 under the terms of the will of John Jacob Astor. An addition to the north was completed in 1855 and another twenty years later, at which time an ornamental story and a heavy balustrade over the cornices were added to the central section, and the main entrance hall was constructed in the center of the building. Today the modified structure houses the Public Theater.

---

changed to The Center for Fiction. In addition to its function as a subscription library, The Center offers programs of literary interest and provides workspace for writers and meeting space for writers and readers. It also presents awards for literary merit.

of Astor's son, William B. Astor, and a stone's throw from the Mercantile Library. The scholar Joseph Cogswell scoured European book markets purchasing titles to supplement the extensive personal collection of books that John Jacob Astor had assembled in his lifetime.[7] The doors opened on January 9, 1854. Unlike the Mercantile Library, which focused on the needs of the general reader, the Astor Library was a research library, attracting scholars from all over the world. However, it was also patronized by ordinary citizens whose curiosity and interest led them to explore the mostly recondite collection. The building was enlarged a year later by William B. Astor, who added an addition to the north, and again in 1879 by William B. Astor's eldest son, John Jacob Astor IV. The architects in charge of the additions matched the original materials and design so perfectly that today the building, which now houses the Public Theater, looks as if it had been one original conception.

By 1850 commercial interests had crept up Broadway nearly to Bleecker Street, and during the next decade, Broadway residences continued to be replaced by shops and workrooms. The side streets gradually began to decline as residents moved to more fashionable precincts like Fifth Avenue, Fourteenth Street, and Gramercy Park.

Some of the fine Bond Street houses became dentists' offices and boarding houses, and on Fourth Avenue, new commercial buildings steadily encroached on what was left of Vauxhall Garden. At the same time, large public institutions made their appearance in the area, and strangers poured into the neighborhood every day, destroying the aura of seclusion that it had once enjoyed.

In 1851 the American Bible Society constructed a six-story building on Eighth Street (across from what would become the site of Cooper Union). Here thousands of Bibles and testaments were printed daily on huge hydraulic presses—700,000 in 1852 alone. The mission of the Society was to distribute Bibles without doctrinal note or commentary, not only to the heathen in distant corners of the world, but to unconverted New Yorkers in tenements, grogshops and jails. The Society's building also served as headquarters for a number of the city's many charitable institutions.[8]

---

7 The Astor Library collection was eventually combined with that of the Lenox Library to form the basis of the original collection of the New York Public Library, which was built with funds bequeathed by Samuel Tilden, one-time governor of New York. The New York Public Library is today one of the world's great research libraries.

8 "Benevolent Institutions of New York," *Putnam's Magazine* 1, no. 6 (June 1853): 673–74. The American Bible Society is now located at Sixty-fourth Street and Broadway.

The same year that the Astor and the Mercantile libraries were opened, construction began on the Cooper Union at Fourth Avenue and Astor Place. The long-held dream of its founder, New York City's beloved Peter Cooper, it was to be a free school for youths who could not otherwise afford advanced training in the practical arts and sciences. The only requirement for admission was a good moral character. Most of its classes were held at night so that working men could attend, but there were also daytime classes in drawing and painting on china for women. It opened its doors to 2,000 students in 1858.[9]

In the 1850s the Bond Street neighborhood was no longer the exclusive quiet suburban enclave it had been ten years earlier, but it was still respectable enough. Some of the neighborhood's most prominent citizens had left for fancier houses uptown, but others, including the William B. Astors and the William Colford Schermerhorns, stayed put. In the winter of 1854, in fact, the most spectacular event of the social season took place at the home of the Schermerhorns at Great Jones Street and Lafayette Place. Six hundred of the city's elite received invitations directing them to appear on the appointed evening in costume—and not just any costume. They were to be dressed as members of the court of Louis XV. The mansion was refurnished and decorated in the manner of Versailles and the servants outfitted with appropriate uniforms and wigs. The guests appeared in such an extravagant display of diamonds and dress that people are still talking about it today.[10]

Because the large public institutions that were moving into the area represented cultural and intellectual pursuits, New Yorkers began referring to the Bond Street neighborhood as "The Athenian Quarter." In addition to the Astor Library, the Mercantile Library, and Cooper Union, nearby neighbors included the Society Library, the National Academy of Design, and the New-York Historical Society, which at the time also served as the city's only art museum.

In 1860 the Tompkins Market–Seventh Regiment Armory building was completed, and the market opened for business. For years, it had been obvious that the city needed a new building to replace the old wooden market that had served the neighborhood since 1830. As it happened, the Seventh Regiment also needed

---

9 Cooper Union still stands, its exterior virtually unchanged. It offers undergraduate degrees in art, architecture, and engineering. Until recently, the school offered free tuition to all students, but because of budget constraints, they have announced that they will charge tuition to graduate students. Students are responsible for their own housing and board as well as fees for supplies and books. The school offers a financial aid program, for which students are encouraged to apply.

10 Lloyd Morris, *Incredible New York* (New York: Random House, 1951), 18–19.

an armory, and somehow the idea took hold that if the soldiers joined with the butchers and others who wanted a new public market, they would have a better chance of persuading the city to build them one. It was a strange alliance; the Seventh Regiment was composed of elite young men who had little in common with the butchers. But the plan worked.

23. Cooper Union About 1861.
Courtesy of the Museum of the City of New York, Print Archives.

This scene shows some of the large institutions that had been established in the neighborhood in the 1850s: the Bible House at the extreme left, Cooper Union in the center of the drawing, and Tompkins Market/Seventh Regiment Armory on the right. Steam rail service became available in New York City in 1837, but the city required that the trains be horse-drawn south of Thirty-Second Street because of the nuisance of noise and spitting ash and cinders. Pictured here, the horse-drawn cars of the Harlem Railroad line in the foreground and the Third Avenue Line in the distance.

The fine new building occupied an entire square block just catty-corner from the Cooper Union. The market was a large open space on the first floor where shoppers could buy butcher's meat, poultry and game, produce, fresh fish, and something new: cooked food "ready for parties, breakfast, dinners or suppers, cold or warm."[11] On the second floor, lavishly furnished rooms provided space for the eight companies of the regiment, while on the third floor there was a drill

---

11   Thomas F. DeVoe, *The Market Book: A History of the Public Markets of the City of New York* 1862; reprint New York: Augustus M. Kelley, 1970), 557.

hall, said to be the largest in the nation, where four companies could perform the maneuvers that prepared men for battle.[12]

In 1863 the Tredwells saw the residential character of their own block transformed. In that year the Liederkranz Society, a German singing group, purchased the three houses to the east of the Tredwells. The Germans cut through the party walls to combine the houses into one large building, which they extended to the back property line. On the second floor they installed a theater whose windows opened onto the Tredwells' back yard. The Liederkranz concerts and masked balls were popular events that attracted large crowds to Fourth Street. The Tredwells were no doubt frequently provided with musical entertainment whether they liked it or not.

By the time Seabury Tredwell died in 1865, the neighborhood was no longer attracting New York's elite. Bond Street itself had finally yielded to commercial development. And just three blocks away from the Tredwells' home, at the corner of Broadway and Bond Street, some 1,000 poor persons came each day to what had once been the home of the eminent physician, Dr. John Francis, to apply for fuel assistance from the Department of Public Charities.[13]

The Tredwells' once fashionable Fourth Street residence was now modest and unfashionable compared to the large mansions and imposing brownstones that had been built further uptown. And the residents of that modest home were, by extension, not nearly as socially prominent as they had once been. *Harper's New Monthly Magazine* noted that even children understood the association of a big house with social status.

> In the earlier days of New York, a three-story house was the badge of the aristocrat.... Now, girls and boys, we are told, are nobodies at a fashionable school, if their parents don't live in four or five story houses with brownstone fronts.[14]

But Seabury Tredwell had seen no reason to change his address just because it was the fashionable thing to do, and after his death, the women of the family may

---

12 In just a few months after the Armory was opened, the men of the Seventh Regiment were called to join the fight at the battle of Gettysburg.

13 "Distress Among the Poor," *Harper's Weekly*, February 15, 1868: 99–101. In 1863 the Commissioner of Charities moved from his office downtown to No. 1 Bond Street, which then also housed the Outdoor Poor Department. In 1869 the office and the department moved to East Eleventh Street.

14 "The Houses We Live In," *Harper's New Monthly Magazine*, 30 (May 1865): 736.

24. DISTRESS AMONG THE POOR
Engraved from a drawing by Stanley Fox from Harper's Weekly Magazine, February 25, 1868. Collection of the New-York Historical Society, negative number 79753D.

During the two decades preceding the Civil War, residents of the Bond Street area gradually moved further uptown. What had been their elegant homes became boarding houses and dentists' offices. In 1863, when the elegant home of Dr. John Francis at the corner of Bond and Broadway became a relief station for the homeless or "outdoor poor" as they were then called, the decline of the neighborhood was complete.

simply not have had the emotional resources to pull up stakes, for they continued to live in the Fourth Street house for the rest of their lives. As time went on, the neighborhood continued to decline. When Gertrude Tredwell died in 1933, saloons and manufacturing lofts were her neighbors, and the nearby Bowery had achieved notoriety as the nation's skid row. But today, the neighborhood is fashionable once again. New York University has appropriated many of the buildings to its use, and high-rise apartment buildings and boutique condominiums have made their appearance throughout the area.

3

Setting the Stage: The Parlors

"The drawing room is a stage upon which parts are performed before a public that applauds or hisses, according to the merits of the actors."
— THE ART OF CONVERSING, 1846

On a fine spring day in 1846, Philip Hone took a walk and was surprised to discover how rapidly the city had changed when he wasn't looking:

> I ... saw many wonderful sights and discovered that I knew no more about New York as it now is than the hermit of Saba. Such a mass of busy population, such noises of "armorers closing rivets up," such creaking of blocks, such puling [sic] of ropes and such caulking of seams![1]

But for the city's "old merchants," there was something even more disturbing than the frenetic pace at which the city was physically transforming itself. The very nature of the mercantile profession was changing. With the expansion of trade, more and more young men were needed to fill positions in the countinghouses. But the young men entering commercial life were a different breed from the old merchants who had inhabited the compact, closely knit town where Seabury Tredwell and those of his generation had built their businesses. The new men were brash, opportunistic, and impatient. They were unwilling to spend years loyally climbing the ladder of one firm, learning every detail of the business. They didn't accept the notion that to be a merchant necessarily presumed a superior moral

---

1 Philip Hone diary, April 27, 1846.

character. And who knew what their family backgrounds were?[2]

To make matters worse, lurking among the simply crass interlopers was the truly venal figure of the confidence man. The merchants were increasingly in danger of being duped by an unscrupulous cheat. It was critical for them to know whom you could trust. One of their greatest concerns was that a confidence man would win the affections of one of their daughters—and Seabury Tredwell had six of them.[3]

The houses of the Bond Street area were fortuitously arranged in such a way that those within could easily protect themselves from unwelcome intrusions. The rowhouses of the 1830s and 1840s were four-and-a-half stories, built on a lot that was usually 25 feet wide, and 100 feet deep. There were two rooms per floor opening off of a side hall that ran the length of the house. The design was not new. In his study of the development of the New York City rowhouse, Charles Lockwood points out that the plan had evolved by the 1820s and would remain basically the same into the 1890s, with some modifications.[4]

In the Tredwells' house, there is a separate vestibule and a second, interior doorway that opens into a long narrow stair hall. Behind the stairway at the end of the hall, there is a small extension, commonly referred to as a "tea room." The stairway is lit by a window at the second-floor landing. On the first floor, two large rooms separated by sliding doors open onto the hall. The family bedrooms are on the second and third floors; the servants' quarters, on the fourth floor. The basement level, which is a half-story below ground, has its own entrance reached by a short stairway from the street. On this level, there is a kitchen and a front room opening onto the stairway hall.

This arrangement of rooms provided for a gradual and wary exposure of the home. Having climbed the high stoop and rung the bell, the caller was admitted

2 Stanley Horlick, *Country Boys and Merchant Princes* (Lewisburg: Bucknell University Press, 1975), 83–84.

3 In his novel *Washington Square*, Henry James tells the story of Catherine Sloper, who was the victim of one such fortune seeker. Catherine and her physician father were fictional neighbors of the Tredwells, having moved to a house on the north side of Washington Square the same year the flesh-and-blood Tredwells migrated uptown to a similar home just blocks away. Henry James had firsthand knowledge of the Washington Square neighborhood, for he was born just around the corner on Washington Place, and his grandmother, like the Slopers, lived on the north side of the Square.

4 Charles Lockwood, *Bricks and Brownstone: The New York Row House 1783–1929* (New York: Rizzoli International Publications, 2003), 14. See also Morrison H. Heckscher, "Building the Empire City: Architects and Architecture" in *Art and the Empire City: New York, 1825–1861*, ed. Catherine Hoover Voorsanger and John K. Howat (New York: The Metropolitan Museum of Art; New Haven: Yale University Press), 179–80.

to the unfurnished vestibule by a servant to whom she presented her visiting card. Here the walls are painted to resemble Siena marble, a fashionable treatment that hints at the elegance of the rooms within. Next the servant opened the interior vestibule door and admitted the visitor to the dimly lit enclosed hall. When the visitor was finally invited to step into the spacious front parlor, with its high ceiling and its elegant appointments, the contrast was dramatic—and impressive.

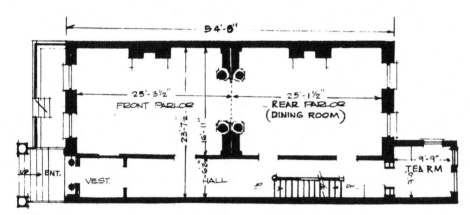

25. FLOOR PLAN OF THE PARLOR FLOOR OF THE TREDWELL HOME.
Courtesy of the Merchant's House Museum.
The floor plan was typical of the rowhouses located in the Bond Street area. The dual parlors, which could be used separately or as one large gala space, perfectly served the needs of the families who lived there.

The thick mahogany sliding doors between the front and back parlor were usually kept closed. Thus the back parlor, which was used primarily as a family sitting room, was out of view of the front parlor. The doors from the parlors leading into the hall were also kept closed, making it possible for servants and family members to move back and forth through the hall without being observed, or their low conversations heard by any visitors who were being entertained in the front parlor. The closed hall doors also made it possible for a servant to politely turn away an inconvenient or unwelcome caller, who would be unaware of what was going on in the parlor.

Because the houses were built in a contiguous row, without side windows, the rooms and halls were dark and airless, especially when interior doorways were kept closed, as they almost always were. By 1835 back stairways had been introduced into some of the new houses. Still, in many homes like the Tredwells', residents daily ran the risk of running into a servant bearing cleaning rags or a chamber bucket on the single staircase. In an attempt to explain the ways of fashionable New Yorkers to his adopted British countrymen, Charles Astor Bristed noted another particularly inconvenient aspect of the floor plan of these urban rowhouses.

> [Up] and down a steep and narrow flight of stairs, whenever the Vanderlyns give a party, every one has to tramp on entering and retiring, for all the cloaking and uncloaking must be done in the bedrooms, as there is no place for it elsewhere. Very inconvenient, you will say; but use is second nature, and the New Yorkers are so used to this climbing and swarming on the stairs, that even in a double house, or a house and a half, or a basement house, three different styles which would all admit of cloaking-rooms on the lower floor, no one ever thinks of having them there.[5]

During the first half of the nineteenth century, New Yorkers had competing impulses when it came to the decoration of their homes. On the one hand, they disdained the pursuit of fashion as being inappropriate for a republican democracy. Harriet Beecher Stowe admonished her readers to avoid pretentious and wasteful expenditures on home furnishings. *Godey's Lady's Book* constantly warned women about living beyond their means. Anna Mowatt's enormously popular 1845 play *Fashion* poked fun at a character who made a fool of herself trying to appear *au courant* and aristocratic.

On the other hand, there was a yearning on the part of many New Yorkers to be *au courant* and aristocratic. A mania for anything French had begun as early as the 1820s when some members of the upper class imported furniture from France to decorate their parlors. Many New Yorkers of means even traveled to Europe to do their shopping or appealed to their neighbors who were travelling abroad to send back everything from *etageres* to alabaster vases.

In 1844 Harriet Colles, who was just getting ready to return to the United States from Paris, received a letter from Mrs. Jaudon, a friend back home in New York City, who asked her to select a number of items from Ringuet, the famous French upholsterer.

---

5   Charles Astor Bristed, *The Upper Ten Thousand: Sketches of American Society by a New Yorker* (London: John W. Parker and Son, 1852), 35–36. There were, of course, exceptions. The Samuel Skidmore home, four doors to the east, was, like the Tredwell house, built on a twenty-five-foot wide lot, but it was deeper, with a front and back stair and three closets located at the rear of the first-floor hallway.

It seems unfair to load anyone abroad with so many commissions, and so much to attend to; but we on this side feel as if everything was so much handsomer, and better, and desirable that comes from Paris; we are selfish enough to forget the trouble we may cause our friends and add orders on orders without mercy.

If you see any pretty piece of furniture, some little fancy thing, I wish you would send it with the Buhl tables or China ornaments. Indeed, anything from Paris that is pretty would be acceptable.[6]

To an extent, the double parlors of the time enabled New Yorkers to have it both ways. The front parlor was a feeble reflection of the *salon de compagnie* based on courtly European tradition, a "gala" space reserved for the entertainment of guests. It was dominated by marble and gilt and precious objects and furniture.[7]

The back parlor, concealed behind the sliding or folding doors, was a more democratic locale: a room where the family could gather around the center table and be themselves. Here is where the old sofa ended up, where there was a certain amount of clutter: needlework in progress, what we would call "craft projects," books, and letter-writing paraphernalia. Here the merchant's secretary bookcase was often located. In 1848, when Sarah Tredwell was thirteen years old, she wrote an exercise in her copybook in which she imagined herself sitting in the back parlor writing a letter to a friend while someone in the front parlor was engaged in playing a harp. There could hardly be a better illustration of the ways the two rooms were customarily used.

However, the boundaries defining the use of the front and back parlors were flexible. The family might decide to receive good friends in the back parlor in an atmosphere of intimacy and informality. Diarists frequently made note of whether they were received in the back or front parlor. Obviously it made a difference. And while the back parlor most often offered a relaxed atmosphere, it could be transformed into a component of the gala space with a little effort. For large parties or balls, for the New Year's Day reception, for weddings, funerals, and christenings, the clutter would be cleared away and furniture, most of which was equipped with

---

6   Emily Johnston de Forest, *James Colles, 1798–1883: Life and Letters* (New York: Privately printed, 1926), 203–04.

7   The historical precedents of the drawing room or parlor are discussed by Edith Wharton and Ogden Codman Jr. in *The Decoration of Houses* (1902; reprint, New York: W.W. Norton, 1976), Chapter 10. For the history of the parlor in the United States, see Katherine C. Grier, *Culture and Comfort: Parlor Making and Middle-Class Identity, 1850–1930* (Washington: Smithsonian Institution Press, 1988).

casters, removed to the hallway, the tearoom, or the piazza (an open porch that extended across the back of many of the homes of the Bond Street area).

26. *The Tea Party.*
Henry Sargent, American (1770-1845), Oil on Canvas, c.1824, 64⅜ x 52⅜ in. Museum of Fine Arts, Boston, Gift of Mrs. Horatio Appleton Lamb in memory of Mr. and Mrs. Winthrop Sargent, 19.12

The flexibility of the back parlor is shown in this painting of a fashionable tea party in progress. Large pieces of furniture have been temporarily removed, and chairs have been arranged around the perimeter of the room to facilitate the circulation of the guests.

In the 1830s and 1840s, families also occasionally entertained at a seated formal dinner, in which case the rocking chairs, small writing tables, work tables, and other signs of family activities in the back parlor were moved out of sight. A dining table was brought in from the hall where it was normally kept and extended to accommodate guests. The Tredwell family table conveniently forms a circular center table when closed but can be converted to a dining table seating as many as fourteen by adding all seven leaves.

For many years of the Tredwells' residency, family meals were generally taken in the front room of the basement. This room, which typically served as a family dining room in the rowhouses of the time, was also used as an alternative sitting room. In a story about a newly married couple preparing to move into their new home in Philadelphia, the bride, a native New Yorker, explains to her befuddled husband that she intends to use the basement room for both sitting and dining.

> [W]e had a basement room in our house in New York, and used it constantly. . . . In Ma's family, as in hundreds of others all over New York, it is the place where we sit when we have no company, and where we always eat.[8]

John Skidmore frequently writes of spending time in the Skidmore's basement dining room of his family's home, reading, writing, pasting items in his scrap book, or napping on the sofa there; frequently he read Shakespeare aloud to his brother. Sometimes the parents joined them. The Skidmores also entertained family members and good friends in the much more informal atmosphere of the basement room:

> Spent Ev'g at home in basement (writing verses). About 8 p.m., Mr. & Mrs. Seabury Tredwell & Miss Julia called. Pa, Ma, and Jim [John's brother] saw them in the parlor. They stayed only an hour and then Jim went for Aunt C.T. & Maggie who with Tom and Sarah came to our house (9¼ p.m.) We had cake and chocolate in basement. They left about ¼ to 11 p.m.[9]

In the winter months, when the upstairs back parlor with its high ceilings was cold and uncomfortable, the family gathered in the low-ceilinged downstairs room, which was more easily warmed by the fire. Paradoxically, this same room tended to be cooler in the summer because of its location partially below ground. However, if a breeze could be coaxed through the parlors by opening the sliding doors between them, the family might prefer to use the upstairs back parlor to sew, read, or write letters in hot weather.

In the 1850s formal seated dinners became more popular, and houses were built with dumbwaiters to facilitate meal service to the parlor floor. The Tredwells installed a dumbwaiter at the top of the stairs leading to the basement, but it is not clear exactly when that feature was added. They also, probably at the same time, converted the tearoom to a butler's pantry with glass-fronted wall cabinets

---

8 "Mr. and Mrs. Woodbridge," *Godey's Lady's Book* 10 (January 1841): 3.

9 John Skidmore diary, January 29, 1858.

to hold china and glassware. These modifications have since been removed. After the dumbwaiter was in place, the Tredwells may have taken many of their meals in the back parlor/dining room, though it is likely that both this room and the basement front room continued to perform double duty as sitting/dining rooms.

Emily de Forest, who was born in the home of her grandfather, John Johnston, at Number 7 Washington Square, remembered that her grandparents

> received at times in the front parlor and at other times in the dining room, as the back parlor was called. Sometimes they dined in the dining room; at others in the front parlor, and again in the front basement room, which was their ordinary dining room.

Once Mrs. Johnston even served a large supper in two of the rooms of the second story.[10]

27. *The Ernest Fiedler Family.*
Francis Heinrich, Oil on Canvas. Courtesy of Nicholas Bruen.
The Fiedlers, who lived at 38 Bond Street, were neighbors of the Tredwell family. The painting of their parlor is a rare contemporary depiction of a New York City domestic interior of the 1850s.

---

10 Emily Johnston de Forest, *John Johnston of New York, Merchant* (New York: Privately printed, 1909), 152.

The residents of these homes also used their furniture in a variety of ways. What we think of as dining room chairs were typically bought in sets of six or twelve and arranged around the perimeter of a room to be brought up to a card table when needed, moved about to create ad hoc conversational groupings or "sets," or pressed into service as dining chairs. Such chairs provided entirely adequate parlor seating when erect posture was the genteel standard for both men and women. "Comfortable furniture" as we know it only made its appearance in the twentieth century when the parlor became the "living room," and people felt free to "lounge" in the presence of others.[11]

The same chairs and small tables that were drawn to the window during a mild winter day to take advantage of natural light might be moved to the fire at night. Even a sofa was sometimes moved from its location along the wall to a spot in front

28. THE TREDWELLS' FRONT PARLOR.
Photography by Bob Estremera.
The mid-nineteenth-century front parlors of the Bond Street area were predictably uniform in their appointments: marble mantles, plaster ceiling and cornice ornamentation, a chandelier, crystal prisms dangling from lighting devices, silken draperies, oil paintings, a pianoforte, mahogany or rosewood furniture, and a fine wool carpet.

---

11 Grier, 119.

of the fireplace. Game tables, card tables, and tea tables were set up as they were needed. Such tables were often designed with folding tops, drop leaves, or tilt tops so that they could be conveniently placed against the wall when they were not in use. Oil lamps were constantly moved around to provide light where it was wanted.

When Frances Trollope complained that the New York City homes in which she had been a guest in 1831 were all alike—"When you have seen one, you have seen all"— she may have had in mind not only the preponderance of the standard twenty-five-foot-wide brick and white marble rowhouse facades, but also the appearance of the ubiquitous double parlors within.[12] The most popular style of architecture for New York City rowhouses in the 1830s and 1840s was Greek Revival. Even houses with a Late Federal exterior, like the Tredwells', frequently had Greek Revival interiors. Freestanding Ionic columns or more modest flat pilasters enframed the folding or sliding doors of the mirror-image parlors, and ornamental plasterwork, which included cornice moldings and a center ceiling medallion, employed Greek design motifs. The Tredwell parlors serve as an impressive example of these Greek Revival interiors. The ceilings are thirteen feet high; a dramatic freestanding Ionic column screen enframes the figured-grain mahogany sliding doors. The identical fireplace surrounds are made of costly black, gold-veined marble imported from Italy. The carved marble Ionic columns support Belgian marble mantels. A false door in the front parlor balances the corresponding door to the hall in the back parlor, an example of artifice in the service of symmetry.

It is the Tredwells' ornamental plasterwork, however, that is most worthy of admiration. The ornamentation is extremely rich; the center medallions are unique survivors of the era. At a little over five feet in diameter, they are much larger than most ceiling medallions found in Greek Revival parlors. Also, rather than being flush with the ceiling as such medallions usually were, their thirty-nine-inch centers are recessed, adding depth and interest. The artisan who created the design, combining the ready-made component parts into an exuberant rhythmic guilloche surrounding the center of radiating acanthus leaves, was a master of his craft.[13]

Owners of these homes did not strive for individual expression in furnishing their parlors. They were more concerned with keeping in step with those of their social class and were not in the least embarrassed about copying their neighbors.

12　Trollope, 262.

13　David Flaharty, "The Viewpoint of a Craftsman: The Old Merchant's House Ceiling Medallions," *Cultural Resources Management* 16, no. 8 (1993), Washington, D.C.: U.S. Department of Interior, National Park Service. The author is the craftsman who was responsible for the restoration of the Tredwells' parlor ceiling medallions during the 1970s.

29. Parlor Ceiling Medallion.
Photography by David Flaharty.
The large matching plaster ceiling medallions are extraordinary examples of this type of interior architectural ornament.

In 1841, Nathaniel Parker Willis observed that

> the twenty thousand drawing rooms of New York are all stereotyped copies of one out of three of four styles.... The proprietor of almost any house in New York might wake up in thousands of other houses and not recognize for a half hour that he was not at home. He would sit on just such a sofa, in just such a recess—see a piano just so placed—just as many chairs identically in the same position.[14]

There was also an abundance of gilt-framed mirrors. The Tredwell mirrors, over nine and a half feet in height, were among the largest to be found. Silk bro-

---

14 Quoted in Charles Lockwood, *Manhattan Moves Uptown* (1976; reprint, New York: Barnes & Noble Books, 1995), 254.

cade draperies in the French fashion typically hung at the windows, imported carpeting covered the floors, and oil paintings and engravings decorated the walls. A set of three Argand oil lamps with etched glass globes and dangling crystal prisms often adorned the mantels.

The Tredwells brought some furniture with them when they moved to the Fourth Street house in 1835. The handmade sofa with paw feet and eagle wing brackets (now relegated to the basement dining room) and the sideboard in the back parlor were purchased in the 1820s when the Tredwells lived on Dey Street. The style of this furniture is variously known as Classical, Empire, or Grecian. Based on ancient Greek and Roman forms, it was large, heavy, and sculptural, emphasizing strong horizontal lines and generally made of mahogany. Up until about 1830, zoomorphic elements, especially animal feet, were common, as were gilded brass metal mounts and elaborate carving. Berry Tracy, who served as a consultant in the restoration of the Merchant's House in the 1970s, maintained that the earlier style of Federal furniture, which had been popular during the colonial period, was

> too lovely, over-wrought and precious … too fragile. What was needed was something more monumental and vital to demonstrate the force and splendor of the New Republic.[15]

The massive weight and bold shape of Grecian furniture filled the bill. Furthermore the style could be seen as a reflection of the belief that the ideals of ancient Athenian democracy had been reborn in the United States. It also demonstrated America's sympathy for the contemporary Greeks who revolted against the Ottoman Empire in the 1820s.

The matched set of twelve dining room chairs also came from the Tredwells' former home on Dey Street. They are attributed to the workshop of the famous American furniture maker, Duncan Phyfe, The height of fashion when they were purchased around 1815, these chairs represent a transitional style between the earlier Grecian furniture and later machine-made forms. Like the sideboard and the Federal sofa, they were made entirely by hand.

During the 1830s there was a dramatic change in the appearance of Empire or Grecian furniture. The new "Grecian Plain Style" still owed its design to clas-

---

15 Berry Tracy, "The Decorative Arts," *Classical America, 1815–1845, An Exhibition at the Newark Museum, April 26 through September 2, 1963*, 17.

sical forms, but now highly figured veneers replaced the hand carving, applied mounts, and gilding that had previously been used as ornament. The scrolling of the furniture and the cutting of the veneers were done by means of power saws in the saw mills on the lower East Side, and the pieces were assembled and finished by hand in the small-scale fine furniture workshops lining Broadway south of Houston Street. Furniture purchased from these shops was "bespoke," that is, made to order.[16] The Tredwells bought a number of Grecian Plain Style pieces for their new house. A Grecian Plain Style horsehair sofa and two pier tables, so-called because they are usually placed against the pier (the wall between two windows), are on display in the back parlor. The mirrored backs between the legs of these tables increased the level of lighting in the dark rooms and enhanced the size of the room as well. But they also had a stylistic purpose. By reflecting the legs, they made the table look even more massive than it was, and of course, an *objet d'art* placed on the shelf in front of the mirror would be doubled as well, making it (in a sense) twice as beautiful. Contrary to popular belief, the purpose of these mirrors was not to enable women to check for dangling petticoats.[17]

A recent microscopic paint analysis revealed that during the 1850s, after the bronze gas chandeliers were installed, a house-wide painting of the rooms was undertaken using a neutral palette throughout.

Crimson silk damask draperies woven with a pomegranate motif hung at the front parlor windows from a gilded shepherd's-crook pole, which the family had owned since the early days of their marriage. Delicate lace undercurtains completed the picture.[18] When candlelight augmented the gaslight at an evening entertainment, the parlor must have shimmered in the light reflected from the silken draperies, the polished surfaces of the figured veneers, the crystal prisms of the mantle lamps, and the gilded mirrors and picture frames.

The manufacture of American carpets was well-advanced by the 1850s, but for the parlors, the Tredwells chose an imported French carpet in a classical design that recalled the wall frescoes of the classical ruins at Herculaneum. This predominantly red and gold carpet has been reproduced exactly. Like the origi-

---

16 Elizabeth A. Ingerman, "Personal Experiences of an Old New York Cabinetmaker," *Antiques Magazine* 84 (November 1963): 576–80.

17 Dressers in the second-floor bedroom are also examples of Grecian Plain Style furniture.

18 The tassels were stolen in the 1990s when the draperies were removed and the parlor walls repainted. During the restoration of the Museum interiors in the 1970s, the restorers chose to use a reproduction of the crimson silk draperies for both the front and back parlors. It is not known what the window treatment of the back parlor windows was in the 1850s.

nal, it was woven in twenty-seven-inch strips, which were sewn together on the floor as it was laid. [19]

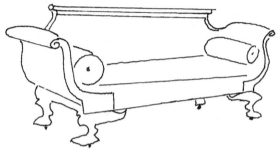

30. EMPIRE (1815-1840)

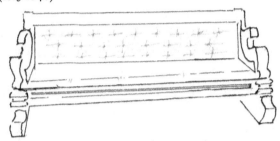

31. GRECIAN PLAIN STYLE (1830-1840)

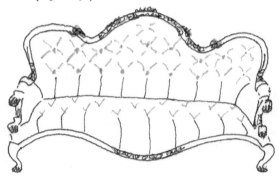

32. ROCOCO REVIVAL (1840-1870)

THREE SOFAS BELONGING TO THE TREDWELL FAMILY
Drawings by Herb Knapp

A history of furniture design is represented by three sofas purchased at different times by the Tredwell family. The most recent sofa was, of course, located in the front parlor; the older models were probably successively relegated to the back parlor and the basement family room.

19　In 1980 Berry Tracy, then Curator of the newly installed American Wing at the Metropolitan Museum of Art and a consultant for the restoration of the Merchant's House, chose to have the Tredwell carpet reproduced for the Renaissance Revival room in the American Wing, where it can still be seen today.

At some time, the Tredwells purchased a new set of furniture for the front parlor and shifted the Grecian Plain Style sofa to the back parlor. Rococo Revival ("Old French" or the styles of French furniture popular during the reigns of Louis XIV and Louis XV) had reached the peak of popularity in New York City in the 1840s. An upholstered suite of French furniture was commonly found in the parlors of the Tredwells' fashionable neighbors, and that is what is on display today in the front parlor.[20] The huge gilded pier mirrors are also in the ornate—some would say gaudy—Rococo Revival style. A large engraving of George Washington saying farewell to his generals hangs in the front hallway, demonstrating how the son of a prominent Tory embraced the new political order.[21]

---

20 The suite now on display is a gift to the Museum from the Museum of the City of New York It formerly belonged to Amos Trowbridge Dwight, a cotton merchant who lived on West Twenty-Fifth Street. Together with the Tredwell family furniture and décor, it provides an authentic representation of the formal front parlor of the New York City rowhouse of the 1850s.

21 Seabury Tredwell also owned Washington Irving's *Biography of George Washington* and a multivolume biography of the signers of the Declaration of Independence.

Lighting the Scene

When illuminating the dark meant lighting a fire of some kind, people made the most of natural daylight while it remained. During the day, women moved from one window to another with their needlework. At twilight, everyone felt a slight sense of urgency as they hurried to finish tasks before they "lost the light."

33. FIRE-SIDE PIETY.
Courtesy of Old Sturbridge Village, Sturbridge, MA.
During the evening, a single oil lamp typically illuminated the sitting room, drawing the entire family together in a circle of intimate domesticity.

When at last darkness fell, it was customary for the family to draw together at a center table around a single light source. As a consequence, families spent a lot of time in close proximity, facing each other, conversing. One member of the family, usually the father, often read aloud to the others. This may partly explain why nineteenth-century letter writers, even those with minimal formal education, were so often surprisingly fluent. Listening to a family member read aloud night after night, they could not help but unconsciously absorb the rhythm and structure of well-formed sentences. Women often knitted as they listened, for knitting, unlike fine needlework, does not require a good light.

It was difficult to move around the house after dark, so people, particularly women, tended to stay put. Climbing or descending a narrow staircase with one hand carrying a candle and the other manipulating a long skirt, a hoop, and petticoats, was not undertaken willy-nilly. Elongated shadows, grotesque companions of the night, played over the walls, stimulating the imaginations of sensitive children, whose activities were constrained because of the dark and who were put to bed early. Adults, on the other hand, were often out at all hours, calling on friends or attending evening entertainments that frequently went on until the early morning. These nineteenth-century night owls made their way along dimly lit streets. In the Bond Street neighborhood, gas street lighting began gradually replacing oil lamps in the 1830s, but even though the gaslight was brighter, the lampposts were a distant 148-and-a-half feet apart. Furthermore, until the early 1850s, the contract with the gas companies specified that streetlights were required to be lit only on nights when the moon was not expected to shine.[1] If clouds obscured the expected moonlight, the only light on many of the streets came from the bobbing red and green oil lamps mounted on the occasional carriage.[2] On a summer evening, friends might elect to sit near an open window to catch a breeze, talking by the light of a single candle or lamp or by moonlight. On the other hand, if an evening party was planned, a great many candles, as well as the gas, would be used, both upstairs and down. To be able to light one's home extravagantly was a conspicuous sign of wealth. Philip Hone observed that on the occasion of a party given by William Backhouse Astor, "The spacious mansion in Lafayette Place was open from cellar to garret, blazing with a thousand lights."[3]

Throughout the nineteenth century, people continued to use candles and oil lamps alongside gas lighting. Candles, of course, had been around for centuries.

---

1 Louis Bader, "Gas Illumination in New York City, 1823–1864" (PhD diss., New York University, 1970). For distance between lights, 190; for moonlight, 246–47.

2 James Dabney McCabe [Edward Winslow Martin], *The Secrets of the Great City: A Work Descriptive of the Virtue and Vices, the Mysteries and Crimes of New York City* (Philadelphia: Jones Brothers & Co., 1868), 47.

3 Philip Hone diary, December 16, 1846.

But by 1835 a plaited, self-consuming wick had been invented, making it unnecessary to remove the charred portion of the wick with a "snuffer" every few minutes to keep the candle from going out. By 1840 stearine or hard wax candles had become available. They were far superior to soft tallow candles that sputtered and guttered and smoked.

One of the chief advantage of candles, of course, was their portability. Their main drawback was that they did not give a very bright light. The Palmer Patent Lamp, located on the Tredwells' piano, was an ingenious effort to brighten candlelight. It was invented by William Palmer in the 1830s. The shaft of the lamp contained a three-wick "magnum candle" resting on a spring-loaded holder. As the candle was consumed by burning, the weight bearing on the spring device lessened, and the candle was gradually elevated, the flame thus being kept level with the shade. The Palmer lamp was said to last for eight hours with no need for tending, and of course the three wicks burned much brighter than that of a single candle. Three or four people could sit around a Palmer lamp, reading by its light. The use of candles diminished in the last half of the century, but there were times when they came in handy and occasions when they were felt to be more appropriate than other forms of lighting. As late as 1902, Edith Wharton and Ogden Codman were insisting that the proper light for a company drawing room was that of wax candles.

> Nothing has done more to vulgarize interior decoration than the general use of gas and of electricity in the living rooms of modern houses....
>
> The light in a gala apartment should be neither vivid nor concentrated: the soft, evenly diffused brightness of wax candles is best fitted to bring out those subtle modellings of light and shade to which old furniture and objects of art owe half their expressiveness.[4]

At the end of the eighteenth century, Ami Argand, a Swiss inventor, had introduced the Argand burner, which created a bright and steady light that burned eight to ten times brighter than a candle, revolutionizing lighting. Argand applied Lavoisier's discovery that flames were fed by oxygen to his invention. The more oxygen that could be brought to the flame, Argand reasoned, the brighter it would burn. So he created a dual-air current burner with a circular wick that

---

4 Wharton and Codman, 126–27.

was enclosed within two concentric metal tubes resting on a circular metal base with a hole in the middle. The entire burner was encased by a glass chimney. Air could thus be drawn through the hole in the base, up the inner tube to the inside of the flame and alongside the outer tube to the outside of the flame. The fuel— oil from the sperm whale—was fed to the wick by gravity from a reservoir located off to the side of the lamp and connected to it by an arm. The Argand burner was employed in every type of lighting: ceiling fixtures, street lamps, stage lighting, reading lamps, and decorative mantle lamps like those displayed on the mantle in the Tredwells' front parlor. (See Figures 8 and 72 for an overhead Argand fixture.)

 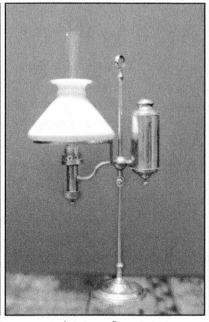 

34. SINUMBRA LAMP.
Courtesy of the Winterthur Library: Printed Book and Periodical Collection.

35. ARGAND LAMP.
Courtesy of the Merchant's House Musesum.

36. SOLAR LAMP.
Courtesy of the Smithsonian Institution Libraries, Washington, DC.

However, the early Argand lamps had two disadvantages: they were expensive to operate, for the whale oil they required was scarce, and the location of the offset reservoir cast a shadow. Over the years, inventors came up with variations of the Argand lamp in an attempt to overcome these objections. The astral and sinumbra lamps, for example, had a circular reservoir that surrounded the burner and thus largely eliminated the shadow. The solar lamp, popular in the 1840s and 1850s, was designed to burn solid fat or lard, a much cheaper alternative to the free-flowing whale oil, which became even more expensive as the whale population declined. The reservoir of the solar lamp which was in the form of an upside-down pear, surrounded the burner; the radiant heat from the burner liquefied the solid fat so that it could be drawn up by the wick. After the discovery of oil in Pennsylvania in 1859, kerosene distilled from petroleum became widely available, and because it was safe, cheap, and burned brighter and cleaner than oil, it soon became the lamp fuel of choice and remained so until the introduction of electric lighting. In a ten-month period in 1862 alone, over 600 patents for kerosene burners and lamps were granted.[5] And conversion of the older lamps to kerosene-burning lamps was a simple matter. By the end of 1862, there were between 4 and 5 million kerosene lamps in the United States.[6]

In 1832, when the Tredwell house was built, the city was already being lit with gas below Grand Street by the New York Gas-Light Company, and in 1833, the Manhattan Gas Company had received a franchise to furnish gas north of Grand. However, actually bringing gas service to all the homes in the area was a long-time effort. Whether or not a block came on line depended on how many subscribers the gas company could count on. In 1848, when the residents of Washington Square North complained to the city that they had not yet been served by street lighting, the gas company explained that there were not enough families on their block who were willing to hook up to the gas mains to warrant installing pipes on the street.[7] Yet in 1845, the Tredwells' neighbors, the Skidmores, ordered two gas mantle lamps for the new home they were building, suggesting that gas was probably being delivered to some of the Fourth Street residents at that time.[8]

But the Tredwells were not among them—not yet. They would not subscribe to gas service until 1855. At that time, they installed bronze gas chandeliers in both parlors. Counterweights made it possible to raise and lower the fixtures, bringing the light closer to the center table if more illumination was wanted there. This was also a useful feature when it came to lighting the fixture or removing the globes for cleaning. A water seal surrounding the outer sliding stem of the fixture pre-

---

5 Roger Moss, *Lighting for Historic Buildings* (Washington DC: The Preservation Press, 1988), 91.

6 Nadja Maril, *American Lighting: 1840–1940* (West Chester, PA, 1997), 23.

7 Bader, 239.

8 Carol Emily Gordon, "The Skidmore House: An Aspect of Greek Revival in New York" (master's thesis, University of Delaware, 1978), 134.

vented leakage of the gas. A gas table lamp could also be connected to the supply of gas by means of flexible tubing connected to the drop finial (seen on the fixture in the Tredwells' back parlor). Yet another way to bring gaslight to eye level was by the use of a gas reading pendant, a rigid metal tube that hooked over one of the gas tips of the gaselier, and through which gas flowed to the tip below, providing light at eye level. However, even in homes receiving gas, portable kerosene lamps continued to be used for task lighting until the gradual introduction of electricity in the 1880s and 1890s.

37. Tredwell Parlor Gaselier.
Photography by Bob Estremera.
The matching bronze gaseliers in the Tredwells' parlors were acquired in 1855 when the family signed up for gas delivery. They were electrified when the house became a museum in 1936 and were restored to their original luster in 2008.

How soon a family adopted gas lighting and how often they used it once they were connected to the gas mains depended on how compelling the advantages of gas seemed to them in comparison to its oft-noted drawbacks. Because gas came through pipes in the wall, fuel did not have to be stored and replenished, nor did the fixtures need constant attention. And gas did offer a brighter light. But gas fixtures were not portable—the gas table lamp was tethered to a ceiling or wall fixture—and some people worried about the effect of gaslight on the eyes when it was used for reading or close work.

Contemporary accounts suggest that the gaseliers in many homes were lit only when company called or for a party. But there were even reservations to the use of gas on these occasions. For one thing, women realized that they looked a lot better by candle and lamplight than they did by gaslight. There was widespread objection to gaslight being harsh and too bright, even though the light produced by a single gas burner was equivalent only to that of a ten or fifteen watt electric light bulb.[9] Thus when all six burners of the Tredwells' gaselier were lit, the fixture put forth only the equivalent of 60 to 90 watts of electricity. That this level of light was thought by many to be too bright gives some idea of just how dim the light produced by candles and oil lamps was. Another objection to gaslight was that it distorted the perception of color. The gorgeous purple satin gown that could be counted on to glow at a candlelit ball appeared to be an insipid grey under gaslight.

Also, the gas supply was often unreliable. For this reason, Philip Hone deemed gas inappropriate for use in private homes (a view shared by many, including Edgar Allen Poe). Hone had once been at a dance in a crowded private home when a drop in the gas pressure caused all the lights to go out.[10] And when the gaseliers were lit, they created a substantial amount of heat—a serious disadvantage during the hot summer months. If all that weren't enough, gas was thought to be detrimental to health because of the impurity of the air it created. Sometimes fixtures leaked, leaving a noxious odor of sulfur. And even when they did not leak, the combustion of gas was believed to create a debilitating atmosphere. On occasion, unaware sleepers had been known to be asphyxiated when a gas light left burning was accidentally extinguished. Many people therefore chose not to have gaslight in their bed chambers. Dr. Dio Lewis, a widely read author of books and pamphlets advocating healthy living, attributed low vitality and disease to the breathing of air that was depleted of oxygen. He particularly condemned

---

9 Moss, 103.

10 Philip Hone diary, December 30, 1836; Edgar Allan Poe, "Philosophy of Furniture," *The Magazine Antiques* 112 (August 1977): 285.

unventilated parlors, with gas burners (each consuming as much oxygen as several men) made as tight as possible, and a party of ladies and gentlemen spending half the night in them![11]

An advantage of the recessed ceiling medallions in the Tredwell parlors was that they provided an open area among the joists where the smoke and fumes from the lit gaseliers could be carried off to a degree.

People also had reservations about gaslight in their homes because they associated it with the lighting of public streets and theaters and the low-life activities that were carried on in those places. In contrast, the traditional center table lamp surrounded by the unbroken family circle was a powerful symbol of domestic security, one that was not easily given up.

In the mid-1880s, with the mass production of electric light bulbs, it became possible to light up a room with just the touch of a finger. However, the transition to lighting with electricity took place gradually.[12] For a time, gas jets and electric bulbs were to be found on the same fixture. Since electric lamps were necessarily connected to wall outlets, the center table with its lamp eventually disappeared, and sofas and chairs, to be near the light source, hugged the wall. Family members were easily able to disperse in the evening, privately pursuing their own interests, if they wished. And what had been one of the most time-consuming and arduous household tasks—maintaining the lights—had been eliminated. Instead of the daily task of scraping wax from candlesticks, filling lamps with kerosene, trimming and replacing wicks, and cleaning soot from glass globes, all that was needed was the occasional replacing of a light bulb. However, the Tredwell sisters who were still living in the house at the end of the nineteenth century did not embrace this extraordinary innovation. Gertrude Tredwell installed a few electric fixtures and outlets in the twentieth century, but the house was not fully wired for electricity until it became a museum in 1936.

---

11 Dr. Lewis's remark is quoted in Catherine Beecher and Harriet Beecher Stowe, *American Woman's Home* (1869; reprint, Hartford: The Stowe-Day Foundation, 1994), 55. Dr. Lewis was the founder of the Women's Christian Temperance Union and an early advocate of physical education.

12 As late as 1945, the East Thirty-Fifth Street police precinct house in New York City was lit by gas. Jan Morris, Manhattan: 1945 (Baltimore: The Johns Hopkins University Press), 72–73.

5

Looking the Part: Fashion

In the fall of 1800 Seabury Tredwell's father paid Thomas Wheeler, an itinerant tailor, five shillings to make Seabury a pair of pantaloons. These tight-fitting long pants, a forerunner of trousers, were gradually replacing knee breeches among fashionable city gentlemen. Although Seabury had been in the city for two years, he was still somewhat under his father's wing, and his wardrobe frequently benefited from his father's generosity and from the skill of the country tailor.

At the turn of the century, all men's clothing, like Seabury's pantaloons, was made to order, but after the War of 1812 and the reopening of trade with Great Britain in 1815, a gradual change occurred in the way men acquired their wardrobes. Enterprising tailors and non-tailors alike took advantage of the opportunity to purchase "dumped" English textiles at low cost and began offering a variety of garments for men. Sometimes these garments were made-to-measure; sometimes they were ready-made. In any case, they were not a product of the artisanal tailor who did all the measuring and cutting and stitching himself but of a bevy of hired cutters and sewers working for a merchant-clothier.[1]

By midcentury, New York City was a cauldron of consumption, and the men's clothing industry was at the center of it. There were over a thousand establishments regularly listed in the city's business directories where men could buy a suit. One of these, D. Devlin, boasted that "near 2000 hands!!" were engaged in producing the coats he sold.[2]

---

1 Micheal Zakim, *Ready-Made Democracy: A History of Men's Dress in the American Republic, 1760–1860* (Chicago: University of Chicago Press, 2003), 41–44.

2 Ibid., 105, 101.

In 1857 what turned out to be the most enduring men's clothier of all opened its doors in a new four-story building at Broadway and Grand Street. The four sons of Henry Brooks, three of whom were among the city's wealthiest citizens, had been doing business at their father's store near the East River waterfront at Catharine and Cherry Streets. The Brooks brothers' new store boasted a gorgeous black walnut interior punctuated by scores of six-by-twelve-foot mirrors and interior columns with golden capitals. A broad staircase led to a decorated rotunda. Here New York's gentlemen could buy coats, vests, shirts, and pantaloons ready-made or made-to-measure.

In the wake of such a superfluity of new clothes, it became socially unacceptable to wear old ones. Time was when men instructed their tailors to "turn" their coats—that is, pick out the stitching, turn the garment inside out and restitch it—so that the worn fabric would then be on the inside and out of sight. Now only new would do. One authority on politeness and fashion warned readers that the man who failed to update his wardrobe risked being pointed out as "a sample of old times."[3]

The style of men's clothing actually did not change very dramatically during the three decades that Seabury lived on Fourth Street. Once eighteenth-century knee breeches and silk stockings had been discarded in favor of the slimmer pared-down silhouette of frock coat, pantaloons, waistcoat and shirt for daywear, men's fashions maintained a relative conservative sameness. Except for colorful patterned waistcoats, particularly popular during the 1840s, suit colors were typically dark and somber and any changes in the cut were subtle. Then in the late forties, an alternative style of jacket became available for men's daywear. The sack coat, or office jacket was introduced at about the same time that the "counting-house" was being replaced by the "office." When paired with matching pants and waistcoat, it foreshadowed the business suit of today. The sack coat was lighter than the frock coat; the sleeves were somewhat baggy at the elbows and looser at the wrists, and the shoulders boxier. At the same time, pants for daywear became looser, and soft hats were introduced, although top hats continued to be worn throughout the century. Another lasting innovation of the 1850s was the introduction of the fly to replace the fall front of men's trousers.[4]

---

3 Henry Lunettes, *The American Gentleman's Guide to Politeness and Fashion* (New York: Derby & Jackson, 1857), quoted in Zakim, 108.

4 Vanda Foster, *A Visual History of Costume: The Nineteenth Century* (1984; reprint, New York: Drama Book Publishers, 1986), 15; Zakim, 109.

**38. SEABURY TREDWELL
C. 1860.**

*Courtesy of the Merchant's House
Museum.*

This photograph of the
elderly Seabury Tredwell
shows him dressed in his best
for the photographer. The
white cravat he is wearing
had passed out of fashion
years earlier, and if you look
closely, you can see that he
is still wearing his hair in an
old-fashioned queue.

In the 1860s, when Henry Van Wyck left for the market on his way to work,
his son remembered that he was

> dressed in a broadcloth, single-breasted frock coat, double-breasted
> black satin vest, white shirt and black silk stock, black broadcloth pan-
> taloons, patent leather button shoes and silk top hat, carrying a cane
> and gloves. Then … walking from the Square to his office, he took off

his coat and put on an office coat, as it was called in those days, and sat in his chair.[5]

39. PARIS, NEW YORK AND PHILADELPHIA FASHIONS FOR SPRING AND SUMMER, 1854.
Courtesy of the Library of Congress.
The frock coat persevered as the standard fashion for men for decades. However, in the 1850s, some men, like the gentleman at the lower right of the drawing, began wearing the recently introduced sack coat for office wear.

Women's fashion participated only minimally in the development of the ready-made clothing industry before the Civil War. Women's outer garments such as cloaks and shawls as well as hoop skirts and caps could be purchased ready-made by 1860, but fashionable dresses and many articles of underwear were still being custom-made well into the twentieth century. Frequent changes in the style of women's fashion kept dressmakers busy.

5   Van Wyck, 122.

The Merchant's House collection of costumes includes forty dresses known to have been worn by the Tredwell women. They demonstrate how one family conformed to the changing silhouette of fashion during the nineteenth century. The earliest dress in the collection is a white cotton dress that belonged to Eliza Tredwell and is believed to be her 1820 wedding dress. It is typical of the classical style that had been popular since the early 1800s. Based on the costume of the ancient Greeks and Romans, these dresses consisted of a narrow column or a drape of fabric falling from a high empire waist. They were often white, made of a thin muslin or cambric. The fashion did not require bulky undergarments, although some women found it necessary to wear an uncomfortably long corset to mold the body into a long, slender shape.[6]

40. Eliza Tredwell's Wedding Dress, 1820.

Courtesy of the Merchant's House Museum.

The cream-colored cotton dress with fitted Empire-style bodice was typical of the classic Grecian style popular in the first quarter of the nineteenth century. Eliza's gown, while simple in line, is decorated at the hem with a wide, cream-colored floral border of tambour embroidery.

6   Foster, 12.

41. Evening Dress, 1830s.
Courtesy of the Library of Congress.
A typical evening dress of the
1830s presented a distinct contrast
to the simple Grecian lines of the
previous period as well as to the
drooping sentimental look that
was to follow.

By the time the Tredwells moved uptown in 1835, fashion had morphed from
the classic simplicity of the Grecian-inspired dresses of the first two decades of
the century into the complexity of what fashion historians call the romantic period. The waist returned to its natural level and was narrowed by a tightly laced
corset. During this period, wider, fuller skirts, supported by several petticoats,
rose to just above-ankle length. Wider shoulders balanced the skirt, and at various times, sleeves ballooned above, below, and at the elbow. To complete this
fussy look, women wore crazy hats and bonnets, adopted complicated hairdos,
and adorned themselves with feathers, ribbons, flowers, and tinkly chains, ear-
rings, and charms.

By 1840, this overly ornamented style had been replaced by a drooping, languid
silhouette. Hemlines dropped to the floor, and women pulled their laces a little

42. FASHION PLATE FROM GODEY'S MAGAZINE, AUGUST 1841.
Reprinted in Fashions and Costumes from Godey's Lady's Book, *ed. Stella Blum. Dover Publications, 1985.*
The long pointed waist, the voluminous floor-length skirt, and the low shoulders are typical of the simple sentimental style of the 1840s. The hair was parted in the middle, drawn to the back of the head and sometimes styled with ringlets in front.

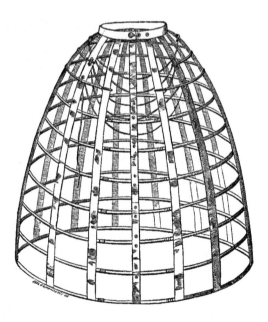

43. DOUGLAS AND SHERWOOD'S NEW EXPANSION SKIRT.
Reprinted in Fashions and Costumes from Godey's Lady's Book, *ed. Stella Blum. Dover Publications, 1985.*
The cage crinoline, introduced in 1856, was a welcome device that liberated women from the burden of multiple petticoats.

tighter under a bodice that came to a point below the waist. To provide the support needed by the bell-shaped skirt, women wore as many as six petticoats. Typically one of the petticoats had a whalebone hoop sewn in or was stiffened with horsehair. Women abandoned most of their jewelry and adopted sleek hair styles, with a part in the middle and the hair drawn to the back. Gradually, the pointed bodice shrank in length, and to balance the ever-increasing fullness of the skirt, sleeves became full and loose, and detachable undersleeves, often with lace trimming, made their appearance.[7]

Skirts had just about reached an unsustainable fullness when in 1856, a collapsible steel frame contraption called a "cage crinoline" was invented by W.S. Thomson. This invention consisted of several hoops of steel increasing in diameter from the hip to the ankle, held together by fabric tapes. The cage crinoline provided a strong foundation for the voluminous skirts and made it possible for women to discard most of their petticoats without compromising their desire to be fashionable. One petticoat worn over the crinoline to soften the steel ridges, and perhaps one flannel petticoat underneath the crinoline for warmth, was all that was needed. Women were now mercifully freed from carrying around pounds of weight in the form of voluminous undergarments.

However, the crinoline did present some difficulties. One had to take care to hike up the hoop in the back a bit before sitting or the entire front would whoop up, exposing the underdrawers that women were now wearing. A sudden gust of wind could result in the same unfortunate exposure. Women also had to learn to judge their distance so that they did not knock over delicate objects or get too close to the fire. The simple act of walking required a somewhat new technique. Gentlemen found the increased amount of space women took up in theaters, omnibuses, and churches annoying, and the crinoline was often the subject of humor and ridicule.[8] However, once a fashionable woman became accustomed to the demands of the new underpinning, she cut an attractive and seductive figure: a curvaceous torso floating over an undulating ocean of fabric.

In the late 1850s, the introduction of aniline dyes, obtained from coal tars, made it possible to produce vibrantly colored silks. Brilliant deep blue and purple

---

7 Karen Halttunen, *Confidence Men and Painted Women* (New Haven, Yale University Press, 1982), 73-80.

8 Men might not have liked the steel crinolines, but young boys did. Edward Hewitt, Peter Cooper's grandson, used to ransack the ash cans with his friends, looking for discarded hoops, which provided fine flat steel wire for their youthful experiments. Edward Hewitt, *Those Were the Days* (New York: Duell, Sloan and Pearce, 1943), 11.

and green and fuchsia gowns were in marked contrast to the pale tints that were characteristic of the earlier period.

A woman who wanted a new dress often selected a style she liked from the pages of one of the popular magazines that published tinted engravings of the latest fashions.[9] Then off she went in search of just the right fabric. A frequent destination for such a quest was A.T. Stewart's Department Store. Established in 1846 at Chambers and Reade, Stewart's was the first of the marble palaces that defined the quintessential shopping experience of the pre-Civil War years. The *New York Herald* called it "the most splendid dry goods store in the world."[10] Customers entering Stewart's for the first time were awestruck by the vast circular hall that opened up before them beyond an arch supported by Italian marble columns. The walls and ceiling were decorated with fresco paintings, and a massive rotunda, a feature that was to become characteristic of stylish retail establishments, rose ninety feet above the ground. Daylight from a skylight in the rotunda streamed over the polished mahogany counters and was reflected by floor-to-ceiling mirrors on the wall opposite the entrance. On opening day, a hundred male clerks stood at the ready.

The impressive interior was an appropriate setting for the merchandise Stewart offered. As the circumference of women's skirts increased, it took more and more fabric to make them. Not surprisingly, textiles comprised the largest category of imports by far,[11] and A.T. Stewart, who managed his own importing, scoured the European markets to secure a wide variety of fabrics and laces of the finest quality for his customers.[12]

Women could order gowns custom-made in Stewart's workrooms, choosing a style from sample gowns on display. More often, women turned over the fabric and trimmings they had purchased to a dressmaker or "mantua maker." The dressmaker who had reached the top of her profession had her own shop where she employed a number of seamstresses and where she displayed models of the latest Parisian

---

9 *Godey's Lady's Book* was the most popular fashion magazine of the nineteenth century. Fashion plates could also be found in *The Columbian Magazine, Graham's American Monthly Magazine of Literature, Art, and Fashion, Frank Leslie's Ladies' Gazette,* and *Peterson's Magazine.*

10 September 18, 1846.

11 Robert Greenhalgh Albion, *The Rise of New York Port [1815–1860]* (1939; reprint, Boston: Northeastern University Press, 1984), 56–60.

12 Harry E. Resseguie, "A.T. Stewart's Marble Palace—the Cradle of the Department Store," *New-York Historical Society Quarterly* 48 (April 1964): 150. .

44. JULIA TREDWELL IN A STUDIO PORTRAIT TAKEN AROUND 1860.
Courtesy of the Merchant's House Museum.

The bell shaped skirt of Julia's dress is typical of women's fashions during the late 1850s and 60s. Note the telltale appearance of the steel rib of the cage crinoline that supports the skirt. The wide pagoda sleeves and the lace undersleeves complete the fashionable look of this period.

fashions. A very common practice, however, was to employ a dressmaker who came to live with the family while she sewed new dresses for the coming season and remodeled old ones. The more women in the family, of course, the longer she stayed. The charge for making a dress was around three dollars, more in the fashionable shops. Using the illustration as a guide, the dressmaker proceeded either by making her own flat pattern, using her customer's measurements and her own drafting skills, or by draping the fabric directly on the customer's body. Until the 1850s dresses were stitched by hand, and while the demanding fitted bodice was stitched by the dressmaker, the customer, working along with her dressmaker at home, might well stitch the long straight seams and hem of the skirt, a laborious time-consuming task greatly simplified by the coming of the sewing machine[13]

Elias Howe was the first American to invent a workable sewing machine. Soon after he patented his machine in 1846, other inventors followed suit with similar models. However, it was not until 1851 that a commercially successful machine, invented by Isaac Singer, was mass-produced. Singer's machine had a great advantage over others in that it employed a foot treadle rather than a hand crank, permitting the operator to use both hands to feed and manipulate the fabric as she sewed. Soon sewing machine treadles began to rattle away in homes and in the shops and workrooms of dressmakers and clothing manufacturers.

Until the latter half of the nineteenth century, when clothes hangers came into popular use, both men's and women's garments were either hung on pegs or folded. In the Tredwell house, storage space for folded garments was provided by the deep shelves and drawers of the built-in cupboards between the bedrooms on each floor and by the sliding shelves of an armoire. Overflow clothing and out-of-season garments were stored in chests of drawers or trunks in one of the dormer rooms on the fourth floor. A closet in the second-floor hallway was probably used for the storage of outer garments, and some outer garments were hung on open pegs in the ground floor hallway.

Women's undergarments included first of all the underdrawers, the crotch seam of which was left open to facilitate the wearer's use of the commode or privy. Next came a chemise, a loose garment like a slip made of soft muslin or linen, followed

---

13　Typically, dresses were made in two pieces, the skirt and the bodice or waist. In the 1850s the basque waist was the most stylish cut, dropping to a "V" falling below the waistline in the center. The charge for a basque waist from a fashionable shop was $4.75. To the charge for the waist, one needed to add the cost of fabricating the skirt and the cost of the fabric, buttons, and trimmings. *Godey's Lady's Book* (June 1854): 572. Mary Ann Wheeler, a dressmaker located at 29 Jones (later Great Jones) Street, charged $3.00 to make a silk dress. *Dressmaker's Account Book*, 1854, Manuscript Division (New York: New-York Historical Society).

by a more or less tightly laced corset, and finally the petticoats or the cage crino-line, and a petticoat topper. Stockings made of silk or cotton or wool, depending on the occasion and the weather, were held up by garters, which might be elastic bands, tied ribbons or an expandable woolen strip, knit with a garter stitch.

The corset was necessary to create the body shape required by the current fashion, its shape and length varying with the styles of the time. Corset-wearing, however, was not just a matter of fashion. Many people believed that females need-ed the extra support that corsets provided. Virtually all middle-and-upper-class women wore them. Special corsets were designed for pregnant women and for nursing mothers, and some women even slept in their "night stays." Little girls of three and four were put into children's corsets. When they reached adolescence, they were fitted with something like an adult corset, which compressed the waist and pushed up the breasts as it smoothed and shaped the entire torso.[14]

Some physicians, dress reformers, and commonsense advisers condemned the wearing of corsets altogether, blaming them for everything from bad breath, pimples, and constipation, to cancer, consumption, curvature of the spine, and insanity. One authority predicted that if fashions did not change, women's inter-nal organs would be so damaged that they would bear an increasing number of idiots, and the whole European race would be extinguished within two or three centuries![15]

More moderate authorities limited their criticism to the minority of women who were known as "tight lacers." According to Valerie Steele, who has made a study of corset-wearing throughout the centuries, many women laced two to three inches smaller than their natural waistlines, but others cinched their corsets as tightly as they could, achieving a reduction of their waistlines by four, five, or six inches. Most women laced more or less tightly, depending on the circumstanc-es.[16] Fashion plates of the time tend to be misleading for they would have us be-lieve that laced waistlines were typically no wider than a handspan, but there is a limit to the extent soft tissue and rib bones can be constricted by lacing. In spite of horror stories to the contrary, there is no evidence of anyone ever having ribs surgically removed to reduce her waist measurement. [17]

Still, while the extent of "tight lacing" is sometimes exaggerated, and while

---

14 For a history of corset-wearing and its social implications, see Valerie Steele, *The Corset: A Cultural History* (New Haven: Yale University Press, 2001).

15 William Sullivan, LLD, quoted in William A. Alcott, *Tight Lacing* (Boston: George W. Light, 1840), 22.

16 Steele, 103.

17 Ibid., 73.

some critics of corsets grossly overstated the medical consequences of any lacing, it was not a healthy practice. At the very least, women developed the bad habit of shallow breathing, since they could hardly draw a deep breath when laced. (It is no wonder that women in nineteenth-century novels are always fainting.) And wearing a corset so weakened abdominal and back muscles that after awhile, a woman who regularly wore a corset really did need its support in order to stand or sit comfortably. But defying both judicious advice and dire warnings, most women continued to consider the corset, in one form or another, an indispensable article of clothing well into the twentieth century.

6

Looking the Part: Health & Beauty

The ideal beauty of the antebellum era was a woman with pale skin, faintly flushed cheeks, bright eyes, and a delicate demeanor. It was hardly a picture of robust health and vigor. It was, in fact, the fragile look of a woman afflicted with tuberculosis. Nevertheless, those who offered beauty advice in manuals and women's magazines insisted that true beauty came from healthful living. They emphasized the need for cleanliness, early rising, adequate sleep, regular exercise, good hygiene, and a positive mental state.

By midcentury, cleanliness had become associated with gentility. Looking clean and smelling relatively good were major concerns of both men and women. And the popularity of water therapy as a cure for illness, "hydropathy" as it was called, served to connect the idea of cleanliness with health as well. Starched, snow-white petticoats, collars, undersleeves, and clean gloves and stockings were requisites for a fashionably dressed woman, and men's removable shirt collars made it easier for a man to appear well-scrubbed. At least he could have a clean collar even if his shirt was not washed after every wearing. It was important that hands, neck, and nails be clean, the nails neatly pared and, in the case of women, buffed until they appeared a delicate shade of pink.

The anonymous author of *The Habits of Good Society* (1860) acknowledged that "our great-grandmothers were not rigid in points of personal cleanliness,"[1] but times had changed, and by 1850 those of the Tredwells' social class bathed regularly. That is not to say that they necessarily got wet all over all at once or even

---

1   *Habits of Good Society* (New York: Rudd & Carleton, 1860), 127.

that they washed every part of their body every day. And they may or may not have used soap. While harsh laundry soap had been around for some time, toilet soap only gradually came into widespread use after midcentury. Until then, gentle soap, perfumed and wrapped in layers of tissue, tinfoil and glazed paper, was considered a cosmetic.[2] Rubbing with a rough towel after rinsing was standard practice, thought to cleanse the skin sufficiently.

Bathing took place in the bedroom where there was a washstand, a towel rack, and a matching china bathing set that included a basin, a ewer or pitcher, a slop jar for receiving dirty water, and perhaps a chamber pot, a toothbrush holder, and a soap dish. An occasional more elaborate procedure might involve a portable tin tub, or a tub on casters, which a servant filled with water, maybe hot, maybe not. Some people felt that bathing in cold water was desirable in order to stimulate circulation of the blood.

Another option was a trip to a commercial bathhouse. Since the latter part of the eighteenth century, commercial bathhouses had offered the opportunity to bathe in pools or tubs or to take a shower bath. Some bathhouses offered vapor (or steam) baths, and some provided additional services such as hairdressing and laundry facilities. The fancier (and more costly) establishments often included such amenities as a teahouse or a reading room. An article in the *New York Enquirer* of May 19, 1827, described one of these establishments, the Arcade Baths, which had recently opened in a three-story building on the north side of Chambers Street in back of City Hall:

> The building is 50 feet front, and 151 feet in depth.... The proprietor, Mr. Tylee, has erected 50 bathing rooms, many of them furnished with tubs of Italian marble, and all lighted with gas. The Arcade, or hall, which has an elegant appearance, runs thro' the gentlemen's baths. The ladies' baths are entirely separate—the entrance is by a separate door, and a furnished parlour is connected with them. The second story ... is appropriated for a reading room, where all the city papers will be found.

On the third floor, the National Academy of Design was then presenting its second exhibition, which included the landscapes of the emerging artist, Thomas

---

2   Richard L. Bushman and Claudia L. Bushman, "The Early History of Cleanliness in America," *The Journal of American History* 74 (March 1988): 1234–36.

Cole. Seven years later, in 1833, the Arcade Baths was expanded to accommodate eighty persons.[3]

45. THE CROTON RESERVOIR, 1842.
Author's Collection.

The distributing reservoir, erected at Forty-Second Street and Fifth Avenue, was part of the system that brought clean water to New York City. Water was piped for forty-one miles from the Croton Dam upstate to the receiving reservoir in what is now Central Park to the Croton Reservoir, from which water was piped to residents' homes. The New York City Public Library now occupies the site.

In 1842, with the opening of the Croton Reservoir at Forty-Second Street and Fifth Avenue, municipal water came at last to New York City. Free water was soon available from street hydrants; private service cost ten dollars a year for a two-story house or twelve dollars for a three-story house like the Tredwells'.[4] A few wealthy New Yorkers immediately arranged to hook up their homes to Croton water, but most people were in no hurry to sign up. With rainwater from the back-yard cistern available from a pump in the kitchen sink, with servants to carry it upstairs for bathing, and with the wherewithal to buy carted water from up island streams for drinking, the Tredwells evidently felt no pressing need for city water.

By the mid-1840s most new housing in New York City included running water and bathrooms,[5] and with the building of a proper city sewer system in the

---

3 *New-York Daily Advertiser*, April 24, 1833.

4 *New York Evening Post*, September 28, 1842.

5 Lockwood, *Manhattan Moves Uptown*, 187.

1850s, the bathroom became a more or less standard amenity for the middle and upper classes.[6] "Bathrooms," however, did not necessarily include a lavatory or sink. The beautiful new homes built in the fifties on Fifth Avenue located the sink in dressing rooms off the bedrooms.[7] Many owners of older homes installed tubs and water closets wherever they could fit them in, but a washstand and basin in the bedroom continued to be used for personal washing between tub baths. Eventually, the Tredwells installed a flush toilet in an enclosure under the second-floor stair and a tub in the pass through closet,[8] but it is likely that they continued to use their china basins and washstands in the bedrooms.

Once running water in homes became available, it was much easier to keep clean, of course, and standards of personal hygiene rose. However, with no deodorant available, indoor temperatures stifling in the summer months, and layers of clothing not necessarily washed after every wearing, people's tolerance for body odor must have been very high.

Not all writers who offered personal advice on health and beauty to women discussed habits of elimination, but the subject comes up often enough to suggest that it was a matter of concern. Before the availability of indoor flush toilets, women used their chamber pots for urination only and sometimes postponed their visits to the privy to a point that was injurious to their health. Freezing temperatures, snow drifts, and summer rainstorms often made a trip outdoors to the back of the garden very difficult, and there is no doubt that the atmosphere inside the privy was particularly brutal in the sweltering summer heat. In 1880 James Bayles, an authority on house drainage, minced no words in describing the privy, even then a reality of rural life.

> I know of nothing more disgusting to sight and smell, more nauseating
> to the stomach or more dangerous to health, than the typical country
> privy, with its quivering reeking stalagmite of excrement under each
> seat, resting on a bed of filth indescribable.[9]

---

6 Before the introduction of the city sewer system, homeowners with indoor plumbing drained water into their privies or the storm sewers. Neither was a satisfactory arrangement. The privies often overflowed because they were not able to handle the amount of water being flushed into them, and the storm sewers, which had not been constructed to handle solid waste, became clogged.

7 Lockwood, *Manhattan Moves Uptown*, 189.

8 These modern conveniences were removed in 1935 when the Tredwell house was turned into a museum.

9 James C. Bayles, *House Drainage and Water Service in Cities, Villages and Rural Neighborhoods* (New York: David Williams, 1880), 267.

But as offensive as the privy was, a misguided sense of gentility about their person may have accounted for women's delayed visits as much as anything.[10] Mrs. Farrar, a popular author of advice manuals, allows as much when she takes up the subject in *The Young Lady's Friend*:

> I cannot dismiss this part of my subject without a few observations on the importance of a daily evacuation of the bowels. The practice of taking medicine to effect this should be avoided; but no pains should be spared in regulating the diet and exercise, so as to obtain it ... knowing how carelessly most young persons treat the subject, and that some even consider it a piece of refinement and a privilege not to pay daily attention to this function of the body, I feel it incumbent upon me to point out the evil consequences of such a course.[11]

The "consequences," according to Mrs. Farrar, included pimples and bad breath, risks no young woman of refinement would want to take.

Bad breath, however, was most often attributed to poor dental hygiene, and regular brushing was recommended, not only to sweeten the breath but to prevent the build up of tartar, which, it was understood, could result in tooth loss. The pages of *Godey's Lady's Book* were frequently devoted to recipes for homemade tooth powders, although commercial powders were also available. Some of the most commonly used ingredients in the homemade preparations included powdered charcoal or cuttlefish bone, precipitated chalk, orris root, and starch. None of the mixtures could have been very palatable, and they may not have been very effective. An article in *Godey's* warned that there were particular objections to the use of charcoal.

> It is too hard and resisting, its color is objectionable, and it is perfectly insoluble by saliva; it is apt to become lodged between the teeth, and there to collect decomposing animal and vegetable matter around such particles as may be fixed in this position.[12]

---

10 George Waring, quoted in David P. Handlin, *The American Home: Architecture and Society, 1815–1915* (Boston: Little, Brown and Company, 1979), 459–60; See also Bayles, 268.

11 Mrs. John Farrar, *The Young Lady's Friend* (Boston: American Stationers Company, 1838), 196–97.

12 *Godey's Lady's Book*, 58 (October 1858): 366.

Not a pretty sight.

Unfortunately, no amount of brushing could remove the damage done by the frequent ingestion of calomel, an oft-prescribed medication that caused excessive salivation, which injured tooth enamel and caused permanent discoloration of the teeth. No one ever smiles in the photographic portraits of the period, made possible by the invention of the Daguerreotype camera in 1839. It would have been next to impossible considering the long exposure demanded by those early cameras, but we can be sure that when the subjects of these portraits did smile, many of them revealed crooked, damaged, or missing teeth.

Dentistry was primitive and painful. One of the first entries in Edward Tailer's diary recounts the occasion when in June of 1848, as a youth of 16, he was taken by his mother to the dentist. He had six cavities filled; it took the dentist five-and-a-half hours and cost twelve dollars. The drills used at the time were hand cranked and slow, with a speed of approximately fifteen revolutions per minute. (By way of comparison, modern dental drills powered by turbine engines can reach speeds of 800,000 RPM). After the cavity was fully opened by the drill, the dentist used tools called "excavators" to scrape out the decay. Filling materials included gold foil, tin, and gutta percha, a latex substance introduced in 1842. Edward visited the dentist fairly often after his visit in 1848, but perhaps significantly, he never went to the same one twice.[13]

Hair care relied heavily on the hairbrush. Lola Montez, author of a widely read 1858 advice book and herself a great beauty, recommended ten minutes brushing, two, three, or even four times a day.[14] Washing long hair was a major undertaking, particularly before the introduction of running water. However, it was generally felt that it was not so much the hair that needed frequent washing but just the scalp, which may have made the job somewhat easier, even if it did not make the hair cleaner. Alcohol-based hair washes were sometimes relied upon to remove the perfumed pomades or hair oils that were then popular. *Godey's Lady's Book* offered a recipe for one such pomade, which was said to ward off gray hair. It consisted of four ounces of hog's lard, four drams of spermaceti (the oil from the

---

13 Edward Tailer diary, June 16, 1848, Manuscript Division (New York: New-York Historical Society).

14 *The Arts of Beauty or Secrets of a Lady's Toilet* (1858; reprint, New York: Ecco Press, 1978), 65. Lola Montez was a Spanish dancer, a sensation in Europe during the 1830s and 1840s. She had many lovers, including Franz Liszt and Ludwig I. When Ludwig was forced to abdicate in 1848, Lola Montez came to America, where she finally ended up in New York City. There she was recognized as an authority on fashion and beauty and gave well-attended lectures on these subjects. She died in 1861 and is buried in Greenwood Cemetery in Brooklyn.

46. A TREDWELL SISTER, C. 1860.
Courtesy of the Merchant's House Museum.

One of the Tredwell sisters (probably Julia) reveals hair that had not been cut for years. It is likely that the photograph was taken to commemorate her appearance as the Biblical Ruth in a tableau or parlor theatrical.

sperm whale), and four drams of bismuth, (an alkaline metallic powder) to which perfume could be added if desired. The mixture was to be applied whenever the hair required dressing.[15] For washing the hair, some advisers recommended cold water only—no soap; others recommended castile soap and water.

Curls framing the face could be achieved by means of a curling iron heated over a candle flame or with "curling papers" or *papillotes*. These were homemade triangles of paper shaped "like the corner of a handkerchief." A tress of hair was placed over the paper with the ends of the hair over the point of the triangle. Both hair and paper were then rolled up together and the corners of the paper were twisted tight over the curl. This was easier said than done. Yet many women slept in these papers. In 1859 a metal curler clasp was invented that was easier to use but less comfortable to sleep in. At night women typically braided their long back hair in a loose single pigtail to keep it from tangling during sleep.

Women who had superfluous hair above their lips or on their arms or chins or who had unattractive bushy eyebrows could, of course, resort to plucking or shaving (with a straight razor) or cutting with scissors, but they could also buy depilatories at the druggist's, and there were numerous suggestions for caustic homemade preparations that would do the job, painful though their application and removal might have been.[16]

In addition to homemade dentifrices and hair pomades, face washes, perfumed lotions, pastes, and salves were often prepared by women at home with ingredients purchased at the druggist's. Advisers warned against the use of poisonous substances like lead, prussic acid, corrosive sublimate, and caustic potash, but since there were no laws regulating their sale, they sometimes found their way to dressing tables.[17] Women were also warned about the eating of harmful substances for cosmetic purposes, for example the ingestion of chalk to whiten the skin and arsenic to brighten the eyes. It is not clear just how prevalent these bizarre practices were. But then, as now, the prospect of becoming more beautiful was a powerful incentive.

---

15 *Godey's Lady's Book*, 59 (October 1859): 338.

16 Virginia Mescher, an adviser to Civil War reenactors, combed contemporary sources offering beauty advice on the use of cosmetics and recipes for homemade preparations. Her study, *Powdered, Painted, and Perfumed: Cosmetics of the Civil War Period and Their Historic Context* (Burke, Virginia: Vintage Volumes, 2003) is available from www.vintagevolumes.com. Mescher found no mention of the need to remove hair under the arms or on the legs in the sources she surveyed.

17 Ibid., 240.

47. MARY ADELAIDE TREDWELL, C. 1848.
Courtesy of the Merchant's House Museum.

Mary Adelaide wears her hair in braids at the back of her head. The hair in front, however, has been cut and styled in curls that frame her face, curls that she achieved by the use of a curling iron or curling papers.

By the mid-1830s the earlier practices of using heavy white face paint and roug-
ing cheeks and lips had been abandoned for a perfectly natural look, and the use
of cosmetics was widely condemned as a deceitful practice. Some women wore
no makeup at all, but many opted for at least a dusting of face powder, and some
risked a subtle application of rouge. However, by the 1850s, coinciding with the
gradual change in women's dress from the drooping silhouette and pale tints of the
1840s to widened skirts and bold colors, the use of cosmetics, particularly rouge,
became more acceptable.[18] The finest of the whitening face powders consisted of
powdered "French chalk" (actually soapstone). Some powders, marketed as "pearl
powders," contained heavy metals like bismuth, which had the disadvantage of
not only being toxic but of turning black when exposed to sulfurous gases. On occasion, such gases escaped from gas lighting fixtures of the period, causing ladies
who were wearing pearl powder considerable embarrassment![19]

Rouge could be used to color lips as well as cheeks, and like face powder, was
widely available in the shops. It came in the form of powder, pomade, liquid, or
pieces of gauze or silk that had been saturated with color. Eyebrows might be dark-
ened with a pomade made especially for this purpose or with burnt cork.[20] To enhance her *décolleté* when wearing a ball gown, the fashionable woman might outline
the veins of her neck and throat with a blue powder applied with a leather pencil.[21]

Even after 1850, a deft touch in the use of all cosmetics was necessary, for an
obviously made-up woman risked being thought "loose." Whatever the antebellum woman did to enhance her looks, while not exactly a secret, was supposed to
leave the gentlemen with the impression that she was a natural beauty.

---

18 Halttunen, 79, 160–61.

19 D.G. Brinton, M.D. and G.H. Napheys, *Personal Beauty or the Laws of Health in Relation to the Human
Form* (Springfield, Missouri: W.J. Holland, 1869), 208–09.

20 Mescher, 50.

21 As early as 1811, a popular beauty manual condemned vein outlining. See *The Mirror of the Graces* (London: Printed for B. Crosby and Co., 1811), 56. Yet in 1869, Brinton and Napheys were recommending a blue-
tinged French chalk for this purpose, and as late as 1911, aristocratic British women, when preparing for a
formal ball, were in the habit of outlining the veins of their throat, neck and temple with a blue crayon. See
Juliet Nicolson, *The Perfect Summer: England 1911, Just Before the Storm* (New York: Grove Press, 2006), 82.

7

Learning the Part

The desire to imitate aristocratic European tradition was at the root of the "fashionable education" provided by the female boarding schools in the nineteenth century. As might be expected, however, this kind of education did not sit too well with some Americans who saw their country as the democratic antithesis of nations ruled by aristocracies. Authors of advice manuals and publications directed to women, like *Godey's Lady's Book,* criticized the superficiality of an education that encouraged young women in the pursuit of fashion and that emphasized the ornamental arts like drawing, singing, and painting. Most critics, however, did not propose a more rigorous study of the branches of a liberal education for its own sake or as preparation for advanced professional studies. Instead, they faulted a system that encouraged young women to have extravagant tastes and that failed to prepare them for the culturally accepted role of wife and mother. Even Catherine Beecher, the educational reformer who founded the Hartford Female Seminary, justified its curriculum because it prepared women to be mothers. "It is to mothers and to teachers," she wrote, "that the world is to look for the character which is to be enstamped on each succeeding generation."[1]

But for many wealthy New Yorkers "a fashionable education" was exactly what they wanted for their daughters and what the daughters wanted for themselves. There were many finishing schools in the city that prepared daughters of the elite to take their place in society. The five older Tredwell daughters attended Mrs. Okill's School on Eighth (then Clinton) Street; Gertrude, the youngest,

---

1   Quoted in Lawrence A. Cremin, *American Education: The National Experience, 1783–1876* (New York: Harper & Row, 1980), 144.

attended Miss Gibson's School on Union Square. Both schools were within easy walking distance from the Tredwell home.

48. CLASSROOM OF MRS. OKILL'S ACADEMY.
Drawing by Maria Tillman, c. 1841. Collection of the Rensselaer County Historical Society, Troy, New York.
In lieu of attending to what must have been a boring French lesson, Maria Tillman made this drawing showing details of her classroom. The occupants of the inclined desks are identified; a venetian blind covers the window, and candle fixtures stand ready to illuminate the room for an evening event. For the soiree of 1840, the rooms were cleared of furniture and served as ballrooms for the dancing that followed.

Mary Okill's school, which was also her place of residence, occupied two adjoining rowhouses that had been connected by cutting doors through the party walls. Here day students like the Tredwell girls joined boarding students from as far away as Mobile and New Orleans. Because it was desirable for women to know a little bit about a lot of things in order to be interesting conversational partners for men, the curriculum at Mrs. Okill's covered the bases: English composition and grammar, philosophy, history, geography, natural science, mathematics, and

French—especially French—at least a smattering of which was considered necessary for true female refinement. Musical training and drawing were offered for an additional fee. Often young women were also trained privately in drawing and dance.

Mary Okill was herself a fashionable lady, the daughter of Sir James Jay, the older brother of John Jay, who became the first Chief Justice of the Supreme Court and later Governor of New York.[2] Upon opening her "Select School for Young Ladies" in 1823, she made it known that she would take particular care to see to the "religious principles, morals, and manners" of her students, and her expertise in these matters was endorsed by Benjamin Tredwell Onderdonk, Seabury Tredwell's relative who would later become the bishop of Trinity Parish.[3] This was no doubt a decisive factor in the Tredwells' choice of Mrs. Okill's for their daughters' schooling.

The first location of Mrs. Okill's school was at 43 Barclay Street, just a few blocks from the Tredwells' downtown residence on Dey Street. But in 1837, Mrs. Okill, following her patrons, moved north to the Bond Street area. This was to be her last move uptown; she died in 1860, having been amply rewarded for her efforts on behalf of the young ladies. Five years earlier, *Godey's Lady's Book* congratulated her for having made a quarter of a million dollars by keeping school.[4]

The method of instruction at Mrs. Okill's was typical. It consisted mainly of rote memorization. Students read aloud, were drilled aloud, and examined aloud in "reviews" based on the text. They also copied poems and essays in their copybooks, and sometimes were assigned original compositions. Students were graded on their oral reviews and their copybook exercises, the latter mainly for neatness and penmanship, with marks from one to four. Occasionally the teacher commented on the work in the copybook, but the remarks were brief and not very helpful: "Style very defective in some respects," or "With this composition, not much fault can be found; neither can it be greatly praised," "Not very good." When Phebe Tredwell was fifteen years old, she wrote an original essay in her copybook on the sinking of the steamboat *The Swallow* in the Hudson River (then called the North River).

---

2 Mrs. Okill's daughter, Mary Helena, married Dennis Hart Mahan, a professor at West Point. Their son, Alfred Thayer Mahan, was the author of *The Influence of Sea Power on History: 1666–1783*, a book that continues to influence the thinking of naval strategists around the world.

3 *The Christian Journal and Library Register* 7 (May 1823): 160.

4 *Godey's Lady's Book* (July 1855).

May 8, 1845

Within a few weeks past our city has met with a dreadful accident, which was the loss of the steamer Swallow. It was in the night, and in the midst of a heavy storm, when the boat was coming down the north River from Albany; she ran on a rock opposite Athens. The front part broke in two and the other part sunk in deep water in less than ten minutes....

It seems almost impossible that such a disaster would have happened. Only the day before, those persons had as charming hopes of a long life as any of our selves, and now they are in the eternal world waiting the day of judgment.... Death in a thousand forms, may come upon us with the same rapidity. And we should therefore live as if every moment was our last.

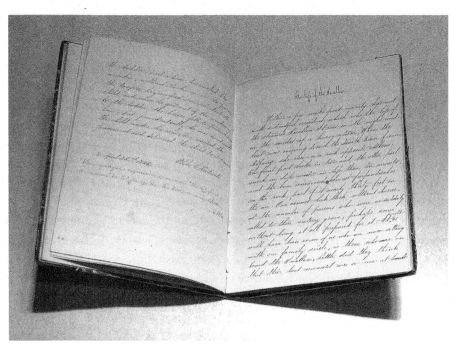

49. Copybook Belonging to Phebe Tredwell, 1845.
Courtesy of the Merchant's House Museum.

The copybook was a popular pedagogical tool in the nineteenth century. Students wrote original essays in their copybooks, but the main activity associated with these books was the copying of sayings and moralistic poems and essays. Such an exercise required little of the teacher and was thought to be an effective way of improving the minds and morals of youth. Neatness counted.

The teacher, ignoring the point of Phebe's sobering reflection, commented only, "I would not say that 'our city' had met with the accident of the loss of the Swallow. North River, being a proper noun, should be capitalized."

"Disgrace marks" in deportment were liberally handed out and recorded on a slate kept for the purpose. Infractions such as making too much noise, talking during class, making others laugh, or turning one's head around to talk to another girl while walking with a group on Broadway could also result in a mark. At the end of the term, the marks were added up and reported to parents.[5]

Day students like the Tredwells were presumably continually perfecting their parlor deportment at home, while boarding students were given the opportunity once a month to make overnight stays in the homes of the school's patrons where they put their social skills into practice. They may also have been grateful for the opportunity to enjoy a variation in the boarding school diet. Maria Tillman, a student from Troy, New York, writing in her diary in March of 1846, lists the school menus for the week: Sunday, cold ham, boiled rice, and beets; Monday, beef steaks, potatoes and beets; Tuesday, beef and macaroni; Wednesday, cod fish, beef, and potatoes.[6]

Mrs. Okill's boarding students were allowed a great deal of freedom to walk in pairs or even alone to the homes of patrons or to the homes of day students or to shop on Broadway for essentials such as sweets, ribbons, pins, and gloves. Such outings were not always without peril, however. Maria Tillman records putting her veil over her face and walking very fast down Broadway because there were so many "loafers" about.[7]

One Saturday morning she and her friend Cornelia ventured to the New York Garden. They were not sure a lady should be seen there without a gentleman, but tempted by the opportunity to sample the ice cream served by the proprietor, Contoit, they decided to take the chance. On either side of the narrow shaded garden, there were white and green wooden booths accommodating four to six persons. Here patrons could enjoy vanilla or lemon ice cream, pound cake, and lemonade. What happened once the ice cream arrived probably made for excited retelling once the girls returned to Mrs. Okill's. According to Maria, a man, "a

---

5 See Maria Tillman diary (Troy, New York: Rensselaer Historical Society) for references to daily life at Mrs. Okill's, including methods of instruction and discipline. Copybooks belonging to the Tredwell girls in the collection of the Merchant's House Museum contain original graded compositions as well as copied essays and poems.

6 Ibid., March 16, 1846.

7 Ibid., June 8, 1846.

real handsome one too," repeatedly passed where they were sitting and then sat down in the next booth.

> He ordered ice cream and paid the man when he brought it. Then he made such a clattering with the spoon to attract our attention and a shuffling with his feet. By this time we were very much frightened and our ice was hurried down in less than no time and we called the man and paid for it. We had to wait to put on our gloves and in that time our next door neighbor passed us twice and once really I thought he was coming in to sit down, as he almost stopped, then he passed us again going towards Broadway and as soon as we thought we might venture out we started with my arm round Cornelia looking in at every little place as we passed as we were afraid that he might jump out at us, but we got safely out and proceeded down to Stewart's Candy Store in Chambers Street.[8]

50. New York Public Garden at Broadway and Leonard.
Published in Reminiscences of an Octogenarian *by Charles Haswell, New York: Harper & Brothers, 1897. Author's collection.*
A favorite New York pleasure garden operated by John H. Contoit, known for its ice cream. Here Maria Tillman and her friend Cornelia met with their exciting afternoon adventure.

---

8 Ibid., July 20, 1846.

On February 27, 1840, Mrs. Okill held a grand musical soiree at the school to showcase the musical talents and social graces of her students. Mary Adelaide Tredwell was then fifteen years old and the only Tredwell sister to be enrolled at Mrs. Okill's at the time. Almost certainly she, her older sister Elizabeth, and her parents were in attendance at this significant social event. Twelve rooms were opened for the affair. The rooms on the third floor were designated as ballrooms for the dancing that followed the concert.

51. Grand Musical Soiree.
Engraving from a drawing by Elton from the New York Herald, February 27, 1840. Collection of the New-York Historical Society.
A grand soiree at Mrs. Okill's Academy was front-page news in February 1840. Young women in the finest gowns their dressmakers could produce performed musical numbers for their proud parents and admiring beaux. The soiree was a great success as evidenced by the fact that "every avenue to the room in which the concert was to take place was crammed from the hall door to the top of the third story stairs."

The importance of the occasion was marked by front-page coverage in the *New York Herald* of February 27. The paper devoted almost as much space to describing the soiree as it did to the famous Brevoort masked ball, which occurred only a week later. James Gordon Bennett, who founded the *Herald* in 1835, made many enemies in New York because of the paper's irreverent approach to the activities of the city's elite. Both Mrs. Okill's musical soiree and the Brevoort Ball came in for the comic hyperbole characteristic of the paper's style when reporting on such events:

> The grand concert, soiree, musical melange, and ollapodrida, that came off on Monday evening, was given by way of eliciting and exhibiting the talent, loveliness, and accomplishments of the charming pupils to their admired, fond, foolish, doting, parents, relatives, and lovers.... The 'bright particular star of the evening' was a sweet girl dressed in striped satin who sang sweetly, and played scientifically both on the piano and guitar.... The only feature that is objectionable, seems to us to be the manner the lovely singer has of opening her mouth too wide.... However, she is a lovely girl and a sweet singer.

The crowd was so "suffocatingly dense" that

> Silks were split, satins were stained, muslins were mauled, chinchillas were crushed, tiaras were torn down. Head geer [sic], and tail geer and all sorts of geer had to go by the board.

In the customary gossipy style of the day, the reporter referred to the guests by their initials, thus managing at once to reveal their identities to those in the know while avoiding the vulgarity of printing their names in the paper.

> Miss W----- was there, a truly beautiful girl, dressed in white, with her hair exquisitely arrayed. Ariel reposed in these ringlets half the night; her brilliant eyes made sad havoc with many hearts.... Miss E----- of St. Mark's Place, a pretty girl, danced admirably with Mr. J----- F----- of Chatham Street.

But at the conclusion of the merry piece with its gentle insults came a brutal *coup de grace.*

Such is a fashionable soiree, growing out of the fashionable boarding school system of education in vogue at present. It is part and parcel of the progress of the present system of fashionable society, and is working its way silently but surely to the complete revulsion in morals, manners, religion, philosophy, and finance, of the whole community.... [Y]oung ladies are educated and taught to sing, dance, flirt, laugh, and act French vaudevilles; but never learn one useful thing that will enable them to perform the part of a good wife and mother.... The consequence is when they are "finished" under the present fashionable system of education, they are perfectly competent to "finish" a husband....

Mrs. Okill was not amused. In 1846 she changed her mind about having a "fancy ball," according to Maria Tillman, because she was afraid of "poor Bennett and the *Herald*." Instead of arraying themselves "like peacocks" in costumes and masks, the girls had to settle for simple white dresses and a modest soiree that was not even mentioned in the *Herald*.[9]

There is no record of the education of the elder Tredwell son, Horace, but we know that in 1840, the year of the soiree at Mrs. Okill's, Samuel, the younger son, at the age of twelve, was enrolled for the first time at St. Paul's College in College Point, twelve miles from the city on Long Island Sound near Flushing. The school had been founded in 1835 by Augustus Muhlenberg, an Episcopalian clergyman. Younger students were educated in grammar school classes and boys fourteen to eighteen were provided an education equivalent to four years of college, according to the school catalogue. Both socially and academically, life was more disciplined for the young men of St. Paul's than it was for the young ladies at Mrs. Okill's.

One of the reasons for locating the school outside of Manhattan was to provide an "asylum from the allurements to youthful dissipation." Inexperienced young men were felt to be particularly subject to the evil predators that lurked on mean city streets. The fear was not only that a confidence man would swindle the trusting youth, but what was worse, would entice him into a life of gambling, drinking, and illicit sex.[10]

Unlike the girls at Mrs. Okill's, the boys at St. Paul's were not allowed to leave the school unaccompanied. Nor were they were allowed to have money or food other than that provided at their meals. Needless to say, "tobacco, gambling, and

9 Ibid., February 23, 1846.
10 Halttunen, Chapter 1.

dirty books" were not permitted. Visitors were not allowed except on Thursdays from two to five. And all the boys were required to wear a uniform consisting of jacket and trousers of dark green cloth, a double-breasted black cashmere vest, and on Sunday, a velvet collar.

Samuel, as a student in the grammar school, would have studied Latin grammar, arithmetic, geography and atlas, English grammar, history, reading, and writing. The older boys pursued a rigorous curriculum: the first year included the study of Latin (Cicero, Livy, and Horace), Greek (Herodotus, six books of the *Iliad*, St. John's Gospel), algebra, plane geometry, trigonometry, natural philosophy, English and modern history. The daily routine consisted of chapel twice a day, recitations for each class conducted in a recitation room with the emphasis on rote memorization, study in a communal hall, and lectures. Samuel Seabury, the grandson of Seabury Tredwell's illustrious half uncle, was a member of the visiting committee that examined the students once a year.[11]

The rigors of St. Paul's may not have been appropriate for Samuel Tredwell, for his name does not appear on the registers after 1840. Rather, we know that he pursued classical studies under the tutelage of two different Episcopalian priests from the age of fourteen to seventeen. The study of Latin and Greek was standard preparation for a young man intending to enter the profession of law, and in December of 1845, after three years of private study of the classics, Samuel began a four-year clerkship in the office of his brother-in-law, Effingham Nichols, his sister Elizabeth's husband. Before the Civil War, there were professional schools for aspiring lawyers or physicians. However, throughout the nineteenth century, it was possible to become an attorney or a physician by apprenticing to a member of those professions. But Samuel did not continue long enough under Effingham's tutelage to become an attorney. Instead, he became a merchant, first in the distillery business, then in china and crockery, like his uncles George and John Tredwell.

Neither Samuel nor Horace ever achieved the success of their father, and only two of their sisters realized the goal of their fashionable education—which was to catch a husband.

---

11 *Catalogue of the Professors, Instructors and Students of St. Paul's College and Grammar School for the Season 1839–40* (College Point, New York: St. Paul's School, 1840).

8

Enter the Guests

ntebellum society in New York City was rigidly exclusionary, but a family's social position was not writ in stone. The values of the new republic meant that it was possible to better oneself—to rise from a lower to a higher social class. And the proliferation of etiquette manuals during the three decades preceding the Civil War was due in part to demand by readers who, though not to the manor born, were confident that they could behave like ladies and gentlemen if only they knew the rules.

Those rules, however, were not easily mastered. Even the members of the elite felt the need to consult experts on the thorny subject of etiquette. Eliza Tredwell owned *The Habits of Good Society: A Handbook for Ladies and Gentlemen,* which was written by an anonymous gentleman and provided guidance to both men and women on "manners of refinement, and rules of good breeding and etiquette."

The etiquette manuals generally devoted several pages to the important subject of ceremonial calling. This obligatory routine in which women paid periodic reciprocal visits to a carefully selected list of acquaintances served to establish and reaffirm alliances among the gentry. Not only could those who made up one's calling circle be counted on for invitations to dinner parties and balls, but more importantly, their children were likely to be safe marriage prospects for one's own offspring. [1]

---

[1] The discussion of the etiquette of calling relies on the following manuals: T.S. Arthur, *Advice to Young Ladies on Their Duties and Conduct in Life* (New York: T.W. Strong, 1851); Mrs. John Farrar, *The Young Lady's Friend* (Boston: American Stationers Company, 1838); *The Habits of Good Society* (New York: Rudd & Carleton, 1860); Sarah Josepha Hale (Buell) *Manners; or, Happy Homes and Good Society All the Year Round* (Boston: J.B. Tilton and Company, 1868); Catherine Maria Sedgwick, *Morals of Manners; or Hints for Our*

Calls were to be made during a specified interval, usually from ten or eleven in the morning until five in the afternoon, and each call lasted from ten to fifteen minutes. Although the calling went on into the afternoon, the calls were customarily termed "morning calls" and the dresses in which women made these calls, "morning dresses." Essential to the practice was a supply of visiting cards, upon which one's name was tastefully engraved in italics. Women carried these cards in small cases designed for the purpose.

52. Eliza Tredwell's Visiting Card.

Courtesy of the Merchant's House Museum.

Proper etiquette required that a married woman use her husband's name on her visiting card. The names of young unmarried females were included on their mother's card.

In order to avoid the risk of not being at home when friends called, women often had an "at home" day when they were known to be available to receive calls. This enabled them to control their wardrobe selection for receiving calls, and in cold weather they could make sure that there was a cheerful fire burning in the front parlor when visitors showed up. The day of the week that served as a woman's "at home" day could be engraved in the lower left-hand corner of her visiting card, and her address might appear in the lower right-hand corner. On the other hand, since those of her calling circle could be expected to know where she lived, the address might be omitted. Sometimes the women of a neighborhood cooperated in establishing a day of the week when they all could be found in their parlors. Friday, for example, was the day when one could expect the ladies of Washington Square to be "at home."[2] Once a call was made, the person called upon was required to return the call, and then that call in turn had to be returned, and so

Young People (New York: G.P. Putnam & Co., 1854); Emily Thornwell, *The Lady's Guide to Perfect Gentility* (New York: Derby & Jackson, 1856); *True Politeness, Etiquette for Ladies* (New York: Leavitt and Allen, 1854).

2   de Forest, *John Johnston*, 154.

on … and on. In addition to these routine calls, one was required to call after having been entertained at dinner or a party or ball (these were called "party calls"), on the occasion of a death in the family to offer condolences, and to extend congratulations for any number of reasons.

Complicating matters was the fact that a woman could choose either to make a personal call or just to leave a visiting card with the servant who answered the door. If leaving a card only, she might employ the grammar of the corners, folding down one of the corners of the card as a shorthand way of leaving a message. The rules varied from time to time, but she might, for example, fold down the upper right-hand corner to indicate the attempt to make a personal visit; the upper left, congratulations; the lower right, leaving town for an extended visit; and the lower left, condolence. Abbreviations for French phrases indicating one's intent might also be noted on the card: "p.c.." *pour condola*—"to condole"; "p.f," *pour feliciter*— "to congratulate"; and "p.r.," *pour remercier*—"to thank, and "p.p.c.," *pour prendre conge*—"to take leave." In the spring of 1857, after hearing that one of his girlfriends had become engaged, Charles Tracy sent her one of his cards marked "p.p.c."

> I meant by that to show her (of course a joke!) that I wished to take
> leave of my old friend, Anita and that in the future I should treat her
> with the respect and consideration due to the future Mrs. Carroll.[3]

A personal call carried more weight than the call at which only a card was left and required that a personal call be made in return. But in effect, if both parties were willing, cards could actually call upon cards in perpetuity, although it was mandatory that the cards be delivered to the servant in person. In this way, women could maintain relationships that, for one reason or another, they did not want to drop or to develop. This dizzying procedure could be set in motion by means of a letter of introduction if one was new in town, or a woman might call for the first time on someone to whom she had been properly introduced by a mutual acquaintance.

To pay a call of condolence, a woman left a card only. As soon as the bereaved family was ready to receive callers, the lady of the house made the rounds, leaving a visiting card bordered in black signaling the family's desire to resume their social duties. If one did not receive a card, it was a sign that future visits were not welcome. Thus a death in the family provided an opportunity to cut down on what

---

3   Charles Tracy diary, May 18, 1857, Manuscript Division (New York: New-York Historical Society).

53. MORNING CALLS.

Fashion plate from Godey's Lady's Book, *February 1858. Author's collection.*
Women might change their costume several times a day. These gowns are examples of what the fashionable woman was wearing on her ceremonial calling rounds in 1858.

Edith Wharton once called "an onerous duty." So did a lengthy stay out of town. Before leaving for vacation, a woman left a card with the notation "p.p.c." Upon the family's return to the city, she once again made the rounds with her cards. If a card was not received, the social relationship was considered terminated. Immediately after a marriage, the bride and groom sent around cards with both of their names, announcing that they would be at home. In this way the new bride established her own calling circle, which might or might not include the groom's bachelor friends. Another way a social relationship could be terminated was by a social superior ignoring the call of a social inferior or by returning a personal call with a card only.

With respect to the timing of calls, Eliza Tredwell's manual advised that ceremonial calls should be returned within three days. Party calls should be made (1) the day after having been entertained at a ball, when a card only could suffice; (2) within a day or two of a dinner party, when it was preferable to call in person; and (3) within a week of a small party, when the call should certainly be made in person. Calls of congratulations (a personal call) and bereavement (card only) were to be made about a week after the event.

Ladies were advised to leave their shawls and bonnets on during the call; gentlemen were to carry their hats and canes into the parlor but leave their umbrellas in the hall. Once seated, a gentleman placed his hat on the floor beside his chair. If another person arrived during the course of a call, the proper thing to do was to leave "not indeed immediately, as if you shunned the new arrival, but after a moment or two." As they left, callers found their own way to the parlor door where an alert servant met them and showed them out.

It's a good thing that the calls were brief, for subject matter deemed suitable for conversation was limited. The manuals advised women to listen discretely, to speak in a soft tone, and to refrain from introducing subjects requiring deep thought. On the other hand, it was thought improper to talk about one's own affairs, especially the amusing behavior of one's children, which was "seldom interesting to others." Discussing problems one was having with one's servants was considered ill-bred. Disagreeable subjects like disease and anything to do with money were also off-limits.

A newly married woman in her twenties could look forward to forty or fifty years of calling—if she lived that long. Week after week, the routine was repeated. The women raised their children, saw them married, became grandmothers, grew old and stout; and through it all, they were borne back and forth in their carriages, climbed the stoops, left their cards, or went inside, emerging ten minutes later having engaged in virtually the same insipid conversation they had the last time they called. Mrs. C.M. Kirkland, writing in *Sartain's Magazine* in 1850, bitterly characterized the requirements of the call:

> The eyes must be guarded, lest they mete out too much consideration
> to those who bear no stamp. The neck must be stiffened, lest it bend
> beyond the haughty angle of self-reservation.... The mouth is bound

to keep its portcullis ever ready to fall on a word which implies unaffected pleasure or surprise.... Subjects of conversation must be any but those which naturally present themselves to the mind.... O, the unutterable weariness of this worse than dumbshow! No wonder we groan in spirit when there are visits to be made![4]

Mary Ann Parker, the wife of a New York City physician, saw calling not only as a social but almost a moral obligation.

Mrs. Hamilton called.... I would rather be out of this fashionable society than in it, but we cannot repel civilities. I must try to keep my heart light and do what is right.[5]

And when women weren't calling, they were in danger of being called upon. Sometimes when a woman was just not up to receiving callers, she directed the servant to tell the caller that she was "not at home." Eliza Tredwell's manual was explicit in warning that this tactic had to be employed at the door, for once admitted to the hall, the guest had to be seen. The caller, fully aware that she might be the object of a polite fiction, would leave her card and be on her way. "We should by no means urge the point, even if we were certain it was not the case; and if by chance we should see the person, we should appear not to have done so, but leave our card and retire." In truth, the caller might be more relieved than insulted by this tactic.

If a woman had an "at home" day, that meant she would receive duty callers on that day only. The rest of the week, she was "not at home." But of course, she welcomed the visits of intimate friends and relatives on any day. Therefore, to enforce an "at home" day, she needed an experienced, savvy servant who recognized her close friends and relatives and could discriminate between them and ceremonial callers.

Although we think of calling as women's work carried on in the domestic sphere, its importance in facilitating business relations among men should not be overlooked. When making a call, a woman carried not only her cards, but her husband's as well. She would leave two of her husband's cards—one for the lady of the house, and one for the husband. (She would not leave one of her own cards

---

4 Mrs. C.M. Kirkland, "The Mystery of Visiting," *Sartain's Magazine* 6 (May 1850): 317.

5 Mary Ann Parker diary, December 27, 1862.

for the husband, because it was "positively improper" for a lady—or her card— to call upon a gentleman.) Thus her husband could reinforce his business connections by the simple expedient of having his wife leave his card. When the merchant arrived home from the countinghouse (or after 1850 from his "office"), it is a safe bet he carefully examined the contents of the hall card receiver to see which business associates' wives had left cards for him. It is also likely that he discussed his wife's calling itinerary with her and made sure she called upon the wives of certain associates with whom he wished to maintain business as well as social ties.

Mastering the subtleties of ceremonial calling was difficult, requiring meticulous record keeping. Women kept a "visiting book" where they recorded the names of those who had called in person, those who had left cards only, and the date when they returned those calls. Ceremonial calling also required a good measure of intuition and a sensitivity to the verbal and nonverbal cues that informed the entire procedure. Eventually, however, the routine became second nature to a genteel woman of the nineteenth century. After all, it was her job.

Ceremonial calls were not the only type of visits that were made, of course. Intimate friends came for longer visits during the day, and what were known as "half-ceremonious calls" were made by ladies who were well enough known to be considered friends, but not intimates. During the evening hours, friendly couples called on each other, and young single men came to court young ladies from whom they had received permission to call. These visits were not exactly unexpected, but one never knew just who might show up, and callers never knew who would be home.[6] A lot of impromptu social exchange as well as planned formal entertainments took place among the families of the Bond Street environs. They spent a great deal of time in each other's parlors.

A letter from Sarah Dawson in New York to her mother in Baltimore reveals how severely the demands of calling and being called upon dictated the course of daily life. Sarah's aunts, Nancy and Maria, who live next door to her, have just returned home from a lengthy stay out of town and are expected for dinner.

> I ordered dinner … sent to market, saw to a great many household affairs … and was most through finishing off settling my accounts in the parlour when our stupid servant let in Mrs. Cruger. I was not in dishabille but still I was not dressed for company. She sat a great while and talking as fast as she could, I listening patiently but wishing her any-

---

6 The telephone was not invented until 1876.

where but where she was.... After I had the pleasure of seeing her out of the house I came upstairs, curled off my hair, put on my lace cape and in short made my toilette for the whole day and was just congratulating myself that I could now take a book and sit comfortably in the parlour when Aunt Nancy came in and begged me to pay a visit to Mrs. & Miss Davis who had come from St. Croix with them ... so down went my hair, on went my Poke and off I went immediately.... Cook gave us dinner exactly at ½ past 3.... Mrs. Eastbourn and Mrs. B. Watts came in while they were removing the cloth. The two visitors stayed until it was most dark and then went away ... Aunt Maria and Aunt Nancy did not go home until ½ past 9. Mr. Cort dropt in and talked as much as usual ... he made his exit about ten since when I have been talking to you.[7]

The most elaborate calling ritual of all took place on New Year's Day when the doors between the parlors were thrown open for the traditional New Year's Day open house. According to an old Dutch custom, on that day the ladies stayed home to receive guests and preside over a lavish buffet table, while the gentlemen sallied forth to make calls. It was, according to one observer, a day when the city streets were alive with elegantly dressed men rushing from house to house, on foot or in carriages, all with a list of calls to be made in hand. The idea was to make as many calls as possible—fifty was standard.[8]

The ladies were bejeweled and beautifully dressed in low-neck silk gowns got up by their dressmakers especially for the occasion. The tables were laden with all manner of delicacies: turkey, chickens, fruits, pickled and stewed oysters, crullers, doughnuts, and little New Year's cakes with mottoes written on them in icing. Alcohol flowed almost as freely as Croton water; guests were offered wine, whiskey, punch, and cherry bounce, a favorite of hostesses since the days of Martha Washington. The recipe for the punch was a complicated mystery, but the cherry bounce

---

7 Sarah Jay Dawson (Mrs. William) to Mary Rutherfurd Clarkson Jay (Mrs. Peter Augustus), May 24, 1833, Special Collections, Jay Family Collection (New York: Columbia University Library).

8 Edward Winslow Martin, *The Secrets of a Great City: A Work Descriptive of the Virtues and Vices, the Mysterious Crimes of New York City* (Philadelphia: Jones Brothers, 1868), 227.

was easy. When the cherries ripened in June, one simply washed them and put a half gallon of them in a jug—stems and all. They were then covered with a half gallon of bourbon—or rum—or gin—and set aside in a dark closet until New Year's when sugar was added, the whole thing strained through cheesecloth, and served. Not a drink for sissies.

In 1861, when John Ward was twenty-two years old, he made the rounds with his nineteen-year-old brother, Press.[9] They decided to make only a few calls (the total turned out to be thirty-three), so they were able to stay for more conversational exchange than was perhaps typical.

John was impressed by the finery of the women—Julia Carville wore a French headdress of gold ornaments and velvet; Mrs. Fisher wore blue to match the blue silk on the parlor walls; and Julia Cutting, a red silk with a long train. He admired a table mat that Miss Minturn had worked for her mother and the four splendid baskets of flowers that adorned the Beekman parlors, which he assumed had been sent to Kate Beekman by "adoring lovers." He talked to Bessie Fish about the sculpture "Babes in the Woods" by Thomas Crawford[10] and to Lizzie Schuschardt about crossing the ocean and admiring the rosy sunsets over Mount Rigi in Switzerland. Mrs. General Jones told him how she detested shopping and always just went to one large shop and bought everything that she could think of and scarcely shopped in Paris at all. He ate tongue and biscuits at the Aspinwalls and peered into the stereopticon at the Cuttings'.[11] Marianne Turner addressed him as "you sinner"; Lucy Baxter accused Press of deliberately cutting her and swore the next time she saw him she intended to march right up to him and put out her parasol or throw her muff to attract his attention. John recommended the singing teacher Cerimeri to Julia Grinnell and talked about the funeral of a mu-

---

9 John Ward diary, January 1, 1861.

10 Crawford's sculpture is today on exhibit at the Metropolitan Museum of Art, New York City.

11 The stereopticon was a viewing device commonly found in nineteenth-century parlors. Using a special camera with two lenses that produced two negatives, photographs were taken of the same scene but from slightly different viewpoints corresponding to the distance between the eyes. These images were then mounted side by side and the whole inserted into the device. When looked at through the viewer, a single three-dimensional image sprang into life. To a nineteenth-century audience for whom photography itself was a relatively new phenomenon, the effect was magical. The stereographs Mrs. Cutting showed John Ward were taken by Henry Bedlow, a member of the Amateur Photographers Exchange Club, which was in existence from 1861–63. Each of the members was required to send to every other member six stereographs a year at prescribed intervals. The club disbanded when two of its members were drafted into service in the Civil War. See William Welling, *Photography in America: The Formative Years, 1839–1900* (New York: Thomas Y. Crowell Company, 1978), 152.

tual friend to Mrs. Hosack, who was in mourning and so not really receiving but only came in just before he left.

54. JOHN WARD (1838-1896), LIEUTENANT, 12TH REGIMENT, N.Y. STATE TROOPS, WASHINGTON, D.C., MAY 1861.

Collection of the New-York Historical Society, negative number 837820.

A neighbor of the Tredwells, John Ward was a graduate of Columbia College, class of 1858. He served in the Civil War at the battles of Fort McHenry and Harper's Ferry, and in 1863 entered Columbia College Medical School. This daguerreotype was made the same year that John recorded his New Year's visits in his diary.

At some of the houses, the talk was of politics, and concern was expressed over the recent secession of South Carolina from the Union. But when John found himself in the "enemies' camp" at the Anson Livingstons, who were Southerners, social norms prevailed and they settled on the subjects of dogs and theatricals. The attack on Fort Sumter and the sobering battle of Bull Run were still in the future. At Bull Run the Union Army would suffer a humiliating defeat in the first land battle of the Civil War, and New Yorkers would realize that there would be no easy victory. But on New Year's Day of 1861, the gaiety of the event was undiminished by serious apprehension of the coming conflict.

55. New Year's Day, New York City, 1868.
Engraving from a drawing by J.W. Erninger, Harper's Weekly, January 4, 1868. The New-York Historical Society, negative number 83404d.
The doors separating the front and back parlors were thrown open to provide a gala space for the observation of the old Dutch custom of the New Year's Day reception.

After returning home to dine, John resumed calling. However, the unfettered hospitality of the day had come to an end; at the Davises', he was obliged to send in his card with the servant, who said he would see if Mrs. Davis would see him. She did, and gladly, explaining that "a visit at this time in the evening means a card of etiquette you know. I told the waiter that if any gentleman wished to see me especially, to bring in his card." John assured her his call was not merely *pro forma*, that he wished to see her *particularly*, and so the demands of etiquette were met. John returned home after visiting six more homes where he just left his card, bringing his New Year's Day calling to an end.

Even children took part in the New Year's festivities. At the age of eighty, Catherine Havens recorded events of her childhood in a child's voice. She remembered what it was like in 1850 when she was ten years old and lived on Ninth Street near University Place and the gentlemen called on New Year's Day. In the entry for January 2 she wrote,

> Yesterday was New Year's Day, and I had lovely presents. We had 139 callers and I have an ivory tablet and I write all their names down in it. We have to be dressed and ready by ten o'clock to receive. Some of the gentlemen come together and don't stay more than a minute; but some go into the back room and take some oysters and coffee and cake, and stay and talk.... The gentlemen keep dropping in all day and until long after I have gone to bed.[12]

The custom had begun to wane by the 1880s. As the city grew, the residences of New York's socially elite were no longer confined within intimate boundaries. "Making the rounds" had become an intolerable burden. And according to Julia Ward Howe, the young men, some of them strangers, had begun to come in squads, "taking refreshments meant for others" and generally making a nuisance of themselves.[13]

But there was more to it than that. Mrs. Howe was too polite to say so, but other commentators have made it clear that often those "gentlemen" who arrived in squads partook of the cherry bounce much too freely, and by the time their afternoon visits rolled around were falling-down drunk. It had been customary for those not wishing to receive calls to hang a straw basket on the doorknob to receive gentlemen's cards. Soon the straw baskets began to appear on more and more doorknobs. Gradually fewer and fewer gentlemen came to call, and eventually even the baskets disappeared.

---

12 Catherine Elizabeth Havens, *Diary of a Little Girl in Old New York* (1919; reprint, Bedford, Mass.: Applewood Books, n.d.), 58.

13 Howe, 32.

9

A Fine Romance

The Tredwells, like other New Yorkers of their social class, were members of a Byzantine network of related individuals whose families had intermarried. Young women's beaux were limited to those men their parents deemed appropriate marriage prospects. As a result, friendly relations often became familial ties. Seabury, for example, and his neighbor, Samuel Skidmore, were first cousins once removed. (Samuel Skidmore's grandfather and Seabury's father were brothers.) In 1858, the Skidmores spent a two-month summer vacation on the Long Island shore, living in the spacious Great Neck home of another of Seabury Tredwell's cousins, Edward L. Tredwell, who was Skidmore's second cousin. Seabury's nephew, George Tredwell, also owned a home in Great Neck. George was married to Frances Lucy Wetmore. George and Frances Lucy were themselves first cousins, for George's mother, Cornelia Wetmore and Frances Lucy's father, Prosper Montgomery Wetmore, were brother and sister. Lizzie Wetmore, Frances Lucy's sister, would marry Samuel Skidmore's son John after a lengthy courtship that began in the winter of 1858.

That year the initial object of John's attention was Mary Louise Mitchell, a young woman to whom he had been introduced at a party. On January 12 he called on Miss Mitchell:

> Spent the evening 8:10 to 10:45 with Miss M.L.M. (alone we were by a happy chance). The evening was one of the pleasantest of my life. Miss M has a sweet face and is a lovely young lady.

On February 2 he decided to pursue the acquaintance and called again. But on this occasion, he got a little more than he bargained for. He arrived at the home of "Miss M.L.M." at around ten minutes after eight and upon entering the parlor, discovered her little sister studying there. Miss M.L.M. soon made her appearance, however, and the little sister made a diplomatic retreat. The young couple was then able to converse alone until nine o'clock.

> Then she invited me into the dining room to take a cup of coffee. There at table we found her brother Sam and her little sister and Mr. L. Luguier and Miss Sarah Mitchell of Manhasset and another lady in black (another sister I believe of Miss M.L.M.) We had coffee and cake. Then we went all of us into the front parlor where L.L.M. and S.L.M, Jr. [brothers of Miss M.L.M.] played together a few minutes on the piano and then left to go upstairs to play chess (Sam apologized to me for doing so.) Soon after, Sarah Mitchell left the room and immediately after her the lady in black, leaving Miss M.L.M. and her youngest sister and me in the parlor. (say 9½ p.m.)
>
> We sat and conversed until about 10 p.m. when M.L.M., S.L.M. [Miss M.L.M.'s parents], Mr. And Mrs. Edwin Post, and Miss M.L.M.'s sister Annie and Miss Maggie Mitchell of Manhasset, who had been to hear Mr. Everett's oration, came in. I stayed about 20 minutes longer and left.

In this entry, we see the way areas of privacy were carved out through the use of closed doors and how various social groups composed and recomposed themselves during the evening. Within the space of approximately two hours, family members, friends, and out-of-town houseguests come together, leave, reappear, and arrive, moving from room to room. However, even with the intermittent presence of twelve others during the evening, John was able to spend almost an hour alone with M.L.M. in the front parlor before the presence of the party in the "dining room" was revealed to him. It is likely that John is referring here to the back parlor, which, as has been noted, often did double duty as a dining room, and was, in fact, sometimes referred to as the "dining parlor."

Soon after his evening at Miss Mitchell's, John turned his attention to Lizzie Wetmore, who lived with her parents at Number 1 DePau Place. DePau Place was a unified row of houses, lining an entire block on Bleecker, with a continuous cast-iron veranda extending across the front of the houses at the second-floor level. Here John often called, frequently bearing a bouquet of flowers from his own garden. The Wetmores and the Skidmores both attended nearby St. Thomas Church, and John took advantage of the opportunity of walking Lizzie home from church whenever he could.

On June 28 he resolved to pursue Lizzie's hand in marriage.

> From the evening of this day & the ensuing night dates my full & final determination to offer my hand to Miss Lizzie N. Wetmore in marriage. I had long admired her & as I suppose (Indeed as I am well assured by others) showed my feelings very often & unmistakably in various ways. But I had always on a little cool reflection been forced into the conviction that I ought not to encourage such feelings & ought to discontinue seeing her often & avoid paying my marked attentions because I had not the means to support myself—much less to support a household & that therefore it was a wrong to both of us to encourage any such ideas on the part of either. Then Love would step in & I for a long time in an uncertain undecided state. Reason warring against Feeling. Cool judgment against warm love. Tonight the latter won its final and decisive Victory.

Shortly afterwards, the entire Wetmore family left the city to spend the next two months at Great Neck, Long Island, where their married daughter, Frances, and her husband, George Tredwell, had their home. During that time, John frequently boarded the steamship *Croton*, making his way up Long Island Sound to Great Neck where his uncle, James Skidmore, also owned a summer home on the shore. There, during the hot summer months, John and Lizzie spent an idyllic summer of moonlight strolls along the beach and time alone on the Tredwells' piazza walking back and forth. The diary entry for August 17 sums it up succinctly and poetically:

> Glorious night. Moon. Comet. Ev'g star. Walk on shore and alone with Lizzie on piazza. Arm in arm.

On the afternoon of July 21, John delivered a written proposal of marriage rolled into a scroll. It was not unusual for a young man to offer his proposal of marriage in writing and for the reply also to be made in writing.

> July 21 After breakfast walked over to Mrs. Tredwell's. Spent remainder of day and evening there. Delivered scroll at 4:40. After tea took stroll to the point (Bayview Point) with Miss Lizzie Wetmore, Ed Wetmore walking not very far from us with his sister Emily. Left Tredwells' about ¼ to 10 p.m. and returned (on front along shore as usual to Uncle James). Bed 10½ p.m.

56. *Yes or No?*
John Everett Millais (1829–1896), Oil on Canvas.
Private Collection, Bridgeman Art Library.
A young woman holds a daguerreotype of her suitor behind her back as she contemplates his written proposal of marriage laid out on her writing table.

Two days later, on July 23, he was again at the Tredwells' where "at 11:17 p.m." Lizzie handed him a written reply in which she accepted his proposal. That evening, he returned her reply, as she had requested. Lizzie was taking no chances. Had the engagement fallen through, it would have been compromising for John to have her letter of acceptance in his possession. If on the other hand, Lizzie decided to turn John down, it would be proper for her to return his scroll along with her written rejection.

On July 29 both John and Lizzie had returned to New York City, and that evening John called on her at the home of another of her sisters, the newlywed Louisa, who lived on Thirty-Second Street. She and her husband, John Jay White, had just returned from their honeymoon. The couples walked to the New Palace Gardens at Fifteenth Street and Sixth Avenue, where they ate ice cream and enjoyed the music, the crowds, and the balloon ascension. That evening as Lizzie and John sat alone in the parlor of the newlyweds, John gave Lizzie another written note. He does not record the contents, but we can guess that he expressed his happiness at her having accepted him.

The next evening he was invited, along with Lizzie, to the Whites for dinner. After dinner they all went to an ice cream saloon and then returned to the Whites' house. In his diary entry for Friday, June 30, he writes, "It was this evening, in the front room, sitting near the balcony in the dark alone, that Lizzie and I became engaged." On second thought, perhaps realizing that he did not yet have the approval of her father, he scratched out the word "engaged" and added "a sort of 'full understanding' (provided her father approves it) but not an engagement was had this evening."

Sometime before September 24, he must have mustered the nerve to speak to her father, for on that date, he writes that a "regular engagement" was entered into, and on October 9, he presented Lizzie with a ring. Three years later on June 6, 1861, they were finally married. She was twenty-three; he was thirty-one.

John and Lizzie's love story has a sad but all too familiar ending. On February 15, 1871, after ten years of marriage, Lizzie Skidmore succumbed to tuberculosis at the age of thirty-three. She left two young children, Samuel Tredwell, eight, and William Robert, four. John moved back to his parents' home on Fourth Street, where his mother and father and his grandmother helped raise his sons. He never remarried.

From what we know, John and Lizzie behaved appropriately during their courtship. Even so, they probably fell short of the rules in one of the most popular manuals of the day. Mrs. John Farrar, author of *The Young Lady's Friend*, was firm in her advice:

> Never join in any rude plays that will subject you to being kissed or handled in any way by a gentleman. Do not suffer your hand to be held or squeezed, without showing that it displeases you by instantly withdrawing it. Accept not unnecessary assistance in putting on cloaks, shawls, over-shoes, or anything of the sort. Be not lifted in and out of

carriages, on or off a horse; sit not with another in a place that is too narrow; read not out of the same book; let not your eagerness to see anything induce you to place your head close to another person's. These and many other little points of delicacy and refinement deserve to become fixed habits.[1]

57. ARCHITECT'S ELEVATION OF THE HOME OF JOHN SKIDMORE AT 39 EAST FOURTH STREET.
Courtesy of the Winterthur Library, Joseph Downs Collection of Manuscripts and Printed Ephemera.
Located just four doors east of the Tredwell home, the Skidmore House was built in 1845, an example of the Greek Revival rowhouse, which by that time had achieved great popularity in New York. The building is still standing, landmarked by the City of New York.

She also advised young women not to receive company apart from the rest of the family, "lest your parlour become a lounge for all the idle youth of your acquaintance." This was advice that was not always followed, even by very proper

---

1   Farrar, 293.

young ladies. In conducting much of their courtship in the parlors of Lizzie's married sisters, who often obligingly left the young couple alone, John and Lizzie managed a degree of privacy that would probably not have been possible in Lizzie's own home, where her parents and at least some of her six brothers and sisters more often than not would have been participant observers.

58. THE WETMORE FAMILY RESIDENCE, DE PAU ROW & BLEECKER STREET.
Watercolor from Dr. John Francis's Old New York, *Collection of the New York Historical Society, negative number 83559d.*
Lizzie Wetmore and her family lived in the grand home formerly owned by the preeminent physician, Dr. Valentine Mott. It was located at Bleecker and Thompson, the corner home of a block-long row of houses unified by a cast-iron veranda. The Wetmores joined many of their neighbors in their move from the neighborhood in 1858.

In 1848 Sarah Bradley, a young woman attending Abbott's Institute, a female academy located near the Tredwell home, noted in her diary that she had just read *Advice to Young Ladies,* one of the more popular conduct manuals. "Some things in it I liked very well, though I doubt if such books do much good."[2] Sarah's point

2 Sarah Bradley diary, November 5, 1848, Special Collections (Hanover: Dartmouth College Library).

is well-taken: to put too much store in the manuals as an accurate description of widespread social behavior is apt to lead us to a picture of the time as more blood-less than it actually was.

In March of 1844, Henry Patterson, who, with his brother, would found Patterson Brothers Hardware in 1848, described an evening spent alone with his fiancé, Eleanor Wright, in her parlor engaged in "eating, conversing, chess playing, and walking the floor." Perhaps it was because chairs were not comfortable, or perhaps people just felt more at ease in motion, but in any case, "walking the floor" was not uncommon when two people engaged in conversation. [3]

Later in the same month, Henry and Eleanor attended a lecture with Eleanor's mother and some family friends. The lecture ended at 9:15 when they all returned to Eleanor's home. Then—

> The company gradually dispersed, and from 11 o'clock till midnite I was alone with Eleanor, a season, short as it was, filled with enjoyment in the mutual interchange of affection. [4]

As we have seen, couples did sometimes find themselves alone, though surely not as often as they would have liked, and undoubtedly they were putting their heads together without regard to Mrs. Farrar. It is hard to imagine how young women would ever reach a "full understanding," let alone a formal engagement, if they strictly followed her advice. Still, the ideas expressed by Mrs. Farrar and others were generally accepted as the ideal and tended to keep relationships between the sexes on a formal footing compared to today. During the years before the Civil War, genteel young unmarried couples may have been reading out of the same book, but they were not sleeping in the same bed.

Unfortunately, no diaries or letters remain to tell us about the courtship of the Tredwell daughters. Although wedding ceremonies were often held in the parlor during the 1840s, both Elizabeth and Mary Adelaide Tredwell were married in St. Bartholomew's Church right around the corner at Great Jones Street and Lafayette Place.

Charles Astor Bristed, writing in 1852, described a wedding that took place in a home very much like the Tredwells' except that the parlor floor consisted of three connecting rooms rather than two.

---

3   Henry Patterson diary, 1844, Manuscript Division (New York: New-York Historical Society), 170.

4   Ibid., 170.

The doors between the rooms are closed as the guests, some sixty in number, gather in the front room. The wedding party, which has been getting ready in the upstairs bedchambers, descends the narrow staircase and assembles sight unseen in the center room.

> As soon as the bridal party is arranged in a semicircle, filling up about half the room, the folding-doors are thrown open, and the company have a very pretty *tableau* fronting them....
>
> And now advances into the semi-circular space between the two groups, Dr. Mabury, the officiating minister.
>
> The marriage service has been completed about five minutes, and people are crowding unmeaningly round the bride and bridegroom, making them formal congratulations, when a shrill whistle is heard without, and the door-bell rings, and straightaway the six groomsmen rush out into the hall, for the company are coming. Company? *What* company? Why, my unsophisticated reader, only the two families were asked to the *wedding* but all the fashionables of New York ... were asked to the *reception*.

The arriving guests ascend the staircase to the bedchambers that have been appointed as dressing rooms, the gentlemen to the third-story front room, the ladies to the corresponding room on the second floor. When every detail of dress and personal grooming has been attended to, the gentlemen descend, picking up their ladies on the way down. When they reach the parlor floor, each lady is turned over to one of the groomsmen, who escorts her up to be presented to the bride. After two hours, the doors to the third room are thrown open and supper is served.[5]

Of the eight Tredwell children, only three married: Elizabeth, Mary Adelaide, and Samuel. Elizabeth married Effingham Nichols, an attorney whose grandfather had owned all the property along the north side of Fourth Street from Lafayette Place to the Bowery. His father was a clergyman in Westchester County, and his uncle, one of the founders of St. Bartholomew's Church. Mary Adelaide married Charles Richards, who, like her father, was a hardware merchant. Considering

---

5 Bristed, 42–44.

the successful matches made by their sisters and the importance society placed on marriage and motherhood, it is fair to ask why the four younger daughters never married.

We can only speculate. We know that their father was wealthy, the founder of a large, successful hardware firm in the city. The Tredwells were an old Long Island family with a number of prominent ecclesiastical relatives—a circumstance that alone would have assured them a respected social standing in the community. Also, judging from the few photographs available, the Tredwell women were not unattractive. The gowns that survive in the Museum's collection show that they were beautifully dressed. They were educated as day students at fashionable female academies and so we can assume they had the requisite social graces. Yet there is a widely accepted notion that with the exception of a few proto-feminists who rebelled against the constraints of marriage, the typical nineteenth-century spinster was an old maid, too unattractive to induce a man of sufficient means and good character to propose.

The sociologist Zsuzsa Berend offers an alternative to the conception of the spinster as either a reject or a rebel. She argues that by the nineteenth century, "the ideal of marriage based on love—mysterious and unintentional love—had gained wide acceptance" and that some women, failing to find their true soulmate chose to remain single rather than settle for someone with whom they were not deeply, romantically, in love. By this time, there was also a fuller understanding that there were ways a woman could be useful outside of marriage, through involvement in charitable activities or as a teacher, for example. Thus the spinster who had refused to compromise her ideals could be seen as a "highly moral and admirable" woman.[6] Some women, of course, felt they had no choice but to marry. Lacking a remunerative occupation or the prospect of inherited wealth, they needed a husband to support them. And there were no doubt other women whose cynical goal was to catch a rich husband regardless of emotional attachment.

In the case of the Tredwell sisters, there is some reason to believe that they may have remained spinsters not because they were never asked but because the right man never came along. Family legend has it that Gertrude Tredwell, the youngest daughter, had a suitor named Louis Walton, but that her father would not give his permission for the marriage because Louis was Catholic. Gertrude is reported

---

6 Zsuzsa Berend, "'The Best or None!' Spinsterhood in Nineteenth-Century New England," *Journal of Social History* 33 (Summer 2000): 935–57.

to have declared that if she couldn't marry Louis, she would never marry—and we know she did not. If this story is true, it is doubtful that Gertrude arrived at such a vision of romantic love all by herself. It seems more likely that it was a vision she shared with her older sisters.

But there is yet another possibility. The younger daughters had an unusual opportunity to observe the obligations and trials of marriage up close. Both of Gertrude's married sisters and their husbands lived in the house with the family longer than was customary, Elizabeth, much longer. She and her husband lived with the Tredwells for fourteen years! For four of those years, Mary Adelaide and her husband were also in residence. During that time Mary Adelaide gave birth to three babies. In 1852, the Tredwells had a full house consisting of fourteen family members and four servants. There were four unmarried Tredwell sisters living at home—Phebe, twenty-three; Julia, nineteen; Sarah, seventeen; and Gertrude, eleven. Elizabeth and her husband, Effingham Nichols, and Mary Adelaide and her husband, Charles Richards, were also living there, and Mary Adelaide and Charles had a newborn and two other children under four. In 1853, the Richardses moved out, but the following year, Elizabeth and Effingham's only child, Lillie Nichols, was born.

In a letter to her younger sisters, who were staying at the country house in Rumson, New Jersey, Phebe recounts the circumstances of Lillie's birth:

> You can imagine what a time we had on Monday. I really thought the little visitor would never come. We had no dinner until 7 oc. The Doctor came at 8 oc in the morning and did not leave until about 8 in the evening. Such a time I never want to witness. I can assure you you were quite fortunate to be in the country. I suppose you are very anxious to see the little stranger.[7]

Phebe acknowledges that the baby is "the best little thing and handsomest little creature you ever saw." However, the overall tone of the letter is more aggrieved than celebratory. The most notable aspect of the birth for Phebe seems to have been the disruption of the meal schedule.

So it may be that Phebe, Julia, Sarah, and Gertrude remained unmarried partly

---

7 Phebe Tredwell to her sisters, November 1, 1854, Nichols Box, Manuscript Division (New York: New-York Historical Society).

because they had seen quite enough of pregnancy, childbirth, and crying babies. It also may be that as time went on, they formed a sisterly bond that they found no overriding reason to break up.

Samuel, the younger Tredwell son, remarried after his first wife died. According to family legend, his second wife was never accepted by the Tredwells because "they did not believe in second marriages." Samuel is said to have remarked that it didn't seem to him as if they believed much in first marriages either.

⤳ 10 ⤳

Let There Be Music

Musical performance was a popular form of entertainment in New York during the nineteenth century. The sound of music filled not only concert halls, opera houses, churches, pleasure gardens, and hotel assembly rooms, but front parlors as well.

The "sociable," an evening entertainment at which polite conversation took place and refreshments were "handed around" by a servant, could be dull a affair. On April 28, 1858, John Skidmore wrote in his diary:

> I then hurried home as I had to go to a confounded "Sociable" at the Tredwells. Not a great many there. The ev'g was decidedly stiff but on the whole passably good for a "sociable." What a frivolous waste of time our social meetings in N.Y. are! They are also to me very unpleasant. I wish I could avoid them without giving offense, but it seems I can't. Pa & Ma, too, want me to go always.

The problem was that the rules of parlor etiquette placed rigid constraints on social exchange. There were, however, several ways such gatherings could be legitimately enlivened. Musical performance was one of them.

Both boys and girls received music instruction. They might take private lessons or be enrolled in music classes offered by music schools. Private female academies like Mrs. Okill's provided both instrumental and vocal training, usually for an additional fee. Musical training was considered particularly important for girls, for the young woman who was blessed with a beautiful voice and had received vocal training enjoyed an enviable advantage in attracting a husband. She was in an even better position if she could accompany herself. The instrument of choice for women was the piano, or pianoforte, as it was then called. However, some girls chose the guitar and a few the harp. Boys typically chose the pianoforte, the flute, or the violin.[1]

59. GROUP SINGING.
Engraving from Frank Leslie's Ladies' Gazette, January 1854, Collection of the New-York Historical Society, negative number 83562d.
Harmonizing to a piano accompaniment provided a pleasant way for ladies and gentlemen to be at ease with one another. They may have found it preferable to sitting stiffly, engaged in formal conversation.

The pianoforte played such an important part in social life that it was the "universal accompaniment" of the parlor according to A.J. Downing, nineteenth-century tastemaker. Its presence did not signify, he said, that the occupants necessarily "knew music," only that they shared the universal desire for it.[2] Even if no one in the family played, it was important that a pianoforte be available so that guests could play.

However, in many homes, the pianoforte was in daily use as brothers and sisters took turns practicing, often playing four-handed compositions together, sometimes one accompanying another singing. (An advantage of the four-handed

---

1   The strings of the pianoforte were struck with hammers, while those of its predecessor, the harpsichord, were plucked by a quill plectrum. As a result, it was possible to modulate the tone of the pianoforte from soft (*piano*) to loud (*forte*), depending on how hard one struck the keys. Thus the name "pianoforte." Julia Koza examined references to music in the stories and nonfictional articles in *Godey's Lady's Book* during the period 1830–77 and found that particular musical instruments were associated with each sex. Julia Ecklund Koza, "Music and the Feminine Sphere: Images of Women as Musicians in *Godey's Lady's Book*," *The Musical Quarterly* 75 (Summer 1991): 103–29.

2   A.J. Downing, *The Architecture of Country Houses* (1850; reprint, New York: Dover Publications, 1969), 42.

composition was that its execution required young men and women to sit close together on the piano bench.) In the evening, family members performed for each other, and sometimes the whole family gathered around the piano to sing three- or four-part harmonies. Singing before bedtime was a practice recommended by Lydia Maria Child in a popular mother's manual: "It has a salutary effect for the whole family to unite in singing before retiring to rest."[3]

In 1863 Julia Lay recalled an idyllic picture of her family enjoying a private moment in the public space of the parlor, listening to her thirteen-year-old son play the pianoforte:

> We were all sitting in the parlor after supper listening to Georgie's play-ing. He does play beautifully. Everyone was as silent as possible except Gracie who was as full of mischief as she could hold. Ollie was shak-ing his head at her. Pa was holding up his hand to keep her quiet.... I sat on the sofa holding Wesey. Johnnie sat by my side. Ollie was in the large rocker, his father in the smaller one. We were all happy and in a tranquil state of enjoyment.[4]

The Tredwells' rosewood pianoforte was manufactured by an American firm, Nunns and Fisher, sometime in the 1840s. It had an "Aeolian" attachment that could make the instrument sound more or less like an organ. A bellows located in a leather case beneath the keyboard could be activated by pumping the long pedal at the left. Air then streamed across a set of reeds housed within, creating the organ sound. One dealer described the tone as "soft and delicate," suggesting that an Aeolian piano was as appropriate for sacred music as the organ.[5] Such an instrument might be seen to meet any objections of playing the pianoforte on the Sabbath, and that may very well be why the Tredwells bought theirs.

Music stores along Broadway did a brisk business selling musical instruments, including pianofortes. But what kept customers coming back again and again was the sheet music they sold. New titles were constantly being introduced by concert artists and published for the amateur market. Music stores like Atwill's, just two doors south of St. Paul's Cathedral, also offered to compile the home musician's

3 Lydia Maria Child, *The Mother's Book* (1831; reprint, Bedford, Ma.: Applewood Books, n.d.), 156–57.

4 Julia Lay diary, February 15, 1865.

5 *Citizens' and Strangers' Pictorial and Business Directory for the City of New York and Its Vicinity: 1853*, ed. Solyman Brown (New York: Charles Spalding & Co., 1853), 3.

collection of favorite pieces in a special binding that enabled the volumes to lie flat on a music rack. These bound collections were among the prized possessions of young ladies. When bound, a variety of songs could be carried around with ease, and guests were often reminded to "bring your music."

60. THE TREDWELLS' PIANOFORTE.
Photography by Bob Estremera.

The pianoforte played an important part in the social life of the families who lived in the Bond Street area. The Tredwells' five and a half octave "square piano" is made of rosewood, with a cast-iron frame and a harmonium attachment that when activated produced an organ-like sound.

It is astonishing with what willingness and apparent self-possession so many people performed solo in front of social gatherings that included both friends and strangers. Like it or not, public performance was an accepted part of social exchange. If one was known to be able to play, it was considered impolite to refuse when asked. On the other hand, it was certainly not good form to force oneself (or one's daughter) on the company.

> After finishing one song, a lady should rise from the piano, even if she
> be brought back again and again.... Nothing can be worse than to go
> on from song to song till admiration and even patience are exhausted.[6]

---

6 *The Habits of Good Society*, 267.

That "the young lady who sings" could be a nuisance is evident from a satirical piece in *Godey's Lady's Book* of June 1839.

> In every neighborhood there is invariably a "young lady who sings."
> This young lady in general has a voice like that of a tin kettle if it could
> speak, and takes more pride in reaching as high as D sharp than if she
> had reached the top of the pyramid of Cheops.

Whenever this lady is invited out, her "mama," according to the author, "brings along a supply of music in four languages and sometimes an ominous green box containing a guitar." The only defense, he concludes, is before accepting an invitation to a party, one should ascertain that "the young lady who sings is not to be one of the number."[7]

But for all the young ladies who were untrained and had no natural talent, there were others, who though they may not have had strong voices, sang well enough to provide real pleasure for their audiences. By her own account, Julia Ward Howe, who lived at the corner of Broadway and Bond Street, was one of these: "My voice," she writes, "had been cultivated with care, and though not of great power was considered pleasing in quality."[8]

Musical performance in the parlor might be planned or spontaneous. Accomplished musicians might be invited expressly for the purpose of entertaining the guests. Such was the case on April 29, 1858, when John Skidmore attended what he called "a little family party at the Whitlocks." Only about thirty guests were present. Among them was Michael Rapetti, the Italian violinist who had conducted the orchestra at the Astor Place Opera House.

> [He] accompanied little Miss Durkee who plays magnificently on the
> piano. (Some good judges say she plays almost or quite as well as Thal-
> berg.) The evening was quite a pleasant one to me.[9]

---

7   "The Young Lady Who Sings," *Godey's Lady's Book*, 18 (June 1839): 279.

8   Howe, 41.

9   Sigismond Thalberg, to whom John compares little Miss Durkee, was an Austrian pianist rivaled only by Franz Liszt in popularity. Usually it is the pianist who is considered the accompanist of the violinist. However, Miss Durkee's astonishing prowess at the pianoforte may have led John Skidmore to perceive her as the more prominent performer.

More often, the parlor performance was an impromptu affair in which an amateur musician, at the urging of other guests, sang parlor songs and accompanied herself (or himself) at the pianoforte. John Skidmore's diary entry for May 25, 1858, reads in part:

> In ev'g went to a very small sociable at the Franklins'. Pa, Ma, Aunt C.T., & Ben went up in a carriage & Maggie T., Mrs. T.S.T. & I in another. We had dancing, singing, &c. Mr. Murray sang. Miss Anna Willis was there. She sang also.

Parlor songs were simple and sentimental with two to three verses, all sung to the same tune. They were generally lyrical, not narrative, designed to evoke emotion. The piano accompaniment was simple enough for inexpert pianists to play. Even so, sometimes lacking the skill to play both treble and bass at the same time, the singer would play only the single notes of the melody with the right hand.[10] The parlor song accommodated a wide range of talent.

The most popular theme of the songs was love of a member of the opposite sex, a friend, or a relative. The lyrics often mourn the death of a sweetheart:

> Eyes bedimmed with tears are streaming,
> Round her deserted home.
> Silent stars are nightly beaming,
> Lending sadness to the gloom.
> While the winds of summer dying,
> Borne from the deep dark wave
> O'er the lands in dirges sighing,
> Murmur with sorrow round her grave.
> "Cora Dean" (1860)

Or of a child:

> Go to thy rest, my child!
> Go to thy dreamless bed,

---

10 Nicholas Tawa, *Sweet Songs for Gentle Americans: The Parlor Song in America 1790–1860* (Bowling Green, Ohio: Bowling Green University Press, 1980), 78.

> Gentle, and undefiled,
> With blessings on thy head,
> Fresh roses in thy hand,
> Buds on thy pillow laid—Fly
> Fly from this dreary land,
> Where flowers but bloom to fade.
> > "My Dying Boy" (1855)

Some lyrics tell of the departure of lovers or relatives on sea voyages that could last for months or years and were fraught with danger:

> Fare thee well, Marianne,
> So fare thee well, my own true love,
> Fare thee well, my dear,
> The ship is sailing, and the wind blows free,
> And I am bound away to the sea, Marianne.
> > "Fare Thee Well, My Own Marianne" (1860)

And then, as now, some songs focused on a lover's broken heart:

> Thou has learned to love another,
> Thou hast broken every vow,
> We have parted from each other,
> And my heart is lonely now;
> I have taught my looks to shun thee
> When coldly we have met,
> For another's smile hath won thee,
> And thy voice I must forget.
> > "Thou Hast Learned to Love Another" (1845)

A number of parlor songs had as their subject the Irish experience. No doubt many a tearful young Irish servant listened on the other side of a closed hall door as a tenor entertained after-dinner guests with a rendition of "The Irish Mother's Lament."[11]

---

11 For subjects treated in parlor songs, see Tawa, Chapter 7 and Jon W. Finson, *The Voices That Have Gone: Themes in 19th-Century American Popular Song* (New York: Oxford University Press, 1984).

The lyrics of these songs, with their exaggerated sentiment and hackneyed allusions, are apt to strike us as ridiculous. Yet for most of the nineteenth century, they were taken seriously; no one dismissed them as trivial or inane. How can this be?

To answer, it is necessary to consider the function of the parlor song. There was more to it than simple entertainment. Karen Halttunen, in her study of antebellum culture, argues that during the 1830s and 1840s the most highly valued quality informing every aspect of social behavior was sincerity. Threatened by the confidence men among them and concerned that they themselves might be guilty of hypocrisy, members of polite society tried to cultivate a "perfectly transparent character" and to project sincerity in all personal conduct.[12] One of the most popular songs of the time, *I Dreamt That I Dwelt in Marble Halls*, demonstrates the importance of sincerity to a nineteenth-century audience.

> I dreamt that I dwelt in marble halls
> With vassals and serfs at my side,
> And of all who assembled within those walls
> That I was the hope and the pride.
> I had riches too great to count
> Could boast of a high ancestral name,
> But I also dreamt, which pleased me most
> That you loved me still the same,
> That you loved me still the same.

The modern listener surely finds the final refrain a little puzzling. Shouldn't it read "that *I* loved *you* just the same"? The singer has it all— servants, riches, family name. What's not to love? Yet she assumes that it is she who is at a disadvantage in the romantic relationship because the trappings of privilege suggest pretension. Fortunately, the lover of her dreams can see beyond her wealth and status to her sincere soul.

When John Skidmore summed up Lizzie's virtues in his diary, he considered sincerity to be on a par with goodness itself.

> My Lizzie I believe to be a good, pious, religious & kind hearted young
> lady—eminently so. For this I admired her—for this I loved her—for

---

12 Halttunen, Chapter 2.

this I offered my hand.... [I] will be content & happy all my days if God bless me also & make me as sincere & good as I believe her to be.[13]

But the display of sincere sentiment had to be conducted within the framework of the rules of etiquette, which demanded, above all, complete physical and emotional self-control.[14] How do you pour out your heart and at the same time exhibit flawlessly controlled self-restraint?

The parlor song provided a resolution of this dilemma. In performing the song without a hint of irony or artifice, the exposed and vulnerable singer revealed the attitudes of his or her heart and displayed the desirable quality of "transparent sincerity." Music intensified the emotion for both the singer and audience, but at the same time the musical contours of the song and the framework of the lyrics provided boundaries that enabled the singer to remain controlled. It is significant that the vocal skills most usually taught were perfect enunciation, singing on pitch, and an ability to suggest sentiment through expressive control of tone and tempo and facial expression. Embellishments such as trills and flourishes, no matter how skillfully executed, were frowned upon, not only because they called attention to themselves and detracted from the meaning of the song, but also because they offered an opportunity for insincere manipulation of the audience.[15]

Young people also sang together on sleigh rides, while traveling on steamboats, and at picnics. And in New York City, some young men practiced the age-old custom of serenading. The boarding students at the many female academies were favorite targets. On September 25, 1846, when two young men serenaded the girls at Mrs. Okill's Academy, Maria Tillman recorded the event in her diary. Unfortunately, the singers were interrupted mid-song by the custodian and the headmistress.

> John Thorp and Richard Wood gave a serenade (by appointment) at midnight.... With the light put out, and the doors closed, I opened my window and waved a handkerchief. This white flag was constantly in motion until a window opened below and the Dowager's head popped out. Adieu, adieu to our serenaders. In the middle of the singularly pathetic

---

13 John Skidmore diary, December 8, 1858.

14 Halttunen, 104–05.

15 Tawa, 79–82.

song "Oh my poor Lucy Neal," they were interrupted and disappeared. The next morning Lizzy received a letter from Douglas saying that he had seen a white flag waving from the battlements but the appearance of the jailer James and the old "Dowager," Mrs. O., caused them to retire.[16]

61. Serenade 12 January 1841.
Courtesy of the Museum of the City of New York, Print Archives.
This pen and ink drawing made by a young man as a gift to his sweetheart shows gentlemen gathering on a snowy evening in preparation for performing the age-old romantic custom of serenading. No doubt the young woman who appears in the lighted window is the object of the artist's affection.

Even those who did not consider themselves fit to perform in public sometimes could not resist bursting into song in private. After visiting Lizzie at her sister's country home on a summer night "brilliant with stars" and with his heart full of Lizzie, John Skidmore walked back to his Uncle James' with his cousin Sam—singing all the way.[17]

---

16   Maria Tillman diary, September. 25, 1846.

17   John Skidmore diary, August 12, 1858.

Parlor Choreography

D ancing dominated New York City social life throughout the nineteenth century. During the antebellum period, balls were held in public ballrooms like Niblos and Delmonicos and in New York City hotels and theaters. In 1842 a ball honoring Charles Dickens took place at the Park Theater, and in 1860 the Prince of Wales was similarly honored at the Academy of Music. On those occasions, the orchestra chairs were covered by a wooden platform, creating a dance floor level with the stage.

But most often, dancing took place in private homes. The diarist, George Templeton Strong, recalled attending "the Ball of the Season" at the home of Mary Mason Jones on December 23, 1845.[1] Mrs. Jones and her two sisters lived in connecting houses on Broadway opposite Waverly Place. On this occasion, Mrs. Jones threw open the doors to her next-door sister's ballroom to accommodate her many guests.

In 1927, when Gertrude Tredwell was eighty-seven years old, she was interviewed by a reporter for the Consolidated Gas Company for a brief feature article in the company's in-house newsletter. She recalled the romantic era before the Civil War when the Tredwell girls and their guests had danced in their own parlors.[2] To make room for dancing in the Bond Street area rowhouses, the sliding doors between the front and back parlors were opened, and furniture was moved to the hall or the tearoom or the piazza. Not everyone was expected to dance, or

---

1   Quoted in Vera Brodsky Lawrence, *Strong on Music: The New York Music Scene in the Days of George Templeton Strong. Vol. 1 Resonances 1836–1849* (Chicago: University of Chicago Press, 1998), 324. Mary Mason Jones was Edith Wharton's great aunt. Her extended family were the Joneses whom everyone is forever trying to keep up with.

2   *To Serve New York* (New York: Consolidated Gas Company, 1927), 10.

at least not all at once. Chairs were arranged along the sides of the room for observer guests. By today's standards, the square footage available for dancing in the parlors of these rowhouses seems small. However, an uncomfortably packed parlor or ballroom was the sure sign of a successful "squeeze" or "jam." According to the *New York Times*

> It was regarded the height of fashion and the supreme of bliss, to fill a house so full with embroidered beaux and belles that they stood upon one another's silken toes in the passages and stairways.[3]

62. THE PRINCE OF WALES BALL, OCTOBER 12, 1860.
Engraving from Frank Leslie's Illustrated Newspaper, October 20, 1860. Collection of the New-York Historical Society, negative number 76593.
During his visit to New York in 1860, the nineteen-year-old Prince of Wales (later Edward VII) was feted at a grand ball at the Academy of Music to which 4000 of the City's elite were invited. At one point in the evening, a portion of the dance floor, which had been constructed over the orchestra and the stage, gave way but was quickly repaired. The ball ended at 4:30 in the morning.

In the winter of 1838, Elizabeth Clarkson Jay, a granddaughter of John Jay, the first Chief Justice of the Supreme Court, was invited to a party at the Hickson

---

3 "The Prince in the Metropolis," *New York Times*, October 13, 1860.

Fields', who lived at the northwest corner of Broadway and Washington Place. The Fields were the future in-laws of her brother, John Jay II. In a letter to her sister Helen, she recounted the details of the event. She had heard that about a hundred people would be there, and although invited to take tea at eight o'clock, she waited until around ten o'clock to appear. Upon her arrival, she sent the coachman in to fetch her brother to come out and escort her into the house, where dancing was taking place in both parlors. She noted that at midnight, a "very handsome" supper was served. However, before the supper could take place, it was necessary for the servants to set up the table in the back parlor, requiring guests to crowd together in the front parlor, the hall, and even on the staircase to make way for the arrangement of the supper.

> [T]hey brought in a table and made it very long in the back parlour, two forms of different ices and jellies, sylabubs and charlotte ruse and all sorts of good things candied horse chestnuts and jelly put in orange skins in the middle of the table. For an ornament they had a ship made entirely of candy and on one of the sails "Victoria" inscribed. It was floating in a sea of trifle, a stuff which is a little thicker than sylabub.[4]

Elizabeth was only thirteen years old when she attended this party. Was her estimate of a hundred guests exaggerated? Perhaps, but in 1855 Edward Tailer noted in his diary that 130 guests were present at his marriage to Agnes Suffern at her parents' home at Number 11 Washington Square North in 1855, and he lists them by name.[5] The homes of the Fields and Sufferns, like those of the Tredwells and Skidmores, were built on lots 25 feet wide and were 100–110 feet deep, allowing for double parlors approximately 16 or 18 feet wide and 50 feet deep.[6]

The most popular dance was the quadrille, a dance for four couples facing each other in a square, employing some of the same figures as the later western square dance. Unlike western square dance, however, the quadrille was sedate and decorous. A volume owned by the Tredwell girls called *Young Lady's' Book* advised:

---

4   Elizabeth Clarkson Jay to Catherine Helena Jay DuBois, January 19, 1838, Special Collections, Jay Family Collection (New York: Columbia University Library).

5   Edward Tailer diary, December 27, 1855.

6   The house of John Skidmore's aunt, Caroline Townsend, at Number 7 Washington Place, where dancing is known to have taken place, was also built on a 25-foot lot. Some houses were slightly smaller, some slightly wider, and some grand houses were built on a double lot.

In the ballroom, all the steps should be performed in an easy, graceful manner: no noise of stamping, on any account be made; the steps should be performed with minute neatness, and in as small a compass as possible; the feet should never be violently tossed about, or lifted high from the ground: the young lady should rather seem to glide, with easy elegance, than strive to astonish by agility; or, by violent action, make it appear, that, to her, dancing is a boisterous and difficult exercise.[7]

The typical double parlors would allow for a square in each parlor, permitting sixteen people to dance a quadrille.

In the winter of 1837, Anna Jay, another granddaughter of John Jay, visited the aforementioned Fields in New York City. In a letter to her brother back home in Westchester County, she described an evening entertainment at the home of Mr. Myers, a German gentleman who had included her in his invitation to the Fields. It is probable that he was the Hanoverian consul, Theodore Myers, who lived at 129 Hudson.

[A]t half past seven, Mr. F., Mrs. F., E & myself stept into the carriage and were driven to Mr. Myers'. The company to the number of fifty or thereabout, were already assembled, and the farther end of one parlor was occupied by the band of musicians; Hungarians, eight in number, with the flutes, violins, a bass viol, clarinets, etc. They played some beautiful operas, also waltzes & cotillions. I never heard such scientific or more delightful music, one soul seemed to actuate the whole number, the instruments were in perfect unison. I enjoyed it extremely.... Most of the gentlemen were Germans, the waltzing was the most graceful I ever beheld; a handsome supper succeeded, and we returned greatly pleased with our evening's entertainment.[8]

Dance manuals of the day suggest that for a private ball a "Holland Cloth" could be stretched over the carpet and tacked down to provide a smooth surface for dancing. This was a strong linen-like fabric, woven in Holland and frequently

---

7　*Young Lady's Book* (Boston: C.A. Wells, 1836), 410.

8　Anna Jay to John Jay, February 9, 1837, Special Collections, Jay Family Collection (New York: Columbia University Library). The Myers' house at 129 Hudson was almost 30 feet wide, allowing for a slightly wider parlor than the standard 25-foot lot, but still not much room for waltzing.

63. COVER OF THE SHEET MUSIC, *THE VARSOVIENNE*.
Courtesy of the Library of Congress
The Varsovienne was a popular dance in waltz rhythm, combining elements of the waltz, the polka, and the mazurka.

used to throw over furniture. Henry James in his memoir, *A Small Boy and Others*, recounts an evening in the 1850s when as a child he was allowed to observe an assembly at the home of his cousins near Washington Square. He remembered that

A great smooth white cloth was spread across the denuded room, converted thus into a field of frolic, the prospect of which much excited my curiosity.[9]

64. THE TREDWELLS' MISSING MUSIC BOX.
Courtesy of the Merchant's House Museum.
The Swiss cylinder-type box with bells was made of inlaid rosewood, 21 x 11 x 9½ in. high. It played "God Bless the Prince of Wales," "The Blue Danube," and opera airs. Such music boxes were frequently found in the front parlor where they could be used as accompaniment to a dance, and they were often advertised as appropriate for the sickroom where they could entertain and comfort an invalid.

People often danced in the parlors on the spur of the moment. One of the guests provided musical accompaniment on the piano, flute, or violin, or the dancers might resort to the tunes of a Swiss music box. These objects were popular parlor ornaments and were sometimes very complex, playing as many as twenty-four tunes. The Tredwells owned a rosewood version that played "The Prince of Wales Waltz." Gustave de Beaumont, who accompanied Alexis de Tocqueville on his American journey in 1831, wrote to his brother that when they were entertained at the Schermerhorns' summer home on the bank of the East River,

9 Henry James, *A Small Boy and Others* (New York: Charles Scribner's Sons, 1913), 44.

> We jumped, danced, gamboled: only music was lacking. But to make
> up, we had a little mechanical music box, which served as orchestra
> the whole time.[10]

These spontaneous dancers didn't worry about the lack of Holland Cloths or
the white gloves that gentlemen always wore at balls and dancing class to protect
the ladies' dresses from their sweaty palms. The carpet didn't present a great problem when dancing a quadrille, since the dance consisted of walking steps. As for
sweaty palms, we assume the girls simply tolerated them.

John Skidmore records numerous occasions when he and his friends took advantage of an unplanned opportunity to dance.

> Spent the ev'g at home. Maggie Townsend [his teenage cousin who
> lived nearby on Washington Place] took dinner at our house (5 p.m.)
> and spent the ev'g. About 8 p.m. Lind Franklin and his sisters (Sarah
> and Eliza) called and spent the ev'g. We had cake and wine, and danced
> "the Lancers" twice.[11]

Evidently on this evening, John's mother took part in the dance, while his father
or one of his brothers provided the accompaniment. The Lancers was a popular
type of quadrille.

These dances were surely not as difficult as they seem from printed instructions
in the dance manuals of the day. But they were not easy, and formal instruction
was necessary. Young people learned the most popular dances from their dance
masters, but some people did not dance at all, and not everyone knew all of the
dances. Elizabeth Jay had agreed to dance with Mr. Kissel after supper, but after
they discovered it was to be a Virginia Reel, he was obliged to turn her over to
another gentleman because "he said he did not understand it."[12]

Children were sent at an early age to a dance master. The most well-known
but by no means the only dancing school was run by Allen Dodworth. For over
four decades, he taught dance to the children of New York City's privileged so-

---

10 Quoted in George Wilson Pierson, *Tocqueville in America* (Baltimore: The Johns Hopkins University
Press, 1996), 141. The Tredwells' music box was stolen in the 1960s and has never been recovered.

11 John Skidmore diary, January 19, 1858.

12 Elizabeth Clarkson Jay to Catherine Helena Jay DuBois, January 19, 1838, Special Collections, Jay
Family Collection (New York: Columbia University Library).

cial class, moving his school northward over the years along with his clientele. In 1851 he moved from a downtown location to 806 Broadway, just north of Grace Church. Dodworth was not just a dancing master; he was a force for the refinement of New York Society. He was himself an accomplished violinist, a founder of the New York Philharmonic, and leader of a band. At his establishment he also offered lectures and concerts. In January of 1858, John Skidmore and his family heard Fanny Kemble read Shakespeare's *As You Like It* at Dodworth's, and in February they returned to hear her read *Hamlet*. Dodworth's also provided space for artists' studios and was the site of group shows and art exhibitions.[13]

For Dodworth, education in the dance involved much more than just learning the steps. To him, dance was "morality in motion," a social force by which "health, morals and manners" could be inculcated in the young. He advised parents to begin their youngsters' dance training at no later than age five, although there were "baby classes" for children as young as three. Three letters of introduction were required for admission to Dodworth's. Classes coincided with the school year; every summer Dodworth and his wife went to Europe to study with the famous European dance masters and learn the latest fashions in comportment and dress so that they could serve as exemplary models for their students.[14]

Mabel Osgood Wright recalled eager little girls and reluctant boys, including the young Theodore Roosevelt ("Teddy Spectacles"), reporting to Dodworth's twice a week in the 1860s. The girls, in white dresses with ribbon sashes and shoulder knots, stood in one line with the boys in another line facing them as their teacher drilled them in the five classic positions of the dance.

> When a sharp hand clap ended the drill, each boy was required to take the girl directly opposite him as a partner for the following dance.

When the boys and girls progressed to the "conscious age" they learned the cotillion, the *polka redowa*, and the most difficult of all the dances, the *Minuet de la Cour*. As their final test, they were required to waltz in a figure eight around chairs placed in the middle of the room, reversing frequently without change of direction. That accomplished, they could be admitted to the evening class for

---

13　Carrie Rebora Barratt, "Mapping the Venues: New York City Art Exhibitions" in *Art and the Empire City*, 69.

14　Rosetta O'Neill, "The Dodworth Family and Ballroom Dancing in New York," *Dance Index* 2 (April 1943): 43–56.

65. COVER OF THE SHEET MUSIC, *THE GIFT POLKA, SOUVENIR TO HIS PUPILS BY ALLEN DODWORTH NEW YORK*, 1852.

Eno Collection, Miriam and Ira D. Wallach Division of Art, Prints and Photographs, The New York Public Library, Astor, Lenox and Tilden Foundation.

Elegant equipages arrive at Dodworth's studio at 806 Broadway where youngsters of privileged New Yorkers flocked for training in dance. .

young ladies and gentlemen, which was in effect an assembly where they put into practice what they had learned under the tutelage of their instructor. [15]

The quadrille continued to be danced throughout the period, but by the 1840s, the waltz and the polka were also popular. In an atmosphere where interaction between the sexes was so rigidly controlled by custom, these round dances actually countenanced the approximation of a face-to-face embrace. Some people frowned on them precisely for that reason. In fact there was an element of society that rejected dancing altogether as the work of the devil, but they were fighting a losing battle. New Yorkers in the antebellum years loved to dance in a square or in the round, and did so whenever and wherever they could.

---

15 Mabel Osgood Wright, *My New York* (New York: The MacMillan Company, 1926), 168.

⟿ 12 ⟾

The Play Within the Play

usical performance and dancing, as popular as they were, were not the only possibilities for parlor entertainment. New Yorkers were avid card players; they liked to play Whist, a card game like bridge but without the bidding. They performed scientific experiments in the parlor involving an alarming array of chemicals. A fire, for example, could be made to burn under water with the aid of "a small quantity of hyper oxi-muriate of potassium, a bit of phosphorus [and] sulphuric acid."[1] They told each others' fortunes, played board games, solved paper and pencil puzzles, and did card tricks. They often engaged in what would today be considered children's activities. Diarists frequently note having played the card game Old Maid, and on Christmas day, 1848, Charles Blour attended a party of about twenty guests that "finished off with blind man's bluff."[2]

The options for parlor entertainment became greatly expanded when in the 1840s New Yorkers literally began turning their back parlors into stages where they performed tableaux vivants, charades, and other private theatricals. Tableaux vivants, or "living pictures" were just that. In a typical tableau, the performers, with the aid of elaborate costumes, makeup, and props, assumed the roles of figures in a familiar painting or sculpture or in a scene from history or literature. They arranged themselves behind a curtain or the sliding mahogany doors of the double parlors, struck their poses and then, as if they were the objects of a fairy tale enchantment, they froze in place, scarcely breathing. A gong or an arpeggio played

---

1 "Parlor Amusements," *Godey's Lady's Book* 42 (December 1854): 561.

2 Charles Blour diary, December 25, 1848, Manuscript Division (New York: New-York Historical Society).

on the piano suddenly announced the forthcoming spectacle. When the curtain was drawn, or the double doors opened, the living representation appeared, much to the delectation of the audience. For thirty seconds, no one batted an eyelash. And then it was over. The curtain dropped; the doors closed; and the performers scurried about, getting ready for the next tableau. Sometimes an announcer read lines from a poem or play indicating the scene that was about to be represented.

66. BLIND MAN'S BLUFF.
From Catherine H. Waterman, The Book of Parlour Games: Comprising Explanation of the Most Approved Games for the Social Circle, *1853. Collection of the New York State Historical Association.*

Today considered a children's game, Blind Man's Bluff was one of the innocent pursuits enjoyed by adults before more sophisticated entertainment became the norm.

A tableau could also depict imaginary or domestic situations. An 1858 manual of home amusements suggests portrayals of "The Music Lesson," "The Duel," "The Burglary," or a three-part series demonstrating the terrible effects of intemperance on the family and the rewards of reform: "The Drunkard's Home," "The Signing of the Pledge," and "The Temperance Home."[3]

---

3   *The Sociable, or, One Thousand and One Home Amusements,* (1858; reprint, Bedford, Ma.: Applewood

Tableaux that depicted a statue or a painting were particularly entertaining, for they challenged both performers and actors to acknowledge the relationship between art and reality in an interesting way. An original inanimate work was admired for its approximation of a living model or scene while the "living" reproduction was admired for its approximation of the inanimate copy! The players were holding a mirror up to a mirror of nature, as it were. The blurring of boundaries between the animate and the inanimate tantalized and titillated viewers.

Tableaux had been part of the theatrical scene in New York City since 1831 when Mrs. Ada Adams Barrymore appeared at the Park Theater in a tableau illustrating a print called "The Soldier's Widow." By the 1840s they had become a regular feature of public events and celebrations.[4]

When Charles Dickens visited New York in 1842, an extravagant ball was held in his honor at the Park Theater where every inch of the theater from the dome over the pit to the fronts and boxes of the four tiers had been decorated. "Wreaths, rosettes, festoons of flowers, coats of arms of the States, portraits of the Presidents, statues from the antique, cupids, psyches, a portrait of Boz, twenty-two paintings of all Dickens' works, stars, and drapery" adorned the front of the tiers. The whole was illuminated by two golden chandeliers holding sixty wax candles, two candelabra of twelve lights each, astral lamps on brackets at the back of the first tier of boxes and on the proscenium pillars, and sixteen gas light chandeliers of four burners each in front of each tier. Sixty-six waiters were kept busy throughout the evening serving an extraordinary variety and quantity of food in the lobbies of each tier.

The highlight of the event, however, was the series of twelve tableaux vivants representing scenes from Dickens' works, presented between the dances. After the quadrille waltz, for example, the gong was sounded, and the dancers were treated to the spectacle of Mrs. Bardell fainting in the arms of a startled Mr. Pickwick just as Master Bardell, Mr. Tupman, Mr. Windle, and Mr. Snodgrass came through the door. The two thousand guests shouted their enthusiasm and approval.[5]

In November of 1864, Julia Lay, the wife of a New York City bookkeeper, whose oldest son, Oliver, would become a prominent New York City portraitist,

---

Books, n.d.), 163–66.

  4 Jack W. McCullough, *Living Pictures and the New York Stage* (Ann Arbor, Michigan: UMI Research Press, 1983), 11.

  5 *New York Herald*, February 15, 1842. For reaction of the audience, see Meade Minnigerode, *The Fabulous Forties* (Garden City: Garden City Publishing Co., Inc., 1924), 281–82.

attended an exhibition of art work at the National Academy of Design at Tenth Street and Broadway where there was a side-by-side exhibition of works of art with tableaux depicting them.[6]

67. View of the Interior of the Park Theater on the Night of the Great Ball.
Engraving from Extra Boz Herald, February 14, 1842. Collection of the New-York Historical Society, negative number 64273.
Twenty-two scenes from the work of Charles Dickens were presented at the ball honoring the beloved author on February 14, 1842.

The success of a tableau based on a scene in literature or a work of art depended upon the audience's ability to recognize the artwork or scene depicted. While the patrons of the exhibition that Julia Lay attended had the benefit of the artwork before them, usually the audience was expected to draw upon their shared knowledge of a well-known painting or work of literature. Before the Civil War,

---

6 Julia Lay diary, November. 15, 1864.

New Yorkers could become familiar with works of art, including copies of Old Masters, in commercial galleries, auction houses, shops, and studios. Collections of art were on display at the New-York Historical Society, the Brooklyn Museum, and Cooper Union. Also, several private collections were periodically opened to the public.[7] There were, therefore, a number of works that people could be counted on to recognize when portrayed in a tableau.

And there was a body of literature as well, with which audiences could be expected to be familiar. The works of Dickens were so popular at the time, for instance, that audiences were sure to recognize a scene from *The Pickwick Papers or The Old Curiosity Shop.*

One of the most popular poets of the time was Lord Byron, who was the author of a lengthy narrative poem, now largely forgotten, about a merchant named Beppo, who was presumed lost at sea. In 1844 George Cayley, a young Englishman on an extended stay in New York, attended a party given by Mrs. Jane Sedgwick, where scenes from "Beppo" were depicted in a series of tableaux.

> In a drawing room with folding doors at one end of it, was there an assembly of genteels.... The room was darkened to a most sentimental extent.... Ejaculations and exclamations began to prevail and bashful young damsels became wondrously self possessed and young gents ... remarkably at their ease under the influence of extinguish'd lamps. Enthusiasm grew higher and higher ... when ... shove, bang went one leaf of the two folding doors, and shove, shove, stick the other, resisting with most determined pertinacity all the efforts of sundry energetic young gentlemen.

Before the stubborn doors could be coaxed to move, the audience was able to discern a half-disclosed scene:

---

7 See Carrie Rebora Barratt, "Mapping the Venues: New York City Art Exhibitions, 1825–1861" in *Art and the Empire City*, 66–81, for a listing of locations where art could be viewed during this period. Notable among the private collections open to the public were those of John T. Johnston, Emily de Forest's father, who maintained a gallery above the stable at the rear of his house at Eighth Street and Fifth Avenue, built in 1856, and Luman Reed, whose collection was housed on the third floor of his mansion and open to the public once a week until his death in 1836. It was then housed at the New York Gallery of the Fine Arts until 1858 when it was given to the New-York Historical Society.

A kneeling cavalier with long curls, black cloak (ingeniously thrown back so as to display the white satin lining) from which his heels peeped out behind.

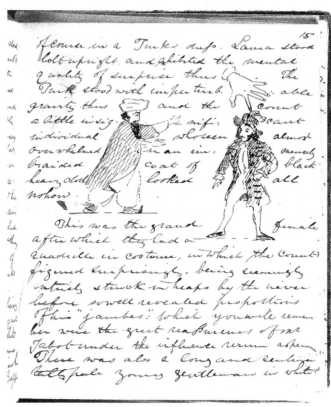

68. A Page from George Cayley's Diary Illustrating His Account of a Series of Tableaux He Attended in 1844. *Collection of the New-York Historical Society, negative number 83557d.*

The merchant Beppo, dressed in a Turkish costume, surprises his wife and her lover, who believe he was lost at sea.

At last the doors opened fully, but the producers, determined that the audience should have the benefit of the full effect, shoved the doors closed and began the "disagreeable preliminary" again. The evening then proceeded smoothly, with intervals of about a quarter of an hour between scenes, filled with

remarks on the last, and wonders when the next tableau would begin, and occasionally a song or two, or interludes on the p'y-a'nner. Thus we went through an operation of about 4 hours long of seeing successive spectacles of Greeks, bandits, Turks, shepherdesses, etc. . . . At last they finished with the scene where Beppo comes and surprises his wife and Count whatsoname. Beppo of course in a Turk's dress.

After this "grand finale," the party finished off with a quadrille. Cayley concluded that it was "a kick up" but hoped that the Lord would preserve him from tableaux vivants in the future.[8]

69. CAYLEY'S VIEW OF THE CAVALIER
Collection of the New-York Historical Society, negative number 83558d.
The kneeling cavalier whose heels "peeped out behind his cloak," is revealed by the half-closed sliding door.

Some of the public presentations of tableaux were not as respectable as those performed in homes, galleries, or theaters. In August of 1847 Hiram Powers, an expatriate artist living in Italy, brought *The Greek Slave*, his marble sculpture of a nude, manacled female to the United States for a two-yearlong tour, which began and ended in New York City. This work of art was an immediate hit; thousands thronged to see it at the National Academy of Design where it was first exhibited, and at the Lyceum Gallery where it concluded its tour. In an age before Sigmund Freud had alerted proper ladies and gentlemen to their baser sexual inclinations, perhaps few viewers would have been conscious of the statue's erotic implications of female bondage. And although initially there was some disquiet over the statue's nudity, this was soon overcome by published moralistic justifications and by the approbation of leading tastemakers like Phillip Hone. In his diary entry for September 13, 1847, Hone noted that the statue attracted crowds of visitors from morning to night. "And so it ought, for it is admirable.... I certainly never saw anything more lovely." Inexpensive reproductions of the statue were

---

8   George G. Cayley diary, January 16, 1844, Manuscripts and Archives Division (New York: New-York Historical Society).

produced for the home parlor where it was displayed as a cultural icon, denoting good taste and refinement.[9]

It wasn't long, however, before enterprising promoters recognized that the tableau vivant allied with Powers' nude sculpture and works like *Birth of Venus* provided the opportunity for the staging of de facto strip teases. Tableaux of such works were performed by "model artists" in disreputable venues, some more disreputable than others, where they attracted what George Foster, writing in 1850, described as a "hard-looking set." One such establishment, the Walhalla, consisted of a dimly lit room located over a dirty hack stable.

> The front is occupied by a rough counter furnished with certain bottles of variously-coloured raw whisky which passes under the various names of brandy, gin, Jamaica or cherry bounce, according to the taste of the customer.... The floor is slippery with mud and tobacco-juice.... A green rag runs across the lower end of the room, and at one corner sit two men, one scraping a villainous fiddle, and the other punishing a rheumatic piano. The music changes to a slow and plaintive air; a little bell jingles, and up goes the rag.[10]

Sometimes the models wore tights and formfitting "fleshings," which covered them from neck to waist, but sometimes their nakedness was covered by only a thin drapery of gauze. Public reaction to such spectacles was one of periodic outrage, resulting in occasional, ineffectual raids by the police. Yet in spite of these unsavory associations, the reputation of the tableau did not suffer, for it continued to be deemed "one of the most refined recreations that a mixed party can indulge in."[11]

The many manuals of instruction published during the 1850s and 1860s provided sample tableaux and suggestions for costuming, scenery, makeup and lighting. Staging a tableau in one's parlor could be quite involved. If the scene called for courtiers and ladies dressed in eighteenth-century apparel, for example, sewing the costumes could take weeks. If colored lighting was part of the plan, globes filled with colored liquid could be placed in front of lamps or candles, or a much

---

9 For a discussion of the impact of *The Greek Slave* on New York audiences, see Thayer Tolles, "Modeling a Reputation: The American Sculptor and New York City" in *Art and the Empire City*, 158–61.

10 George G. Foster, *New York by Gas-Light and Other Urban Sketches* (1850; reprinted in *New York by Gas-Light and Other Urban Sketches*, edited and with an introduction by Stuart M. Blumin (Berkeley: University of California Press, 1990), 77–78.

11 Preface to *The Sociable, or, One Thousand and One Home Amusements*.

70. THE GREEK SLAVE.
Hiram Powers. Courtesy of the Library of Congress.
The marble statue attracted crowds of appreciative viewers when it was displayed at the Dusseldorf Gallery in 1858.

more difficult procedure, that of creating colored fire, could be employed. Both required purchasing chemicals such as nitrate of strontia, sulphur, and chlorate of potash. To create colored fire, the chemicals had to be carefully mixed according to a recipe and ignited in a flat iron pan. Scenery could be simple and suggestive or complicated enough to require the skill of a carpenter. Makeup required water colors and brushes, fine chalk, dry rouge, burnt cork, India ink, and perhaps a collection of false moustaches and wigs.

The manuals also offered detailed directions on exactly how to arrange the performers. For example, William Gill's *Parlor Tableaux and Amateur Theatricals* gives the following directions for staging the tomb scene from *Romeo and Juliet* (two gentlemen and one lady).

> At the back of the stage, a small platform or box about 5 x 2′ should be placed, painted in imitation of stone. Juliet is seated upon the center of the platform, her lower limbs extended towards the left, her face looking in the same direction at Friar Laurence, who stands beside the tomb with a terrified expression on his face.
>
> Her right arm is raised, extended toward the right, holding the veil which she is throwing off her head, and her left arm extended towards Friar Laurence who stands at the left. She wears a white silk or satin dress with low neck and long sleeves. Necklace of pearl beads, and a long white lace veil extends over her shoulders and arms and held up in her right hand.
>
> Romeo lies upon the floor with feet towards the right, face turned upwards very pale with eyes closed, left hand lying upon his breast, right arm at his side. He wears a crimson or white waist and trunks, crimson mantle with lace collar and cuffs.[12]

One thing that may have partly accounted for the popularity of tableaux vivants was that they sanctioned behavior that under ordinary circumstances would be absolutely impermissible in polite society. They permitted men to stare steadily at women (in dresses with "low necks") for a full thirty seconds, and made it possible for women to enjoy the attention. Still, for the parlor performers, and their audiences, unlike the voyeurs of the Walhallah, the tableau's primary purpose

---

12 William F. Gill, *Parlor Tableaux and Amateur Theatricals* (Boston: J.E. Tilton and Company, 1867), 194–97.

was, as William Gill suggested, "to develop a love of the beautiful and to provide healthful amusements."[13] Tableaux also provided complicated projects to occupy the time of nineteenth-century women, for it was they who poured over the manuals, planned the entertainments, sewed the costumes, scoured the house for props, applied the makeup, and cajoled the men into constructing scenery, helping with the lighting, and taking the gentlemen's parts. Tableaux vivants continued to be popular well into the twentieth century as domestic entertainment, and even today they live on in the field of photography, in avant garde performance art, and in the theater where they sometimes are used to stage significant scenes.

Another form of dramatic play found in nineteenth-century parlors was the charade, a guessing game. To perform a charade, a two-part word was first selected. Then clues for each part of the word were given, and finally the word as a whole was acted out. Suitable words were suggested by the manuals devoted to parlor amusements: "watchman," "eyeglass," "rainbow," for instance.

Charades were originally performed silently, but in the 1850s they sometimes took the form of a mini-drama, with the actors speaking lines. In any case, the audience was eagerly involved. Sometimes charades were a spur-of-the-moment activity performed in dumb show, or they might be elaborately planned playlets with three scenes. Often, like the tableau, the dramatic charade employed costumes, makeup, lighting, scenery, and props. Unlike the usually serious and morally elevating tableaux, however, charades were often occasions of much hilarity. Household objects like dishpans, brooms, mops, and jelly molds were pressed into service, and exaggerated mannerisms, ludicrous getups, and low melodrama prevailed. Whatever else one might think about this form of parlor amusement, gatherings at which charades were performed were anything but "stiff."

---

13 Ibid., 8.

The Dinner Scene

During the years that Seabury and Eliza Tredwell entertained dinner guests in their home on Fourth Street, two methods of dinner service were practiced: the Old English method, which was the traditional way of serving a formal dinner, and service *à la Russe*, which was introduced to New Yorkers during the 1830s. Whichever method was used, the antebellum formal dinner was a lavish production, conducted within an elaborate framework of rules and procedures.

In the Old English method, multiple serving dishes covered by domes and filled with soup, fish, and a variety of vegetables were already on the table when the diners sat down. A silver-plated caster set, which held condiments, was placed in the middle of the table; salt cellars and serving spoons, at the corners. Everything was arranged with diagrammatic precision.

While details of the service varied somewhat over the years and even from home to home, the rules for dining prescribed by Mrs. L.G. Abell, the author of a popular midcentury etiquette manual, are typical for a dinner served in the Old English style:[1] As soon as everyone is seated, the hostess, with the help of a waiter, serves the soup from the tureen in front of her, filling the soup plates that have been stacked at the side of the tureen. When the diners finish the soup, the waiters remove the soup plates and the tureen and bring on plates for the fish, which has been placed in front of the host and is carved by him and served by the waiters. Once diners finish with the fish, the waiters remove the fish plates and bring on clean plates and as many as four platters of game, roasts, fowl, or ham. The host

---

1   *Woman in Her Various Relations* (New York: J.M. Fairchild & Co., 1855).

then gives a signal, and waiters remove the domes of the vegetable dishes. The host carves the meat set before him and gentlemen guests carve whatever bird or meat has been placed near them. When the carving has been accomplished, the host and hostess, beginning at their respective right hands and proceeding down one side of the table, ask the guests what they would like. A waiter then offers a plate to the carver responsible for the designated meat dish and serves it to the diner who has requested it. Other diners help those around them to nearby vegetable dishes and pass dishes to those who are out of reach. When one finishes eating the first selection of meat and vegetables, he or she signals the waiter to remove the plate by placing his knife and fork parallel to each other on the plate. After the waiter has brought on a clean plate and knife and fork, the host or hostess asks the guest what meat he or she would like next. The procedure of serving is repeated—and repeated yet again, if appetites warrant, though a person must take care not to appear gluttonous, restricting the choice of vegetables to two per meat dish requested.

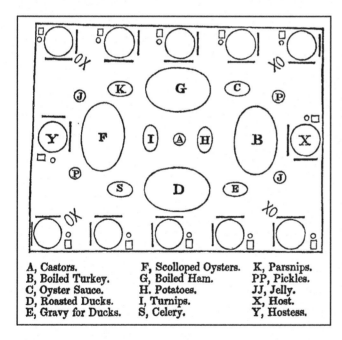

A, Castors.
B, Boiled Turkey.
C, Oyster Sauce.
D, Roasted Ducks.
E, Gravy for Ducks.

F, Scolloped Oysters.
G, Boiled Ham.
H, Potatoes.
I, Turnips.
S, Celery.

K, Parsnips.
PP, Pickles.
JJ, Jelly.
X, Host.
Y, Hostess.

71. TABLE SETTING FOR OLD ENGLISH STYLE OF SERVICE.
Reprinted in the 2001 Dover republication of Miss Beecher's Domestic Receipt-Book *by Catherine Beecher, originally published in 1858.*

Filled serving dishes were in place on the table when the diners sat down. Salt stands and large crossed serving spoons were set at the corners. Old English Service was gradually replaced by Service *à la Russe*.

When all the guests appear to have had their fill, the hostess signals the waiters to clear the table. One of the waiters then brushes the tablecloth free of crumbs with a silver crumber, or two waiters might together remove the tablecloth by rolling it from one end of the table to the other, revealing a clean tablecloth underneath.[2] At this time the waiters bring on the finger bowls, and diners dip the corner of their large napkins in the bowl, dab their lips, and then dip their fingertips in the bowl and dry them on their napkins.

Finally, the dessert course consists of a number of sweet dishes like puddings, pies, tarts, and jellies. After the dessert service, the table is cleared, the second cloth and a baize cloth table protector are removed, and fresh fruits and nuts are served directly on the mahogany table surface.

Service *à la Russe* was said to have been introduced by the Russian ambassador to France in 1810. It was very popular in Europe, and some fashionable New York City hostesses adopted it in the 1830s. The author of Eliza Tredwell's etiquette book suggests that when serving *à la Russe*, the soup plates be filled by the waiters just before the diners arrive so that all can begin eating at once. After the soup, however, the waiters bring on the various dishes in sequence and offer them to each diner in turn. All of the carving is done by the servants offstage, and the meat and vegetable serving dishes and platters are not placed upon the table. After the various courses are served by the waiters, the dinner proceeds in much the same way as in the Old English method with the crumbing or removal of the tablecloth. All of the dessert dishes are placed on the table, and after the second cloth is removed, fruits and nuts are served.

The host and the guests who were expected to carve a roast or a fowl when the Old English method of service was employed were probably happy to be relieved of this responsibility. However, service *à la Russe* was not immediately popular with American hostesses or their guests. Philip Hone objected to it on very practical grounds:

> [O]ne does not know how to choose because you are ignorant of what is coming next, or whether anything more is coming. Your conversation is interrupted every minute by greasy dishes thrust between your head and that of your next neighbor.[3]

Gradually, however, the new method was adopted, sometimes with modifications.

---

2 Instructions for removing the tablecloth from Thomas Cosnett, *Footman's Directory and Butler's Remembrancer* (1825), quoted in Louise Belden, *The Festive Tradition: Table Decorations and Desserts in America, 1650–1900* (New York: W.W. Norton & Company, 1993), 30.

3 Philip Hone diary, January 26, 1838. Hone refers to the new method of service, as do some others, as service *a la Francaise*.

72. THE DINNER PARTY.
Henry Sargent, American (1770-1845). Oil on Canvas, c. 1821. 61 5/8 x 49 ¾ in., Museum of Fine Arts, Boston. Gift of Mrs. Horatio Appleton Lamb in memory of Mr. and Mrs. Winthrop Sargent, 19.3.

The separation of the spheres sometimes extended to the social realm. Depicted here, an all-male formal dinner party that took place in the home of one of the members of the Wednesday Club, a Boston gentleman's club. The meal has progressed to the fruit and nuts, which will be served on the bare table.

In 1850, when the John Paines, who lived on Fifth Avenue near Nineteenth Street, gave a dinner party to welcome the new minister of the Unitarian Church, Mrs. Paine made sure that ignorance of what was coming was not a problem. The minister's daughter, Mabel Wright, described the dinner as it was recounted to her by her mother.

Menu cards, decorated by Mrs. Paine … then a novelty in private houses, were placed at intervals along the flower-trimmed table that was covered with rich damask and glittered with silver and glass. The napkins themselves were so large that they covered the widest crinoline…. Very stiff and prim that card looks today, and the offering of food is quite appalling—beginning with large, fat Chesapeake Bay Oysters it meandered through nine courses until it reached a solid wall of plum pudding.[4]

Service *à la Russe* involved less food than the Old English method of service, which put a premium on an abundant display of food to signify the host's affluence. But however the dinner was served, the amount of food offered was, as Mabel Wright suggests, "appalling." Of course, diners were not expected to eat or even sample everything, except the soup, which according to one etiquette book should never be declined. "If you do not eat it, you can toy with it until it is followed by fish."[5]

Since the new method no longer required the host and some of the guests to carve and serve the food, there was no longer any need to talk about it. A person only needed to nod to the waiter in the affirmative or negative when presented with a dish. In fact, the less notice taken of the food the better, for it was now not considered good form to comment on it at all. Genteel diners could thus demonstrate their indifference to their appetites while they freely indulged themselves.[6]

To transform the back parlor into a formal dining room, the servants began early in the day removing the rocker along with the sewing tables and other small pieces of furniture from the room. The dining table was extended by the addition of its many leaves and set with snow-white damask cloths and napkins and the family's finest silver and china.

The sideboard was a ubiquitous piece of furniture in the dual sitting-dining rooms of the urban rowhouse. During the formal dinner, its function was to hold clean plates, flatware, and the crystal that was going to be needed during the dinner service and to provide a surface for wine, water, and dishes waiting to be served. The small serving table usually held plates and flatware for the dessert ser-

---

4 Wright, 12.

5 *True Politeness: A Handbook of Etiquette for Gentlemen* (New York: Leavitt and Allen, 1848), 43.

6 See John F. Kasson, *Rudeness and Civility: Manners in Nineteenth-Century Urban America* (New York: Hill and Wang, 1990), Chapter 6, for dining etiquette in the nineteenth century.

vice and whatever china and glassware that would not fit on the sideboard. During the intervals between dinner parties, the sideboard provided a display area for cut glass and crystal and storage space for flatware, linens, and liquor bottles.

73. THE TREDWELLS' MAHOGANY SIDEBOARD.
Photography by Bob Estremera
Brought from their home downtown when the family moved into the Fourth Street house in 1835, the sideboard was a fixture of the rear parlor-dining room throughout the family's residency.

By midcentury, Americans could purchase matching silver place settings as well as a number of specialized pieces of silverware. Manufacturers' catalogues offered for sale coffee spoons, salt spoons, sugar shells, asparagus tongs, ice tongs, bar spoons, egg spoons, oyster forks, pickle forks, mustard spoons, sugar shovels, sugar tongs, jelly spoons, crumb knives, cream ladles, and gravy ladles.[7] A variety of silver enhanced the beauty of the dining table, and once it was no longer the custom to present a table loaded with serving dishes, there was plenty of room

7   Dorothy Rainwater, "Victorian Dining Silver" in Kathryn Grover, *Dining in America: 1850–1900* (Amherst: University of Massachusetts, 1987), 179–81.

for menu cards, place cards, and elaborate decorative accessories. A hostess might combine silver candelabra with a central floral arrangement, or epergnes laden with grapes dripping from the crystal tiers.

The dinner party was a field of social landmines. Dinner-party manners were the ultimate measure of gentility, and the possibility of making a *faux pas* was great. Punctuality was of the utmost importance. Having been relieved of their wraps (but not, in the case of the ladies, their gloves), the guests made their way directly to the hostess and greeted her. Only then could they take notice of others who had been invited. With no preliminary warm-up in the way of a cocktail hour (a twentieth-century innovation) things got off to a quick start. About ten minutes after the hour at which guests had been invited, the hostess led a procession into the dining room on the arm of the most distinguished gentleman guest, who was seated at her right. The host brought up the rear, escorting the most distinguished lady guest, who sat at his right. During the brief interval before dinner, the host had discretely assigned gentlemen their partners for the procession into the dining room. Elderly and married people always took precedence over others, and hostesses took care to separate couples when making seating arrangements so that private conversations would be less likely. Ideally, everyone at the table participated in the same conversation. For this reason, the number of guests was typically limited to eight or ten.

Before beginning with the soup, ladies removed their gloves, placed them in their laps, and spread the large napkins, partially unfolded, over them. Diners were advised always to make a choice when the carver asked what they wanted and not to talk too much—nor too little. Food offered to others was not to be touched (waiters wore gloves to keep their bare thumbs off the rims of the plates). And teeth marks on anything were considered the height of vulgarity. Thus one was to break bread into bite-size pieces and even fresh fruit, after being pared with the fruit knife, was to be eaten with a fork.

Some of the rules for dining are rather startling, until one realizes they were simply reminders that times had changed and former practices were no longer acceptable. "On no account be guilty of the disgusting practice of gargling your mouth and ejecting water into the finger glass." "Always feed yourself with the fork; a knife is only used as a divider."[8] Who would be so uncouth as to gargle with the water in the finger bowl or to put the knife in the mouth? Yet when Seabury Tredwell was a boy, that's what people did.

---

8 *True Politeness,* 47.

Neither hostess nor guest was to take notice of mishaps. They were bound to happen at even the most well-run party, of course, and so the sight of spilled red wine slowly spreading across the damask went unremarked upon by hostess and guilty guest alike. Ideally, a well-trained servant quietly laid a napkin over the mess while the conversation continued. However, according to the Swedish writer, Fredrika Bremer, who traveled throughout the United States in the 1850s, there wasn't always a lot of conversation to interrupt:

> Is there anything in this world more wearisome, more dismal, more intolerable, more reckless, more sumptuous, more unbearable, anything more calculated to kill both soul and body, than a big dinner in New York?... People sit down to table at half past five or six o'clock; they are still sitting there at nine o'clock, and being served with one course after another... eating and being silent. I have never heard such a silence as at these great dinners.... I was yesterday at one of these big dinners— a horrible feast! Two elderly gentlemen, lawyers, sat opposite me, sat and dozed while they opened their mouths and put in the delicacies which were offered to them.[9]

When at last the meal came to its conclusion, the hostess rose, the men rose, and all the ladies filed into the front parlor—the youngest among the men closing the sliding doors behind them. Now it was time for feminine chatter in the front parlor and serious drinking and frank talk among the men at table. The host, however, kept a sharp eye on his guests and suggested that the men "join the ladies" in time to prevent a level of inebriation that might lead to improper behavior. Coffee was served to all, and finally the lengthy dinner party ritual came to an end—at least for the time being. The guests were expected to make a "party call" within a few days, and of course to reciprocate with a dinner invitation of their own.

---

9 Fredrika Bremer, *The Homes of the New World; Impressions of America*, trans. Mary Howitt, Vol. 1 (New York: Harper & Brothers, Publishers, 1858), 100.

~ 14 ~

Domestic Dramas

Eliza Tredwell was twenty-three years old when she married in 1820. A little more than a year later, she had her first baby, and over the next twenty years, she had seven more. This was fairly typical for women during the three decades before the Civil War. Although the birth rate had begun to decline around 1800, middle-and upper-class women usually gave birth to their first child in the first year or two of marriage and then at two-to three-year intervals, eventually bearing four to seven children.[1] Thus women spent some twenty years of their lives shadowed by a foreboding of the pain they would endure during childbirth and the very real possibility that they might die. Anxiety only increased with each succeeding pregnancy as women worried not only about themselves but about what would happen to their children should they not survive.

Physicians were taking the place of midwives in middle- and upper-class urban families like the Tredwells by the 1830s. However, as a rule, they were not consulted until the time of delivery. Only then was someone hastily sent to summon a doctor. Husbands were typically present at the birth (it was not until much later that they would be deemed a nuisance in the delivery room). Also sometimes present, in addition to the husband and a doctor or midwife, were the woman's mother, perhaps her mother-in-law or a married sister, a trusted friend, and the "monthly nurse," who would help care for the mother and infant for a month after delivery. Over time, the number of female supporters diminished in favor of the professional doctor and nurse and, of course, the husband, who offered what-

---

1   Sylvia D. Hoffert, *Private Matters: American Attitudes toward Childbearing and Infant Nurture in the Urban North, 1800–1860* (Urbana: University of Illinois Press, 1989), 6–7, 207–09.

ever comfort he could.[2]

Mary Harris and Andrew Lester, a dry goods merchant, were married on December 20, 1847. She was nineteen years old. Three weeks before their first wedding anniversary, with the birth of their first child imminent, Mary confided her anxiety to her diary:

> I know that I shall soon be in pain and in peril and that perhaps the bed of pain may be the bed of death. My anticipations are chiefly of recovery and of hours of happiness with my beloved husband and the little one whom God may give us, but I hope I may be prepared for either event.[3]

A week later, on December 7, 1848, at 9:15 in the evening, she gave birth to an eight-and-a-half-pound baby boy. Present were her mother, a midwife, a neighbor, and a nurse, all of whom stayed all night. In the spring of 1851, Andrew recorded the birth of their second child. At that time Mary had dispensed with all of her female supporters; only a doctor and her husband were in attendance. Three years later, when her third child was about to be born, Mary decided to forego the doctor. "She did not wish me to leave her … I did not go for anyone," wrote Andrew. "We were alone all the time." He was expected at a church meeting that evening, but noted that he was "too tired."[4]

Over the next twelve years, Mary delivered three more babies with only her husband to help her. Andrew became quite adept as a midwife. He was perfectly capable of supporting the baby's head during birth, cutting the umbilical cord, and delivering the placenta, which is about all a doctor would do. He did, however, send for a doctor after the birth of their last child in 1865, when Mary appeared to be more exhausted than he felt was normal.[5]

Doctors had some means at their disposal that midwives—and husbands—did not. They had a more thorough understanding of anatomy. They could employ the use of ergot, a fungus that would accelerate labor, although its use was potentially dangerous. And they sometimes administered opium, which provided a modicum of relief from pain. They were also trained in the use of obstetrical

---

2 Ibid., 63.

3 Mary Harris Lester diary, December 10, 1848, Manuscript Division (New York: New-York Historical Society).

4 Andrew Lester diary, January 5, 1853, Manuscript Division (New York: New-York Historical Society).

5 Ibid., February. 21, 1856; August 24, 1862; October 3, 1865.

forceps.[6] However, should things go very wrong, a nightmarish scenario could quickly develop that even the most skillful doctor was incapable of resolving. If the use of forceps proved ineffective, the alternative was a craniotomy, in which the infant's skull was crushed to permit removal of the infant from the uterus, or an embryotomy, the piecemeal dissection and removal of the infant.[7]

With the discovery of the anesthetic property of ether, labor became easier for a few women. In America, its first use during childbirth was in 1847. The patient was Fanny Longfellow, wife of the poet. She already had two children and so knew what she was missing. She (and her husband) declared the experiment a success. However, as strange as it may seem, the idea of alleviating the pain of childbirth was a controversial issue in the American medical community. In fact, the Longfellows had to employ a dentist to administer ether to Fanny, for no doctor could be found who would do it.[8]

Charles Meigs, professor of obstetrics at Jefferson College, one of the most prestigious medical schools in the nation, was an influential and adamant opponent of the use of ether in childbirth. He believed that its use would interfere with God's desire to punish women for Eve's role in tempting Adam. He declared that labor pain was "a most desirable, salutary, and conservative manifestation of life-force." He also believed—and convinced his students and other doctors—that the pain of childbirth served to bind women more closely to their children.[9] Eventually and gradually, sympathetic doctors and women themselves would win the debate, but not until countless mothers had suffered unnecessarily.

Having previously been safely delivered of a number of children was no assurance that things would go well the next time. Surely there was no doctor more aware of the inadequacy of his profession when it came to delivering babies than Dr. Daniel Whitehead Kissam of Huntington, Long Island. Dr. Kissam was married to Seabury Tredwell's oldest sister, Elizabeth. She died at the age of thirty-six giving birth to a stillborn infant, the couple's eighth child.

It was customary for a mother to confine herself to her home for one month

---

6   Hoffert, 65, 77–78.

7   John Ward medical notebook, 1863–64, February 17, 1864, Manuscript Division (New York: New-York Historical Society). See also Hoffert, 86, and Judith Leavitt, *Brought to Bed: Childbearing in America, 1750–1951* (New York: Oxford University Press, 1986) 44–45.

8   Hoffert, 82–83.

9   Charles Meigs, *Obstetrics: The Science and Art* (Philadelphia: Blanchard and Lea, 1856), quoted in Hoffert, 87–88.

after the baby was born. There was no proscription against a pregnant woman appearing in public, but it was considered vulgar to appear to recover too soon after delivery.[10] In fact, the danger of childbirth was not over once the baby was born. Puerperal or "childbed" fever could strike suddenly three or four days after delivery. It was a virulent staphylococcus infection of the womb from which women seldom recovered. Eleanor Patterson was one who did. Her husband recorded the crisis in his diary:

> Eleanor was taken with the pains of labour last Sunday, early in the morning—I immediately summoned Dr. Bayard & the nurse, Mrs. Absly, & at eleven o'clock a.m., she was delivered of a male child weighing eleven pounds. She suffered much & was greatly prostrated, but got on very well, until Tuesday night, when she was taken with remittent fever, which continued with great violence until Friday evening, when it began to abate, & is now nearly gone. The child is doing well. I was obliged to go to the Doctors every night for four nights in succession, which kept me up very late, and made me nearly sick.[11]

The monthly nurse made sure that the new mother got enough rest during recovery. She was particularly helpful to a first-time mother, who was bound to feel overwhelmed by her new responsibilities. If all went well, after the first week, the mother could expect a steady stream of visitors, whom she received sitting up in bed. They called to admire the baby and to rejoice that mother and child had made it through what everyone acknowledged was a "perilous hour."

When the cause of infectious disease was misunderstood and antibiotics were unavailable, the mother frequently shared her bed with a feverish child, and there was nothing much anyone could do to make him well. Parents waited and prayed that their sick children would recover. Often they did not. Scarlet fever, whooping cough, dysentery, diphtheria, pneumonia, measles: these diseases took a terrible toll. And the loathsome disease of smallpox was still a threat, for although vaccination for smallpox was possible, many people refused to subject their children or themselves to what they considered a suspect and risky procedure. Even a minor cut or scrape could develop into a life-threatening infection.

---

10 Hoffert, 26–30, 116–17.

11 Henry Patterson diary, March 19, 1848.

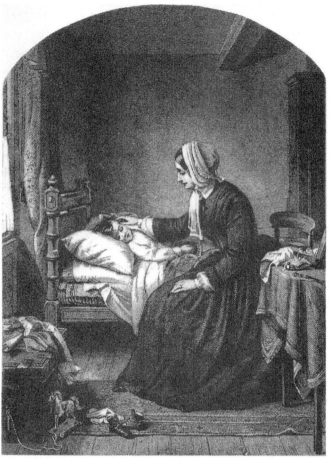

74. THE MOTHER'S BLESSING.
Engraving from Godey's Lady's Book, March 1858. Author's collection.

Mothers spent many anxious hours nursing their children. Lacking effective medical measures, they were helpless to influence the course of childhood disease. Scarlet fever claimed many children, and because it was highly infectious, sometimes all the children in the family succumbed within a matter of weeks.

From the time of their birth, children were looked upon as a contingent blessing. Mary Lester, after having been safely delivered of a healthy son, commended her "dear child" to God and prayed that "if his life is spared" that God would enable her "to train him up in the way he should go."[12] This is not to suggest that parents became inured to the death of their children. Those who recorded the loss of children in their diaries express a profound sense of grief. When Henry

12 Mary Lester diary, December 18, 1848.

Wadsworth Longfellow and his wife Fanny buried their seventeen-month-old daughter in September 1848, Fanny wrote that she "struggled almost in vain with the terrible hunger of the heart to hold her once more." She imagines she hears the child crying at night and dreams of her sitting by her side. As she listens to her other children at play, she thinks how they will look when dead. "Their gleeful voices agonize me."[13]

Children themselves were aware of their own mortality. One evening in 1855, as Julia Lay was getting her two younger boys ready for bed, Georgie, the five year old, remarked about his little brother: "Ain't Johnnie a sweet little boy? Maybe God will want him some day. Maybe God will want me too one of these days."[14] Georgie had no doubt been told about his older sister, Mary, whom the family called "Buty" and who was in heaven with God.

When Buty was four, her mother was afraid she had scarlet fever, so she did the only thing she knew to do; she soaked Buty's feet in water. As it turned out, the child recovered. But two years later, in 1853, she became ill again. On Tuesday, January 25, Julia noted that Buty had been "alarmingly" sick all day.

> I have given her nauseating medicine and hung over her in an agony of anguish, wept and trembled for fear she should be taken from me. I have prayed that she might be spared. She is better of the croup, her cough is loosened and she is out of danger. God has heard my prayers.

But by Thursday, Buty was still very sick, and there could be no doubt that this time it was the "dread disease."

> Jan. 27 Buty all broke out with scarlet fever. Very sick though her throat is not so bad. Some delirious. Very high fever.

> Jan. 28 No better. Her throat worse. She growing weaker. Has not eaten a particle today nor all night.

> Sat. 29 Some better. Am encouraged, hoping she will recover.

> Sab. 30 Very much worse as the croup has appeared. We sent for the Dr. before light this morning. Have had a very sad day. All day she has been very sick.

---

13 Quoted in Hoffert, 175.
14 Julia Lay diary, July 20, 1855.

Mon. 31 Still very, very ill all day and I am coming more and more assured that she will not be mine very long. Sister Mary and John Rodgers came with a little babe. Had to leave in the morning being so much alarmed about the child getting the fever.

Feb. 1 Worse and worse and I am despairing of her recovery. I never spent such a night of sorrow in my life as my little darling daughter was rolling and tossing in agony all night and I was walking the floor in such distress, feeling so unwilling to give her up. My grief was insupportable. I could not feel reconciled to so great a bereavement as she, my only daughter, so beautiful and interesting, so full of life and animation, should have to lie down in the cold grave where I could see her no more. Oh how can I bear it. My loss, my great loss.

Wed. 2 No better although the Dr. says so yet I feel that she is drawing nearer to death. I have given her up and am feeling more resigned to the will of God, who doeth all things well. He will do what is best. Why need I complain, but how hard.

Feb. 3, 1853 There is no hope left. The death rattle is heard and my sweet child will soon be in the Saviour's arms free from anguish and suffering—but how awful to hear her groans and agony, but she will soon—go.

The scene is over. She died at 10 o'clock quite easily and all that is left of my beautiful little Mary is wedged in death and yet so exquisitely beautiful.

Until the year she herself died, Julia never failed to write in her diary about "her darling child" on the dates of Buty's birth and death.

Children who died from scarlet fever suffered for a week or ten days. But sometimes death came quickly—without warning. On May 16, 1847, a servant arrived at Maria Todd's door with a frantic note from her daughter, who lived in Brooklyn. Maria's grandson, nine-year-old Willey, lay gravely ill. By the time Maria and her husband were able to hire a carriage and get to Brooklyn by ferry, Willey was dead. Maria recorded the sad event in her diary.

His little spirit had fled to the world above. His Savior had kissed his life away with only ten hours sickness from health to death. The day before he had been dress'd in his soldier clothes and marched as Captain of the company, and we are left to mourn.

They brought Willey's body back to Maria's house where he had been born. She was comforted by the fact that at his tender age, Willey had already read *The Pilgrim's Progress*, and loved to read the Bible.[15]

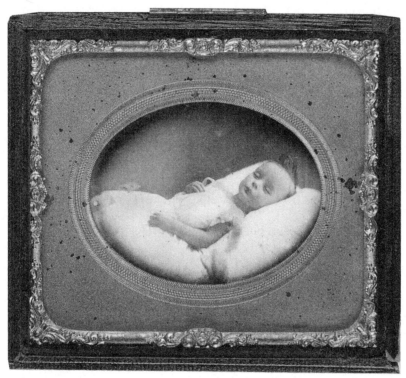

75. POST-MORTEM PHOTOGRAPH OF GEORGE DIETER, JR., C. 1850.
Collection of the New-York Historical Society, negative number 83783D.
The practice seems unbearably painful today, but it was customary in the nineteenth century to have a photograph taken of a deceased child. It may have been the only photograph of the child that the family had to remember him by.

It was not only the children who died prematurely. The fact is that everyone was living on the edge. Mourning crepe on front doors was a common sight as

15 Maria Todd diary, May 17, 1847, Manuscript Division (New York: New-York Historical Society).

were funeral processions on city streets. Julia Lay noted in her diary on February 10, 1852, that she and her son Olly had met with six funeral processions within the space of half an hour as they walked down Broadway on their way to buy a piece of music.

The death notices appearing in the *New York Herald* of January 4, 1855, tell the story:

> Jan. 3 of congestion of the brain, George Henry, aged 4 yrs. 4 mos and 15 days.
>
> January 3, Mrs. Hannah Graham in the 80th year of her age.
>
> January 3 Nicholas Stouvener, aged 30 years, 11 months.
>
> January 4 after a short illness, Mrs. Eliza, wife of John Stanley, aged 31 years and 25 days.
>
> January 3 of consumption, Oliver Haring, aged 37 years.
>
> January 4, Francis, youngest son of Joseph and Harriet D. Myers, aged 8.
>
> January 4 after a short but severe illness, Bridget, wife of Patrick Tracy, aged 32 years.
>
> January 4, Fairy Queen Alling, daughter of Eliza Ann and Theodore Alling, aged 1 year, 3 months and 10 days.
>
> January 4, Daniel Sharkey, aged 60 years.
>
> January 4, Matilda Riddle, aged 51.
>
> January 4, Carrie infant daughter of Charles R. and Harriet Ann Miller.
>
> January 4, of scarlatina, Elisha Galladett, son of Joseph G. and Mary Jane Merritt, aged 1 year, 8 months and 12 days.

Today we would consider all but Mrs. Graham to have died before their time. Remarkably, Seabury and Eliza Tredwell raised all eight of their children to maturity. No parents could have realistically expected to be so lucky.

One is struck in reading nineteenth-century diaries how much sickness there was and how often it was life-threatening. On August 22, 1845, Henry Patterson wrote in his diary:

Dr. Wright is attending Theodore. He has the bilious remittent fever and is very sick. We have been much afflicted this summer. One or the other of my family have been sick and I spend my night times around the bedside.

Of all the infectious diseases, the one that claimed the most lives in the nineteenth century was tuberculosis, or consumption, as it was called. Anyone, including children, could contract the disease, but the death rate among young adults was particularly high. A person could be sick for years with tuberculosis, during which time he or she gradually wasted away. In the fall of 1861, Mary Church, the sister of John Ward's best friend, Ben Church, lay dying of the disease. John sent her a bottle of port by Ben. This was not such a strange gift as it might seem for an invalid, for alcohol was a popular treatment for tuberculosis. Just before Christmas of 1861, Mary succumbed. John recounted the details of her death as told to him by Ben:

> On Saturday, Miss Mary remarked that her memory was failing and that she could not remember what time it was. In the morning, a change came over her face and the doctor declared she was dying.... At 11 she asked the doctor who was feeling her pulse how much longer she had to live. He replied, "Longer than you would wish, Mary, about an hour." "I wish the hour were over," she replied. Dr. Elliot went to get Mr. Smith, a clergyman. He offered up a prayer for the dying. Mrs. Church asked her how she felt and she said happy but remarked, "My eyesight is failing. I do not see too clearly." "I am afraid, Mary," her mother replied, "that you will never see better in this world." She bade them all farewell. Mr. Smith offered the final prayer and with one gasp which distorted her mouth a little, drawing the lip in, she passed away. Sid Morse stepped up and said, "Doctor, is it all over?" "Yes," he replied.

Writing in 1852, Lydia Sigourney, a popular nineteenth-century poet who had run a female academy in Hartford from 1814–1818, wrote an essay titled "My Dead," in which she paid tribute to her former students who had died prematurely from tuberculosis. Out of a total of eighty-four young women, twenty-six had perished. [16]

---

16 Lydia Sigourney, "My Dead" in *Letters to My Pupils*, 2nd ed. (New York: Robert Carter & Brothers, 1852), 205–337.

A cure for tuberculosis would not be found until 1944.

Doctors didn't know what caused people to be sick. What was worse, they didn't know that they didn't know. It would be many years before the medical community understood the role that microscopic organisms played in causing disease and infection. In the meantime, various erroneous systems of belief led doctors to prescribe positively harmful treatments and medications—what were known as "heroic measures." Bleeding or venesection was one of these. It was based on the notion that an overactive circulatory system caused blood to accumulate, leading to inflammation, which caused disease. The doctor used a razor-sharp lancet to cut into a vein in the arm or leg or sometimes in the neck to drain blood from the circulatory system. In addition, he may have drained blood from local tissue by using leeches (segmented worms with jaws and teeth and a sucker on each end). Getting the leeches to attach themselves could be difficult. Sometimes the doctor placed an overturned wine glass holding the leeches on what he presumed to be the inflamed area of the patient's body. Mrs. Farrar recommended using blotting paper in which holes had been cut to direct the leeches to the patient's bare skin.[17] Once the leeches attached themselves firmly, the bloodsucking began. The procedure took an hour or two. The leeches were painless, but doctors admitted that patients found the creatures repugnant and that children were terror-stricken by them.

When the doctor treated Eleanor Patterson for puerperal fever, it is likely he bled her on each visit, for it was believed that only copious bleeding could effect a cure. In 1842 Dr. Meigs described the treatment of one of his own patients, a twenty-year-old woman who developed puerperal fever on the fourth day after delivery:

> I took away, between 1 and 6 o'clock on the first day of the attack, 52 ounces (1500 ml) of blood, without which, I think, she must have died. (I relate this case from my notebook as a fair specimen of the mode of practice, in such attacks, which I have for years been in the habit of pursuing.)[18]

Another authority on the treatment of puerperal fever, Dr. George B. Wood,

---

17 Mrs. John Farrar, *The Young Lady's Friend* (Boston: American Stationers Co., 1838), 76.

18 Charles Meigs, "Introductory Essay," in *Treatment of Puerperal Fever & Crural Phlebitis* (1842), 336, quoted in John L. Wilson, M.D., *Stanford University of Medicine and the Predecessor School: An Historical Perspective*, Part 1, Ch. 5, "Medical Care and Public Health: 1800–1850" (Stanford University), http://elane.stanford.edu/wilson (February. 7, 2009).

recommended that after one or two of these large bleedings, fifty to 150 leeches be placed on the abdomen. Dr. Meigs agreed that this procedure would be useful, though he emphasized that the lancet should be the first remedy. Puerperal fever patients were also given calomel, a mild laxative that was prescribed for every ailment imaginable.[19]

"Cupping" was another widely used treatment. It consisted of heating a glass cup, thus creating a vacuum within, and placing it on the patient's body. The skin was drawn up, a blister raised, and it was believed a therapeutic increase in blood circulation occurred.

Some doctors did reject such "heroic measures." As early as 1835, Jacob Bigelow, a homeopathic physician and professor at Harvard, observed that "the amount of death and disaster in the world would be less if all disease were left to itself."[20] And by the time that John Ward was a student at Columbia College of Medicine in 1863–64, many of his professors referred to heroic measures as "the old way" and seldom recommended them. Yet most doctors continued to inflict bleeding, purging, and cupping on their hapless patients. In 1918 many doctors turned to bleeding in a desperate attempt to save lives during the great flu epidemic in which 675,000 Americans died, most of them within twenty-four weeks. And even as late as 1937, Edith Wharton, who could afford the best medicine had to offer, was bled during her final illness.[21]

With the availability of general anesthesia, surgical procedures that had not been possible earlier began to be performed. But of course doctors, lacking a knowledge of microorganisms, saw no reason to provide a sterile environment, and patients frequently died of postoperative infection as a result. Infection after surgery was simply taken as a matter of course. In 1864 John Ward was invited by his mentor and professor, Dr. Peters, to observe the removal of the breast of a Mrs. Loper. The operation took place in the upstairs bedroom of the patient's home on Forty-Fourth Street. There were no surgical gowns or masks or gloves then, no imperative to sterilize instruments or to scrub hands and nails. Three other

---

19 Dr. Wood's treatment with leeches quoted in Wilson, Part 1, Ch. 5, p. 2 as is Dr. Meigs's reaction. George B. Wood, *A Treatise on the Practice of Medicine*, Vol. 1 (Philadelphia: Gregg, Elliot, and Co., 1847), 690. Charles Meigs, *The Philadelphia Practice of Midwifery* (Philadelphia: James Kay, Jun., and Brother, 1842), 372.

20 Quoted in John M. Barry, *The Great Influenza: The Epic Story of the Deadliest Plague in History* (New York: Viking, 2004), 29.

21 John Ward medical notebook, January 21, 1864. For bleeding of flu patients in 1918, Barry, 355; number of deaths, 450. For bleeding of Edith Wharton, Hermione Lee, *Edith Wharton* (New York: Alfred A. Knopf, 2007), 748.

young assistants were in attendance in addition to John. One administered the ether, one tied the arteries, and one washed the wound (and got his shirt bloody). John's job was to wash some sponges and thread some needles. Once the breast was removed, Dr. Peters threw it into a basin and John took it upon himself to transfer it to a bucket. There is no indication in John's medical notebook as to the further disposition of the breast or the outcome for Mrs. Loper.[22]

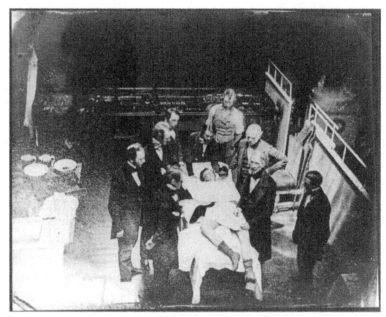

76. Reenactment of the First Surgery Performed with Anesthesia.
Courtesy of the Library of Congress.
On October 16, 1846, ether was used for the first time to anesthetize a patient during surgery, but no photograph was taken to commemorate the historic event. Several years later, the original surgeon, Dr. John G. Warren (facing camera with his hand on patient's thigh) and some of his colleagues posed for this reenactment of the operation to remove a tumor from the neck of the patient. Doctors in street clothes and the obvious absence of a sterile field are breathtaking evidence of the primitive nature of surgery before the awareness of microorganisms that caused post-operative infection.

Understandably, many people turned to alternative practicners: homeopaths, herbalists, or purveyors of water cures. Some people became their own doctors, relying on cookbooks that included recipes for remedies or the advice of expe-

22 John Ward medical notebook, January 27, 1864.

rienced "old ladies." Many naively trusted the claims of the promoters of patent medicines like Moffat's Vegetable Life Pills, which were guaranteed to cure "every human disease. Flatulency, palpitation of the Heart, Loss of Appetite, Diarrhea, Fevers, Rheumatism, Gout, Dropsy, Asthma, Consumption"—whatever ailed you—"yielded readily" to Moffat's pills.[23] At least Mr. Moffat probably did no harm.

---

23 *Citizens' and Strangers' Pictorial and Business Directory for the City of New York and Its Vicinity: 1853*, 85.

The Stage Manager's Assistants: Who They Were

Ann Clark, Bridget Murphy, Mary James, and Mary Smith—according to the New York state census of 1855, these four women resided in the Tredwell house. They left no diaries or letters, but we know this about them: They were the Irish girls, the servants without whom the gentility and elegance we have come to associate with wealthy nineteenth-century urban families would have been impossible.

They would be gone before the next census, replaced by others. Domestic servants rarely stayed long in one household. Sometimes they were dismissed for breaking the china or burning the roast once too often; sometimes they were let go when the family moved to the country for the summer. Some were lured away by the promise of higher wages; some left in a huff over a perceived wrong. Sometimes they turned to factory employment in the needle trades; sometimes they left domestic service to marry and start families of their own. In 1855 domestic servants constituted by far the largest occupational class in New York City.[1] The expansion of trade and the consequent growth of middle-class wealth meant that many New York City families were able to employ at least one servant. The elite merchant families, however, needed from four to seven to do the staggering amount of household labor involved in maintaining their elegant homes and wardrobes.

Domestics were up before dawn and sometimes worked well into the evening with only one afternoon and maybe one evening off each week. When they were in the house, their time was never their own. Two of them typically shared an attic room, and their accommodations were sparse. It is believed that the four Tredwell

---

1   Robert Ernst. *Immigrant Life in New York City, 1825–1863* (New York: King's Crown Press, 1949), 214–17.

servants occupied two of the dormer rooms on the fourth floor, the other two rooms serving as storage areas for clothing. Ghostly silhouettes of stovepipe vents on the walls indicate that the Tredwells' servants' rooms may have been heated, though on a cold winter day, the temperature in the uninsulated attic would have presented quite a challenge to any heating stove. A brass call bell at the head of the fourth-floor stairs insured that the servants could be summoned at any hour of the day or night.[2] Catherine Beecher, the author of a popular household manual, recommended that servants not be required to share a bed, suggesting that in some cases, at least, they did.[3] Furnishings included at the minimum an iron bedstead, a washstand and chamber pot, hooks for hanging clothes, and trunks (the trunks they brought with them) for storage. In addition they might have had the use of a castoff chest of drawers, and a chair or two. The pay was meager. Between 1849 and 1860, domestics earned between one and two dollars a week.[4] And they were often treated with undisguised disdain or even contempt. As a group they were the objects of cruel humor.

77. SERVANT CALL BELLS.
Courtesy of the Merchant's House Museum.
The call bells were suspended on the kitchen walls and connected by wires to thumb pulls beside each of the fireplaces upstairs. Because the bells are of different sizes, they rang with distinctive tones, enabling the servants to know in which room they were wanted without having to look to see which bell was ringing.

Yet they came in droves to take jobs that American women did not want. Even before the famine years of 1845–54, conditions in Ireland were harsh, and hundreds of thousands of its citizens emigrated to America. During the famine,

---

2   One of the servants' rooms in the Tredwell house has been furnished as it would have been in the nineteenth century. It is the only living space of the nearly 38,000 domestic servants living in Manhattan in 1855 that is open for public viewing. See photograph on p.page 166.

3   Catherine Beecher, *Treatise on Domestic Economy* (1841; reprint New York: Source Book Press, 1970), 199.

4   Christine Stansell, *City of Women: Sex and Class in New York, 1789–1860* (Urbana: University of Illinois Press, 1987), 272n.; Faye E. Dudden, *Serving Women* (Middleton: Wesleyan University Press, 1983), 65–66, 95–98; Hasia Diner, *Erin's Daughters in America: Irish Immigrant Women in the Nineteenth Century* (Baltimore: The Johns Hopkins University Press, 1983), 71.

they came in unprecedented numbers. Many of them were young women travel-ing alone, something rarely seen in other immigrant groups. They were mostly from rural areas, where they lived a life of drudgery, scratching out a bare exis-tence. Even after the threat of famine had passed, emigration continued to be an attractive option for Irish women. Traditionally independent and assertive, they were willing to hazard a harrowing ocean voyage and take jobs as domestics in a strange land to improve their economic condition.[5]

In 1850 officers of the Irish Emigrant Society established The Emigrant Sav-ings Bank to help the Irish in New York send remittances back to Ireland. In 1857 eighty percent of the depositors had been born in Ireland, and most of them were women. The letters they wrote to their sisters and cousins and friends back home told of abundant opportunities in the United States, and the money they sent back to Ireland provided the means for their relatives to join them. It seems incredible, but between 1845 and 1854, over nineteen million dollars in remittances was sent to Ireland by the Irish in America, about two-fifths of it in the form of prepaid tickets. Steerage fare at midcentury was about twenty dollars. This, plus another five dollars for expenses was what it cost to "bring out" a relative.[6]

Over the years, the Frederick Van Wyck family employed six Irish sisters. As soon as one saved enough money to marry, another sister came from Ireland to take her place. Thus the young women of one Irish family gradually realized their dreams for a better life. To the Van Wycks, the girls were all pretty much the same; they called them all "Maggie."[7]

This outpouring of assistance was possible because the Irish domestics had few expenses. Although they were expected to provide their own clothing, they didn't need to pay for a room or transportation, nor did they need to buy fuel or food. And while some of them were known to spend foolishly on fashionable frip-peries, others faithfully put aside a portion of their wages, and some saved almost everything they earned.

---

5   For an exploration of Irish cultural patterns that made emigration and domestic service a desirable option for Irish women, see Diner.

6   Marion R. Casey, "Friends in Need," *South Street Seaport Magazine* (Spring 1996), 2–4. In 1995, the Emigrant Savings Bank discovered the ledgers in which details about their early depositors were recorded. These records, now located in the Manuscripts and Archives Division of the New York Public Library, serve as a rich source of information about Irish immigrants in the nineteenth century.

7   Van Wyck, 58–59. Van Wyck was a wealthy dry goods merchant with a home on Twelfth Street. The Van Wyck family employed seven servants.

In 1854 the Tredwells employed four servants. The household then consisted of the parents, the four younger Tredwell sisters, Phebe, twenty-five; Julia, twenty-one; Sarah, nineteen; and Gertrude, fourteen, as well as the oldest daughter, Elizabeth, her husband Effingham Nichols, and their newborn infant daughter, Lillie. As the oldest of the unmarried sisters, Phebe had by then taken over much of the responsibility of managing the Tredwell home. It may be that the arrival of Lillie and the thought of the extra work involved was the motivation for one of the servants' precipitous departure. In any case, shortly after the baby's birth, Phebe wrote to her sister, Sarah, who was staying at the family's farm in New Jersey, that "Rose has gone away. I have not anyone in her place. Hope to get someone tomorrow."[8]

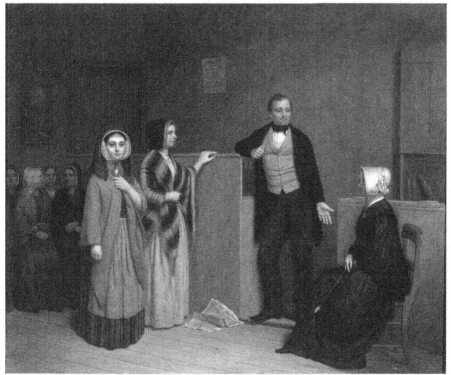

78. THE INTELLIGENCE OFFICE.
William Henry Burr (1819-1908), Oil on Canvas,1849. Collection of the New-York Historical Society, negative number 1959.46.
A woman in search of a servant scrutinizes two applicants chosen by the proprietor of the Intelligence Office for her consideration. The girls stand by mutely as the salesman makes his pitch.

---

8   Phebe Tredwell to Sarah Tredwell. November 17, 1854 (Merchant's House Museum Archives).

In order to "get someone," it is likely that Phebe went to an intelligence office, an employment agency where potential servants could be interviewed by prospective employers. By the 1820s such offices were well-established in New York City, but they were often unscrupulous in their dealings, taking advantage of both employers and applicants, falsifying references, and promising positions that never materialized. Some even sent unwitting girls to houses of prostitution. As a result, many benevolent intelligence offices were founded under the auspices of such groups as the Irish Emigrant Society and the Sisters of Mercy.[9] Phebe was looking for someone with a "character," that is, a reference from a former employer that would indicate that the applicant was honest, sober, and willing to follow orders. Ideally somebody else had already done the time-consuming and frustrating job of training the new girl in the fundamentals of housekeeping: how to make a bed, how to answer the door, or how to serve a meal. Apparently Phebe did find someone to take Rose's place, for the next year's state census lists a full complement of four servants. They had all been in the United States for at least three years and presumably had some experience. The oldest was 31; the youngest, 17.

For Phebe and her neighbors, "the servant problem" was a constant. It was difficult to find suitable servants and difficult to keep them. Nothing in the Irish immigrants' experience had prepared them to deal with objects like visiting cards, Brussels carpets, or silk draperies. Once employed, they usually proved to be deficient in a variety of predictable ways. They were louder than their employers thought they should be; they were quick to take offense, unkempt, and often guilty of drinking. Some of them were so set in their ways they stubbornly refused to deal with unfamiliar conveniences like the hand-cranked wringers that eliminated the heavy work of wringing wet clothes and linens by hand. Jokes about "Biddy" were legion. Cartoons depicting Biddy's ignorance of the ways of civilized urban society were a staple of the popular press. Biddy was said to descend the stairs backwards because in Ireland she was used to climbing a ladder to her loft bed. Mabel Wright remembered that her family hired an Irish servant who did exactly that.[10] But were there really Irish girls who answered the door by yelling through the keyhole or who washed their feet in the soup tureen?

---

9 For a description of the intelligence offices and their operations, see Dudden, 79–87 and Daniel E. Sutherland, *Americans and Their Servants: Domestic Service in the United States from 1800 to 1920* (Baton Rouge: Louisiana State University Press, 1981), 70–72.

10 Wright, 12.

BRIDGET.—"Indade, Misthress Smith isn't in the House. She tould me to tell you so, this very minit, when she set her eyes on you."

PEGGY.—"Please, Ma'am, Cook is dressin' for the ball to-night, and says would you lend her a brooch, and a pair of bracelets, and a scarf, and a wreath.

79. THE MISERIES OF MISTRESSES.
From Harper's New Monthly Magazine, *January 1857. Collection of the New-York Historical Society, negative number 72096.*
Irish servants were consistently ridiculed in the press, characterized as brash and ignorant, incapable of grasping the most rudimentary aspects of genteel social behavior.

One source of tension that employers and servants were incapable of resolving was their difference in religion. The Irish girls were Catholic; their employers, overwhelmingly Protestant. A strong anti-Catholic bias in the culture reinforced employers' nativist suspicions about their servants. Some were convinced that "female Jesuits" pretending to be domestics were sent by the church to spy on American families. Some feared that a servant might carry their baby off to the priest to be secretly baptized. Others more realistically feared that their servants would teach their children to say Catholic prayers and perhaps even indoctrinate them in Catholic beliefs.[11]

---

11 Dudden, 68–70.

Paradoxically, a major reason for the employers' disdain for their "girls," as they were all called, no matter what their age, was that the Irish spoke English. This made them seem less alien than in fact they were. As a result, their exasperated employers concluded that their servants were simply recalcitrant or slow-witted. Nevertheless, Irish servants were much in demand and were often able to drive a hard bargain when negotiating for a position. They argued over wages, the tasks they would be expected to perform, the amount of time off they would receive, and even "presents" they might expect. But when Phebe and her "new girl" came to an agreement, there was no contract, no solid guarantees on either side, and little chance that they would see eye to eye on anything.

80. SERVANTS' QUARTERS.
Courtesy of the Merchant's House Museum.

One of the dormer rooms occupied by the Tredwells' servants. The room has been furnished according to advice offered in domestic manuals of the period, using some furniture owned by the Tredwell family. Paint analysis has shown that the walls were painted with a light blue limewash. This was a common treatment for servants' quarters in the 1850s.

∽ 16 ∾

The Stage Manager's Assistants: What They Did

W hen there were four servants employed, as was the case in the Tredwell household, it is likely that one was the cook; one a housemaid, charged with taking care of the parlors and bedrooms; one a "second girl," who helped the housemaid; and one the waitress or kitchen maid, who helped the cook and waited on the table. During the years from 1849 to the mid-fifties, when the Tredwells' older daughters were in residence with their small children, a nursemaid would have been employed as well.[1]

The cook was usually the eldest, the most experienced, and the most highly paid. It was her job to confer with the mistress of the house about menus, to prepare the meals, and to keep the kitchen and storerooms clean and in order with the aid of her assistant. Her domain was the kitchen; her main tool, the cast-iron cookstove.

The kitchen space of the Tredwell house was somewhat diminished by alterations made when the house was turned into a museum. The size of the kitchen itself (16'4" x 20') has not changed, but a pass-through pantry between the kitchen and the front family dining room has been converted to restrooms for visitors. In addition, two large storage closets—one opening into the kitchen, one into the

---

1   The description of the servants' duties and their probable routine is based on the following contemporary household manuals: Catherine Beecher, *Treatise on Domestic Economy*, Sarah Josepha Hale, *The Good Housekeeper* (Boston: Otis, Broaders, and Company, 1841; reprinted as *Early American Cookery, or, the Way to Live Well While We Live* (Mineola, N.Y: Dover Publications, Inc., 1996), Eliza Leslie, *The House Book: A Manual on Domestic Economy* (Philadelphia: A. Hart, 1850), Mrs. William Parkes, *Domestic Duties; or Instructions to Young Married Ladies on the Management of Their Household, and the Regulation of Their Conduct on the Various Relations and Duties of Married Life* (New York: J.J. Harper, 1828).

family dining room—have been combined into a space that now houses a small modern kitchen. It was in these spaces that the wide variety of staples, cooking equipment, and table linens was stored.

By the time the Tredwells moved into their Fourth Street home in 1835, cast-iron cookstoves were being manufactured in the United States. During the 1840s and 1850s their popularity increased as stove technology improved, and by the end of the Civil War, the transition from the open-hearth to the stove was complete.[2] The Abendroth stove on exhibit is one of the few pieces in the house that did not belong to the Tredwell family, but it is typical of stoves found in the homes of well-to-do-New Yorkers at midcentury.[3] It was fueled by anthracite coal, which was placed in the central firebox. Hot air circulated around the two ovens, the temperature being controlled by a set of dampers located on the front of the stove. There are eight cookholes on the stovetop.

From what we know about the Tredwell family, it seems doubtful that they were among "the first by whom the new was tried." We do know that Seabury Tredwell bought a coal cookstove in the fall of 1857 for $37.76, but we don't know whether this was the Tredwells' first stove or an upgrade. For at least some years after they moved in, their cook probably wrestled with heavy kettles that hung over the open fire and bent over footed pots that had been placed over embers burning on the hearth.

The cookstove had many advantages over the old-fashioned open hearth. It eliminated the need for a great deal of stooping and the dangerous shifting of heavy pots over an open fire. It required less fuel, and the fact that one could cook foods at different temperatures at the same time made it possible to turn out the variety of dishes served at the elaborate dinner parties that were in vogue by midcentury. Yet there were drawbacks. Starting a fire in the stove with anthracite coal was not easy, and cooking required a set of skills unfamiliar to housewives and Irish cooks alike. While manipulation of the dampers permitted the cook to regulate the temperature of the cookstove ovens, there were no thermostats nor oven thermometers to tell her when she had the temperature right, and if the dampers were not adjusted correctly, the fire could easily go out. Also the ovens in the cookstove were

---

2 For the evolution of the cookstove, see Ruth Schwartz Cowan, *More Work for Mother* (New York: Basic Books, 1983), 53–62.

3 The founder of the Museum wanted to show the House as it might have appeared when the Tredwells first lived there and so, rather than exhibiting a cast-iron stove, opted for displaying the open-hearth with a cast-iron pot hanging from a trammel. The stove currently on display was installed during a restoration of the house in the 1970s.

much smaller than the roomy brick oven that was part of the open-hearth setup. This was frustrating to a cook accustomed to baking a large number of loaves of bread or pies at once. And because iron rusts easily, the stove needed to be wiped with a damp cloth at the end of every day and thoroughly dried. Periodically, it was necessary to perform the disagreeable job of "blacking the stove" —rubbing it all over with a waxy stove polish. But culinary expectations were rising. One-pot stews and soups simmered in a kettle would no longer do.

81. OLD AND NEW KITCHEN TECHNOLOGY.
Photography by Bob Estremera.
The Tredwells' cook worked during a transitional era when the age-old open-hearth was gradually giving way to more modern technology. In the Tredwells' kitchen, the traditional beehive oven built into the brick wall surrounding the fireplace coexisted with a modern cast-iron stove.

Cooking three meals a day for a large family was hard enough; preparing a multicourse meal for a formal dinner party required experience, quick hands, and a cool head. Extra help was usually hired—assistants in the kitchen and extra waiters (three were required for a dinner party of ten). Down in the kitchen, the cook had to order about an unfamiliar staff while juggling her pots and pans over a temperamental stove, but somehow she managed to turn out dish after dish and send them upwards to the parlor floor where formal dining took place.

By the 1850s builders were including dumbwaiters in new homes,[4] and the Tredwells, like many other families living in older houses, decided to improve their dining service by installing such a convenience. They located it in the hall across from the kitchen where it would rise to the parlor floor just at the top of the basement stairs, outside the butler's pantry. After the dumbwaiter was in place, the servants no longer had to carry dishes up and down the stairs. They simply retrieved the dishes from the dumbwaiter and shuttled them to the butler's pantry, to the table, and back again. The ideal was to have course after course magically and silently appear with absolutely no hint of the sweaty flurry of activity taking place in the overheated kitchen below or in the pantry outside the dining room. Servants who could pull this off were worth their weight in gold, and housewives were willing to put up with a lot to keep them. Often, of course, they were not able to pull it off; everyone had a tale of a dinner disaster to tell.

Even after a modern cast-iron stove was installed, a cook who had learned to cook on an open-hearth back home in Ireland probably continued to use the beehive oven for baking, finding it more reliable than a newfangled stove. Also housewives believed that bread baked in a brick oven was of better quality than that turned out by a stove.

Bread was eaten at every meal; fine white homemade bread on the table was the sign of a good housekeeper. Bread from commercial bakeries was available, but it was considered déclassé to buy it. It was unhealthy and tasteless according to Sarah Joseph Hale, the editor of *Godey's Lady's Book* and an authority on domestic matters. In her cookbook, *The Good Housekeeper* (1841), she gives thorough instructions for baking seven loaves of bread at once in a brick oven, or enough for a family of four or five persons.[5] The seven loaves, according to Mrs. Hale's calculations, would require twenty-one quarts of flour and somewhat more than four quarts of warm water. The kneading of the dough, a physically demanding chore, was done by hand in a large wooden kneading trough and continued for about one-half to three-quarters of an hour. The entire bread-making process, including allowing for the rising of the dough, took about four-and-a-half hours.

Providing homemade bread, cakes, pies, and baked puddings for a large fam-

---

4 Lockwood, *Bricks and Brownstone*, 167.

5 Hale, 24–32.

ily like the Tredwells would certainly have required two full days of baking each week whether done in the brick oven or the cast-iron stove or both. To heat the beehive oven, the cook built a wood fire on its floor and continued to feed the fire until she judged the firebrick inside hot enough to radiate the necessary amount of heat. Heating the oven to the right temperature to bake bread would take about an hour. She then let the fire die and swept the ashes into the slot at the front of the oven where they dropped into a bucket for removal later. Using a long-handled flat wooden spatula called a peel, she slid the loaves into the hot oven. If there were several foods to be baked, she began with the one requiring the hottest temperature and continued with those requiring progressively lower temperatures as the oven cooled down.

82. THE TREDWELLS' PERFORATED TIN-PANELED PIE SAFE.
Photography by Bob Estremera.
Food secured in the pie safe was protected from vermin, but just to be safe, the wooden legs were placed in cups of water preventing ants and roaches from climbing up in search of a meal. As a result of this precaution, the bottoms of the legs of the pie safe are severely degraded. The perforated tin panels permitted circulation of air inside the safe.

From the beginning of the Tredwells' residency on Fourth Street, ice was being cut from lakes and ponds, stored in ice houses along the upper Hudson River, and shipped to New York City where it was delivered by wagon to families who owned a "refrigerator," which at the time meant a zinc- or tin-lined wooden box with a compartment that housed a block of ice.[6] In one of the most widely read domestic manuals of the day, *The House Book: A Manual of Domestic Economy* (1850), the author, Eliza Leslie, declared that "refrigerators [were] conveniences which no family should be without." In fact, she recommended two, one for dairy and one for meats.[7] The Tredwells no doubt had at least one, which they may have kept in the extension outside the kitchen, or even in the cellar, as Catherine Beecher recommended.[8] It would not have been located in the kitchen because of the heat. Of course the block of ice delivered by the iceman gradually melted, which meant that the cook's assistant had to empty the drip pan into a bucket and dispose of the water. But a refrigerator meant that milk and butter could be available at all times and the danger of eating tainted meat was diminished.

Cooking three meals a day for a large family and four servants and cleaning up afterwards must have kept the cook and the kitchen maid busy all day and into the evening. There were no shortcuts then. The availability of commercially prepared food was limited, and poultry was often purchased with its feet and feathers intact. Most mechanical hand tools, with the exception of the geared Dover eggbeater, did not commonly appear in kitchens until later in the century, even though many patents were secured much earlier.[9] There were no detergents and no steel wool, only hard-to-rinse bar soap that had to be shaved into the dishwater and abrasives like sand and powdered brick for scouring the tin and cast-iron cookware.

Yet in spite of her heavy burden of work in the kitchen, it was customary for the cook also to be in charge of the most onerous job of all—the laundry. During the time that the Tredwells were in residence in the city, they may have sent the bed and table linens and men's shirts out to a washerwoman who took in laundry or to a commercial steam laundry after those enterprises became available. However, much of the Tredwell women's washable clothing, including their chemises, petticoats, collars and undersleeves, as well as their washable dresses, was probably done at home. But clothing and linens were not washed after every wearing. Undergarments and men's shirts were draped over a chair or hung on a line out-

---

6 In time, the "refrigerator" came to be called the "ice box." With the advent of mechanical refrigeration in the twentieth century, the term "refrigerator" again came into use. See Merritt Ireley, *Open House: A Guided Tour of the American Home* (New York: Henry Holt and Company, 1999), 69.

7 Leslie, 243.

8 Beecher, 373–74.

9 Susan Strasser, *Never Done: A History of American Housework* (New York: Henry Holt and Company, 1982), 44–46.

side to be aired. Washable dresses were spot-cleaned with a variety of concoctions made at home from ingredients purchased from the druggist. When beds were changed, the top sheet was put on the bottom, a fresh sheet was put on the top, and only the bottom sheet was laundered. (There were, of course, no fitted sheets then.) Even so, the amount of dirty laundry that accumulated in a week was staggering. It was placed in heavy brown linen bags awaiting washday.

The washing was done according to a procedure that required Herculean strength and stamina, and in the Tredwell home probably took place in the downstairs extension off the kitchen where a washbench and four wooden tubs were set up. First, laundry was carefully sorted, for dyes were impermanent and colored clothing needed individualized attention. White articles were soaked overnight and then scrubbed on a washboard in a tub of hot sudsy water, wrung out, and thrown into yet another tub of suds where they were turned wrong side out and washed again. They were then put into a boiler, a special iron or copper pot, sometimes oval in shape, and boiled on the stove for at least half an hour. Some families had a special "laundry stove," but there is no evidence that such a stove was ever installed in the Tredwells' laundry. Instead, the kitchen stove would be pressed into service and a cold supper served on laundry day.

While the laundry was boiling, it needed to be periodically stirred with a dolly or washing stick to keep the harsh soap from yellowing the fabric. After the boiling, the clothes were lifted from the boiling water with the washing stick or a long wooden fork, and carried to the washtubs where the dirtiest spots were scrubbed with the bar soap on a corrugated washboard. Then the clothes were rinsed, wrung, and finally thrown into a tub of water to which a blue dye had been added. The "bluing" gave white fabric a blue cast, making it appear whiter. After one final "hard wringing" (or if the article was to be stiffened, a dipping in starch followed by yet another wringing), the washing was finally done. There was, of course, more laundry than could be accommodated in the tub or boiler at one time, so loads of laundry were circulated from tub to tub to boiler to tub to tub—one load replacing another at each step. Wash water might be used for several loads, but clear water was recommended for each boiling.

In 1847 the invention of a hand-cranked wringer that could be attached to the side of a washtub made it unnecessary to wring the clothes by hand. And the introduction of running water and drains, which occurred for well-to-do New York City families in the 1840s and 1850s, made doing the laundry less difficult, but still far from easy. The Tredwell servants were fortunate in that even before the house was connected to the city water supply, a pump in the kitchen brought

83. THE JOLLY WASHERWOMAN.

Lilly Martin Spencer, American (1822-1902). Oil on Canvas. Hood Museum of Art. Purchased through a gift from Florence B. Moore in memory of her husband, Lansing P. Moore, Class of 1937.

The artist portrays her own servant doing the laundry. Although she seems to be enjoying her work, one suspects her happy mood may have derived more from having her portrait painted than from the arduous chore of scrubbing clothes on a washboard. While the cartoonists specialized in exaggerated portrayals of servants as ugly, sullen and aggrieved, this painting presents an overly romanticized picture of a servant simply brimming with joy.

water indoors from the 4000-gallon underground cistern in the backyard.[10] Nevertheless, that water had to be carried from the sink to the stove to the tubs and finally, before the introduction of drains, disposed of out-of-doors. Carrying water to where it was needed and disposing of it was one of the servant's hardest jobs.

Laundry was hung on clotheslines in the back yard or spread out on the grass to dry. The next day, the servants tackled the ironing. In an era before synthetic fabrics, when starched and wrinkle-free clothing and linens were a mark of gentility, everything had to be ironed, including undergarments and bed sheets. Even when laundry was sent out, it was sometimes returned "rough dried" or slightly damp, to be ironed at home. Some families owned a hand-cranked mangle, which used no heat but smoothed the linens between two rollers. Fussy housekeepers required that the linens be ironed after mangling, but some were satisfied with sheets and tablecloths that had merely been mangled.

The ironing was done on a table preferably large enough for two women to iron at once, and on which a heavy woolen pad covered by a clean "ironing sheet" had been laid. A padded "skirt board" measuring about five feet in length and tapered at one end was helpful in ironing the voluminous skirts and petticoats. The garment was slipped over the board, which was then laid between the table and a chair. A "bosom board," shorter in length, served for ironing men's shirts.

Before beginning the ironing, the servants dampened the articles to be ironed by flicking water over them with their hands. They then rolled or folded them and set them aside until they were uniformly damp.

A hot fire was built in the stove, and the irons, which weighed between eight and ten pounds each, were heated on the top of the stove. To judge the temperature of the iron, the servant held it close to her face or lightly touched it with a spit-moistened finger and listened for just the right degree of sizzle. Too hot and the fabric scorched; not hot enough and the wrinkles wouldn't come out. As she took the iron from the fire, the ironer rubbed a bit of beeswax or candle wax over its surface. When the iron cooled, after ten minutes or so, the ironer returned it to the stove and picked up another. Three irons were recommended for each person ironing. Because the handles were cast iron, they heated up right along with the rest of the iron, of course, so the ironer needed to use a thick pad to protect her hand. Later, detachable wooden handles were introduced, eliminating the

---

10 The cistern was fed by rainwater that drained from the eaves. It was used only for laundry, cleaning and bathing; water used for cooking and drinking was purchased from cartmen who obtained it from up island streams.

need for the pad. Considerable pressure was needed to smooth the fabric, often requiring the use of both hands as the ironer leaned into the board, putting her entire weight behind her effort.

As the ironing progressed, articles were hung on a clotheshorse so that they could dry thoroughly before being folded and carried upstairs to be stored. Meanwhile, more dirty laundry was steadily accumulating in the big brown linen bags.

Details of the servants' daily routine varied from household to household, depending on the number of persons employed and the preferences of the family. However, whatever the routine, each servant's responsibilities were clearly defined and performed on a strict schedule, especially in a home with a single staircase, like the Tredwells'. The family and their servants had to move about in carefully timed patterns to keep out of each other's way. Household manuals suggest what this fugal performance might have looked like on a typical winter morning.

Before dawn, while the Tredwells slept behind closed doors, the servants awoke in their frigid rooms, dressed, and quietly descended the dark staircase to commence their day. While the cook built a fire in the stove and began preparing the breakfast, the kitchen maid collected what she needed to start a fire in the family dining room. Building and tending the fires was difficult and dirty work. It was possible to keep a coal fire going perpetually, and some families did, but Miss Leslie advised against it. "A perpetual fire is almost perpetually dull and ashy ... a grate always choked with cinders and ashes is a sign of bad housekeeping."[11] It is likely that one of the servants, probably the kitchen maid, was tasked with building the fires when and where they were needed. As a rule, a fire would not be kept going in every room.

To start a fire in the cold grate, the servant set aside the fender then spread a thick coarse cloth in front of the fireplace. She raked out the crust at the back of the grate with the poker, took out all the cinders with her hands, and emptied the ashes from the tray underneath the grate into a bucket. She then swept out the grate with the hearth brush. Once a week she washed it out with a wet cloth. After opening a window, she began laying the fire with coal she had brought from the cellar, using pieces of charcoal for kindling. Having burned an old newspaper

---

11 Leslie, 136.

to warm the air in the chimney, she doused the charcoal with kerosene and lit it with a friction match. Then she put the blower in place. This was simply a metal cover that fit over the fireplace opening, leaving a space at the bottom between the grate and the floor. The blower didn't really "blow" anything, but its presence created a draft when air slipped underneath it and through the grate on its way up the chimney. This encouraged the coal to ignite thoroughly. The servant then made sure the scuttle kept beside the fireplace was filled with coal so that the fire could be replenished at eleven o'clock and again at six o'clock in the evening if it was to be kept going. After sweeping the hearth, she removed the blower, replaced the fender, and closed the window. Then she took the buckets, the ashes, the hearth brush, the cloths, and the kerosene can to the cellar, dumped the ashes into the ash barrel, stored everything else, and returned to the kitchen. Now it was time to wash, put on a clean apron, and set the table.

Meanwhile, the housemaid and the second girl were busy on the first floor. They cleaned the back parlor first, so that when the family vacated the family dining room after breakfast, the parlor would be available to them. One of them started a fire. The other carried last night's lamps downstairs where later in the day she would trim the wicks, clean the globes, and refill the reservoirs. Then they swept lint from the carpet with a whiskbroom and dusted furniture, mantelpiece, windowsills, moldings, baseboards, and decorative objects. When the bedroom call bell rang in the kitchen, they knew it was time to carry hot water in the polished brass water cans up to the bedrooms for bathing.

As soon as the family members were dressed and seated at the breakfast table, the chambermaid and her partner were free to resume their work. While the housemaid finished cleaning the back parlor, the second girl carried the "chamber bucket" upstairs to the bedrooms. She emptied the chamber pots into the decorated, lidded tin bucket and cleaned them with water from the slop jars (containers designed to receive dirty wash water from the washbasins) and a colored rag reserved for that purpose. She then emptied the slop jars into the chamber bucket and carried it down to the back yard, where she emptied it into the privy. She left it outside for the kitchen maid to attend to after all the dishes were washed that evening. Scalding the chamber bucket was one of the last things the kitchen maid did before retiring.

With the family still at the breakfast table, both servants now headed upstairs to the bedchambers. Sometimes a servant had laid a fire in the bedchamber late in the previous evening so that the room's occupant could light it herself in the morning and go back to bed while the room warmed up. In a well-run household, the bedsheets and blankets would have been spread over chairs by the bed's occupant upon arising. The windows would also have been opened so that the room could be ventilated and the bed aired. The servants, standing on either side of the bed, turned the feather bed over, shook it to distribute the feathers, and smoothed it from top to bottom. They tucked in the bedsheets, replaced the blankets and the spread, put the bolster back, and plumped the pillows. They then covered the bed with an old sheet and the water pitchers with towels to keep off the dust they were about to stir up as they swept and dusted the room

When they were finished sweeping and dusting, they poured fresh water into the pitcher on the washstand, the water pitcher, and the tea kettle that was kept on the footman, a metal tray that hooked over the fireplace grate. They put fresh towels on the towel rack, neatly arranged the items on the dressers, gathered their equipment, and headed downstairs.

Now the ladies of the house were free to leave the back parlor for their bedchambers if they wished. There they could take up their needlework, arrange their wardrobes, read their Bible, or write letters. By this time the kitchen maid had finished cleaning the family room on the kitchen floor, and that room, too, was available for sitting. This was a good time for Mrs. Tredwell to confer with her cook regarding the day's menus or any problems that might be brewing in the kitchen. At the same time, the chambermaid and second girl could finish up any work left to do in the back parlor. Then they could clean the front parlor so that it would be ready to receive any visitors who might call after ten o'clock. A retired gentleman at home like Seabury Tredwell complicated matters somewhat, as retired gentlemen tend to do, but there was almost always some reason for him to be about and around town and thus out of the servants' way. Once the parlors were presentable, the children's rooms could be cleaned.

In addition to the daily routine, once a week the servants gave each room a more thorough cleaning. They covered all the furniture with sheets and sprinkled damp tea leaves on the carpet before sweeping it. They cleaned upholstery with a horsehair brush and polished the rosewood and mahogany with linseed oil. They washed the marble mantels and carefully dusted all the ornaments and books with a dust brush. Upstairs they scrubbed the bedsteads with soapsuds as a precaution against bedbugs.

Household manuals recommended that the house be turned upside down and inside out for a seasonal cleaning twice a year. During the winter, a great quantity of dirt and soot was produced by the open fires needed for heat and light, and warmer weather brought its special brand of filth. Streets were so dusty that householders paid to have their streets watered, but still that did not keep the dust from blowing in through the open windows along with desiccated horse manure, for there was no wire screening until after the Civil War. Lace curtains filtered out some of the airborne dirt and kept out some of the insects, but of course the curtains became filthy and had to be frequently laundered. Since the Tredwells closed their city home and moved to the country during the hottest summer months, fall cleaning was less arduous than the spring commotion. Miss Leslie noted that it would probably be necessary to employ at least three additional persons to help with the seasonal cleaning. At least two of them would have to be men who could provide the muscle power for what was, to say the least, "heavy" cleaning.

During the one or two weeks of spring-cleaning, brick walls in the kitchen and cellar were whitewashed. A professional was called in to clean the chimney, and when he was finished, the servants thoroughly scrubbed out the fireplace. They then put in place a decorative grill to cover the fireplace opening for the summer. The servants and their temporary helpers took pictures down from the walls and cleaned the glass and the gilded frames. A worker standing on a ladder cleaned the large parlor mirrors. The windows were washed inside and out and rubbed with a buckskin and whiting. They scrubbed walls and woodwork. They untacked carpets, hung them on a clothesline, and beat them thoroughly. They laid them out on the floor, scrubbed them, and when they were dry, rolled them in tobacco leaves to keep out the moths, storing them in the attic. Featherbeds were emptied of their feathers; their coverings were washed and then restuffed. Blankets, too, were washed, as were the curtains.

In the fall, when the Tredwells returned to the city, the house was thoroughly swept and dusted. Draperies and blankets were returned to their places, the Holland Cloth covers were removed from the furniture, and the carpets relaid. After unpacking their trunks, the family settled in for the winter.

When someone in the family was sick, as was often the case, the servants' tasks multiplied. The women of the family did the nursing, but the servants responded to the increased need to empty chamber pots due to the use of purgatives, emetics and bloodletting as medical treatments. They carried food upstairs, fetched cool fresh pillowcases, bowls of ice, warming pans, and extra blankets.

They helped lift adult patients, and ventured out, sometimes in the middle of the night, to summon the doctor.

84. THE FIRST PLACE.
A. Erwood, Oil on Canvas. © Geffrye Museum, London. Purchased with the assistance of the Art Fund and the MLA/V&A Purchase Grant Fund.

Many of the women who emigrated from Ireland and found employment as domestic servants were young, some not yet out of their teens. They were separated from family at a tender age and thrust into an unfamiliar environment that sometimes proved overwhelming.

Besides the servants, there were others whose services were required to make the household run smoothly. There was the dressmaker, who lived with the family for a short period while she fitted and sewed dresses; the delivery men, who brought ice, milk, coal, and water to the door; the woman with the dog cart, who came from her scrabble garden in what is now Central Park to take away the garbage to feed her pigs; the coachman, who rented the family a carriage when it was needed; the knife sharpener, who announced his arrival with a whistle; the bell hanger, who repaired the servant call bells; and the chore men, who made household repairs. Life was not easy for any of them, but none worked harder than the four Irish women, far from home, who cleaned and cooked and scrubbed and ironed and day in and day out hauled water upstairs and down.

Waiting to Go On

E ven after attending to her wardrobe, stirring up pots of cosmetics in her kitchen, and making obligatory social calls, the nineteenth-century woman still had time on her hands. Much of that time was spent in the privacy of her bedroom.

Ideally it was "a room of her own." In reality, of course, with adult children living at home, even for a time after they married, and maiden aunts and grandparents also frequently in residence, space was often at a premium, and the ideal was not always possible. Nevertheless, separate rooms for husband and wife were the norm, and couples living in urban rowhouses like the Tredwells typically started their married lives in separate bedrooms and returned to that arrangement as soon as the realignment of the family made it possible. Unmarried adult females often shared bedrooms and even beds.

Behind the closed door of her room, a woman could loosen her stays, take a deep breath, and alleviate the strain of always "being on." Here she engaged in the most private aspect of her daily activities, her religious devotions. The nineteenth-century gentlewoman was a model of piety, and the Tredwells were even more deeply devout than most.

Seabury Tredwell's father was one of four farmers who in 1802 purchased two acres and ninety-seven square rods in what is now Manhasset, Long Island, to build Christ Church. His grandfather on his mother's side was a Congregational minister who converted to the Anglican faith and became a priest in 1730. Seabury's cousin was also an Episcopalian priest, and two of his Aunt Phebe's grandsons were Episcopalian bishops: Benjamin Tredwell Onderdonk, bishop of the diocese of New York, and Henry Ustick Onderdonk, bishop of the diocese of Philadelphia. But it was his mother's half brother, Samuel Seabury, who was the family's most prominent ecclesiastical connection.[1] The eminent cleric, after whom Seabury Tredwell was named, was the first bishop of the Protestant Episcopal Church in America.

85. Lithographed Religious Motto.
Courtesy of the Merchant's House Museum.

Hung above the bedroom mantel, the reassuring passage from the Twenty-Third Psalm may have been the first thing Eliza Tredwell saw upon awakening. Mottoes, including Bible verses, proverbs, and folk sayings were popular wall decoration. They were originally worked in cross-stitch on perforated paper, but after the popularization of chromo lithography at midcentury, the lithographed versions became very popular.

As communicants of St. Bartholomew's Episcopal Church, the Tredwells were evangelical (or low church) Episcopalians. They believed that the entire human

---

1 Bishop Benjamin Tredwell Onderdonk was the subject of a scandal that rocked the Episcopalian Community in 1844. Bishop Onderdonk's offense was overly familiar behavior towards his female parishioners. Specifically, he was accused of repeatedly thrusting his hands into their bosoms. Four women testified against him at an ecclesiastical trial in which he was suspended without possibility of appeal even though he was widely supported by the New York diocese. Actually the dispute had more to do with a conflict in the Episcopalian community. Onderdonk represented those who followed the Oxford Movement, which strove to return the church to its Catholic roots; those who opposed him viewed this movement with alarm. The fact that his brother, Henry Ustick Onderdonk, Bishop of Philadelphia, was removed for intemperance, did not help his case. There is no written record to reveal the Tredwells' reaction to the Onderdonk scandals. Interestingly, as low church Episcopalians, they would not have agreed with Bishop Benjamin T. Onderdonk on theological grounds, but the scandal surrounding the namesake of Seabury's father and grandfather must have caused them great distress.

race was depraved and that individuals were reconciled with God by the death of Jesus Christ. Salvation was to be achieved by faith alone, not by good works, and sinners who were unrepentant would suffer a hell of fire and brimstone.[2] Because they believed that the writing of the Holy Scripture was directly inspired by God, a close reading of the Bible was the cornerstone of their daily devotion. The Bibles and prayer books in the Merchant's House collection are so worn and fragile from constant use that they cannot be displayed.

But it was not only devotional reading that occupied the time of genteel women. They spent many hours reading novels and stories as well, even though the conduct manuals cautioned them again and again about the corrupting influence of fiction. According to the authors of the manuals, the only books a lady should read were those that improved her morally or intellectually. One adviser enumerated the consequences of novel reading:

> [o]bscured, feeble intellect, a weakened memory, an extravagant and fanciful imagination, a demoralized conscience, and a corrupted heart.[3]

Most women simply ignored this advice. They did not, however, rush to read the new novels that would become classics of American literature. It was not Herman Melville's *Moby Dick* (1851) or Nathaniel Hawthorne's *House of Seven Gables* (1851) or even *The Scarlet Letter* (1850) that captured their imaginations but rather the sentimental novels penned by women writers like Maria Cummins, Catharine Maria Sedgwick, and Susan Warner. In 1855 Hawthorne complained to his publisher,

> America is now wholly given over to a damned mob of scribbling women, and I should have no chance of success while the public taste is occupied with their trash—and should be ashamed of myself if I did succeed. What is the mystery of these innumerable editions of *The Lamplighter*

---

2 During the life of Seabury Tredwell, the rectors of St. Bartholomew's were committed Evangelicals, as was Dr. George Milnor, rector of St. George's, where the Tredwells worshipped before their move to Fourth Street. Dr. Samuel Cooke, rector of St. Bartholomew's from 1851 to 1888, was said to be an "evangelical of Evangelicals," who preached "with such commanding force and fervor that at times his hearers were moved like a wind-swept sea." E. Clowes Chorley, D.D., L.H.D., *The Centennial History of Saint Bartholomew's Church in the City of New York, 1835-1935* (New York: The Rector, Church Wardens and Vestrymen of Saint Bartholomew's Church in the City of New York, 1935). 100-101.

3 Daniel Wise, *The Young Lady's Counsellor* (New York: Carlton & Phillips, 1852), 189.

and other books neither better or worse?—worse they could not be, and better they need not be, when they sell by the hundred thousand.[4]

The Lamplighter, the treacly tale singled out by Hawthorne for contempt, sold 40,000 copies the first month of its publication in 1854. But it was Susan Warner's *The Wide Wide World* (1850) that was America's first bestseller. The story is typical of the genre. It follows the life of little Ellen Montgomery from childhood to adolescence. Separated from her dying mother early on, she is subjected to the harsh treatment of various unfeeling relatives, until at last, strengthened by her religious faith, she overcomes her misfortunes. In the end, the reader is made to understand that Ellen will find happiness when she is a little older as the wife of the irreproachable John Humphreys. Many a tear was shed over the pages of *The Wide Wide World*, which was surpassed in popularity only by Harriet Beecher Stowe's antislavery novel, *Uncle Tom's Cabin* (1852), whose author Abraham Lincoln famously called "the little lady who made this big war."

When it came to British literature, Charles Dickens, popularly known as "Boz," was everybody's favorite.[5] In 1842, at the age of twenty-nine, with six books to his credit, Dickens made his first visit to New York City, where he was showered with adulation. Shortly after the ball given in his honor, Elizabeth Jay wrote to her married sister Helen, who was living in Ohio:

> Every thing is Boz, Boz, nothing but Boz. I even dream about him. Everyone who has not already read his books are now reading them. The people talk of little else. I saw Laura today. She showed me an illustrated copy of The Old curiosity Shop which she is reading to her mother.[6]

And before Dickens, there was Sir Walter Scott. So popular were Scott's Waverley novels that in 1833 residents of Sixth Street from Broadway to Washington Square petitioned the City Council to name their street Waverley Place. (The current misspelling, "Waverly," is due to a long-ago transcription error in the

---

4 Quoted in F.O. Matthiessen, *American Renaissance: Art and Expression in the Age of Emerson and Whitman* (New York: Oxford University Press, 1941), x-xi.

5 "Boz" was a pseudonym used by Dickens for his book *Sketches by Boz*, not one of his more widely read books today.

6 Elizabeth Clarkson Jay to Catherine Helena Jay DuBois, February 28, 1842 (New York: Columbia University Libraries Special Collections, Jay Family Collection).

municipal records.)[7] When Elizabeth Jay's cousin Anna wrote her brother, John Jay II, about her New York trip to visit her friend Ella Fields in February 1837, she recounted that the day after they had danced at the Myers', she and Ella went to visit Miss De Peyster where they spent two hours reading aloud, most likely in Miss DePeyster's bedroom—one hour from Scott's novel *The Abbott*, based on a year in the life of Mary, Queen of Scots. The other hour was devoted to the more serious work of David Hume, an eighteenth-century philosopher.

86. GIRL READING.
George Cochran Lambdin American (1830-1896), Oil on Canvas, 1872. 29 ½ x 25 in., St. Johnsbury Athenaeum, St. Johnsbury, Vermont. Gift of Horace Fairbanks

As suggested by the unfurling lily on the windowsill, the young woman may be absorbed in a serious work of non-fiction that will expand her horizons and contribute to her maturing intellectual development. On the other hand, her attention may very well be engaged by a sentimental novel penned by one of the "scribbling women" authors of the time.

Beginning in the 1830s, advice and instructional manuals began to pour off American presses. Some were addressed specifically to young women, some to young men, some to wives and mothers. There were etiquette manuals, books on

---

7   Luther Harris, *Around Washington Square* (Baltimore: The Johns Hopkins University Press, 2003), 94.

household management, cooking, health, and beauty. There were instructional manuals on needlework, letter writing, dancing, and parlor pastimes. In fact, virtually anything one wondered or worried about, including delicate medical and sexual matters, was the subject of a prescriptive publication.

Another source of advice was *Godey's Lady's Book*, an immensely popular women's magazine of the nineteenth century. *Godey's* was edited for many years by Sarah Josepha Hale, remembered today as the author of "Mary Had a Little Lamb" and the proponent of Thanksgiving as a national holiday. An author in her own right, Mrs. Hale was an untiring supporter of women's education and a true believer in the virtues of domesticity, which were promoted throughout the pages of the magazine. In addition to its advice columns and articles on a variety of subjects, *Godey's* offered poetry, short fiction, and in every issue simple music for a parlor song written for the pianoforte.

But it was the fashion plates, detailed engravings of the latest styles, that were the most highly anticipated feature of *Godey's*. Women were hired to tint these drawings with watercolors. The pictures were then inserted into the magazine underneath a sheet of tissue to protect them. Readers carefully studied these illustrations and sometimes tore them out to take with them when shopping for fabric or consulting their dressmaker. (See Godey's Fashion Plate illustration on page 56).

Godey's also published instructions for what was called "fancywork"—ornamental needlework as well as what we would today call "crafts." Women spent hours embroidering their petticoats and their pillow cushions and in making dried flower wreaths, match holders, penwipers, reticules, needlebooks, and wall pockets, for example. These objects were both useful and decorative and were given as gifts or sold at charity fairs sponsored by schools and churches. Natural objects such as leaves, seeds, flowers, pine cones, shells, fish scales, and seaweed were often used in creating fancywork. In her girlhood diary, Queen Victoria recorded making a "seaweed album" for the Queen of Portugal.[8] In the Merchant's House collection, there is just such an album as well as dozens of sheets of dried seaweed. The Tredwell sisters collected these specimens by pinning up their skirts and wading into the waters of the Jersey shore. First they submerged a sheet of blotting paper underneath the floating seaweed, then carefully lifted the sheet out of the water

---

8   Beverly Gordon, "Victorian Fancywork in the American Home: Fantasy and Accommodation" in *Making the American Home: Middle-Class Women & Domestic Material Culture, 1840-1890*, ed. Pat Browne (Bowling Green, Ohio: Bowling Green State University Popular Press, 1988), 52.

with the seaweed spread out upon it. While the paper was still wet, the delicate tendrils could be teased apart with a needle where necessary. Like the dried flowers mounted and framed for hanging on the wall or those preserved under a glass dome, the sheets of seaweed provided the opportunity for a contemplative look at an object of God's creation—and this may have been, at least in part, the secret of their attraction to those who collected them. On the other hand, women often took delight in transforming natural objects into something quite different from their natural state: in their hands lobster claws became toothpick holders, for example.

87. SEAWEED ALBUM BELONGING TO THE TREDWELLS.
Courtesy of the Merchant's House Museum.
Painstaking pastimes of nineteenth-century women included many varieties of fancy needlework as well as projects such as the making of hair jewelry and creating an album of dried seaweed.

Although fancywork may seem trivial when viewed from a twenty-first century perspective, it was taken quite seriously, not only by the women who created it, but by men, who were meant to appreciate it. In 1845, when Andrew Lester first visited the home of Mr. Harris, a business colleague, Mrs. Harris made a point of showing him many specimens of her and her daughter's fancy worsted work with the needle—very pretty indeed and some cabinet of shells, skillfully arranged.[9]

We don't know just how important the worsted wool work or the shell collection was to Andrew's decision to propose to his colleague's daughter, but two years later, Mary Harris and Andrew Lester were married. It may be that competence in fancywork, like the ability to sing or play an instrument, was considered an asset when it came to securing a proposal of marriage. At any rate, fancywork was "woman's work," a necessary element in providing a beautiful home, and therefore not to be taken lightly.

88. Unfinished Berlin Work Begun by a Tredwell Sister.
Courtesy of the Merchant's House Museum.
Tiny glass beads strung on thread were used to create this project. The canvas is printed with a floral pattern to guide the needlewoman. Evidently she tired of her work, and the brilliant pillow cover never materialized.

---

9   Andrew Lester diary, January 17, 1845.

∼✺ 18 ✺∼

The Final Curtain

On March 7, 1865, Seabury Tredwell died at the age of eighty-four. He had outlived all of his siblings, most of his nephews and nieces, and all three of his much younger business partners. The cause of death listed on the death certificate was Bright's Disease or irreversible kidney failure. The disease was the subject of a medical lecture attended by John Ward in 1864. The professor outlined the final stages:

> Patient feverish and has intense pain in back. Suppression of urine....
> In a day or two, patient becomes confused. A low muttering form of
> delirium, then coma for a few days, then death.

And the treatment:

> Heroic bloodletting alone will relieve. Leeches and cups over kidneys,
> then catherize until urine produced, Then stop bleeding.
> Antimony also may be administered.[1]

A death at home took an immense emotional toll on family members, especially when it was drawn-out and gruesome, as it so often was. Those who had no choice but to sit by and watch their loved one suffer, sometimes for weeks, with no possible hope of recovery and without effective pain relief, often viewed the end as a welcome release. Christian families, who comprised the residents of the Bond Street neighborhood, devoutly believed in the promise of the resurrection, a

---

1 John Ward medical notebook, January 29, 1864.

confidence that helped steady them in their ordeal. Just two days before Seabury's death, his daughter Julia received a letter from her cousin, Timothy Tredwell:

> I am deeply pained by the news of your dear father's illness, and his sufferings occupy much of my daily and nightly thoughts and sympathies.... I had hoped that his closing days would have continued serene and peaceful and that quiet and happy days would yet be spared to him. I trust, if his age will permit, he may even now recover ... but if the good God orders otherwise, let us hope that he will mitigate his sufferings though the sanctifying mercies and merits of our blessed Saviour, who suffered for us that we by his patient example might be led to lean on him [and] thereby live with him forever in heaven.[2]

As soon as the doctor confirmed the death, servants moved quietly through the house, closing the shutters, speaking in whispers. Then with the house in semi-darkness, one of the servants was dispatched to the undertaking firm of Cantrell and Son to let them know that their services were needed. Upon arriving at the house, the undertaker affixed a swath of crape or "door badge" to the front door, a signal that a death had occurred and that the privacy of the bereaved family within was to be respected. Crape, a dull, crinkled silk fabric, was used to drape the doors, mantel, and chandeliers and to cover the mirrors of the parlors. It had been associated with mourning since colonial times.

During the first half of the nineteenth century, the responsibilities involved in the burial of the dead, formerly assumed by a variety of persons like the cabinetmaker, the livery stable keeper, and family members and friends, were gradually consolidated into the occupation of undertaker. At the time of Seabury's death, however, the laying out of the deceased was still done at home, sometimes by the undertaker but sometimes by family members with the help of close friends or a nurse. The viewing of the dead also took place at home, usually, but not always, in the parlor. On Christmas Day, John Ward called at the home of his best friend, Ben Church, where he viewed the body of Ben's sister, Mary, who was laid out in a coffin in the second-floor bedroom where she died.

> I was shown into the parlour and Ben took me up to see the remains. She was laid out in the room (over the parlor) where she died—already

---

2   Timothy Tredwell to Julia Tredwell, March 3, 1865 (New York: Merchant House Museum Archives).

in the coffin, a very handsome one of rosewood. Her left hand lay across her breast, holding flowers and looked like a piece of exquisite sculpture. Her mouth was covered with a piece of linen.[3]

Embalming was practiced during the Civil War to facilitate the shipment of war dead to their homes for burial, but it was not otherwise widely available in the United States at the time of Seabury's death. A few undertakers offered the option of embalming by chemical injection, and a popular household manual published in 1846, *The Skillful Housewife's Book,* even offered do-it-yourself instructions. The book was something like an early version of *Hints From Heloise.* Along with household tips such as how to waterproof shoes, make black ink, and kill weeds in gravel, there is this astonishing advice:

> Preservation of the Dead: The beneficial effects of this are experienced in the case of keeping bodies for the recognition of friends. A solution of alum in hot water, in the proportion of two pounds to a pint, is injected through the right carotid arteries and veins throughout the whole body. In summer three quarts of the solution are required, and in winter less. This is to preserve the body in its original state.[4]

It seems highly doubtful that any housewife, no matter how skillful, ever really tried this at home.

There were, however, several other alternatives available to retard decomposition of the body, giving time for distant relatives to arrive in time for the funeral. In 1848 the first patent for a metallic coffin was granted. An advertisement for such coffins claimed they were "airtight and a corpse may be preserved perfectly in one of them." However, the most widely used method for preserving the remains involved the use of ice, and there were a number of ice coffins patented in the years leading up to the Civil War. Of course, the family could choose to have the body buried without delay—within a day or two—and this was often done in the hot summer months. Sometimes it was necessary to close the casket because of the condition of the body. However, it was preferable for the mourners

---

3 John Ward diary, December 25, 1860. A spasm at the moment of death had caused Mary's mouth to be drawn to the side, thus the piece of linen covering it.

4 L.G. Abell, *The Skillful Housewife's Book, or, Complete Guide to Domestic Cookery, Taste, Comfort and Economy* (1852; reprint, New York: The Lyons Press, 2001), 203.

to be able to view the deceased if at all possible. Early models of the metallic coffin had a glass window over the corpse's face; later models were equipped with a glass top, through which one could view the entire body. Some ice coffins also used glass plates to permit viewing of the body.[5]

It was customary for someone to keep an overnight vigil during the time the deceased remained in the home. John Skidmore and his brother Ben had been asked to perform this service for the young son of the Beekman family. In his diary, John noted:

> June 7 Tony Beeckman died this morning about 5 o'clock. Ben & I sat up with the body at No ----- East 15th St. from 11 p.m. to 6¼ a.m. Long hot night. Room very close. Air became very offensive before daylight. Room very small. Cockroaches &c &c.[6]

One hates to think what the "&c &c" might signify.

During the interval between Seabury's death on March 7 and the funeral on March 11, his family stayed in their bedrooms, the basement-floor family dining room, or behind the closed door of the back parlor. The outside door to the foyer was left open so that when mourners called to leave their cards and view the body, they would not have to disturb the family by ringing the doorbell. A servant posted by the interior door of the foyer admitted visitors, who left their cards in the hall card receiver. They would not call again until Eliza Tredwell returned the visits and indicated that she was once again ready to receive visitors by leaving her black-bordered calling card with "Thanks for kind inquiries" written at the top, .

At 12:30 on March 11, 1865, friends and relatives gathered in the front parlor where prayers were said before proceeding to St. Bartholomew's Church for the funeral. Afterwards, the casket was placed in a waiting carriage and a procession of mourners followed it to the cemetery. Meanwhile, the undertaker removed the drapery and folding chairs from the parlors and aired out the rooms.

After the burial, the family returned to the house where they received their friends' condolences and offered refreshments to the mourners.

Then the family began a lengthy period of mourning, the most visible aspect

---

5   Robert W. Haberstein and William M. Lamers, *The History of American Funeral Directing* (Milwaukee: Bulfin Printers, 1962), 266-67, 316-17. The advertisement quoted for the airtight coffins appeared in the *Pulaski [Tennessee] Citizen* in the years 1858 and 1861 www.uark.edu/campusresources/archinfo/SCHACmason.pdf.

6   John Skidmore diary, June 7, 1858.

of which was a dress code. Men could signify their grief merely by wearing a black armband for a period of several months. The rules for women were more elaborate, and varied according to social class, religion, personal temperament, and the etiquette manual they happened to be consulting.

The length of time for mourning depended on the relation of the bereaved to the deceased. Widows were required to mourn the longest. Generally, during the last half of the century, they were required to wear mourning for at least two full years. There were three stages: The first was a period of "full" or "deep" mourning lasting for a year and a day during which time widows were expected to wear all black with black trim or no trim at all, along with a weeping veil of crape which might reach to mid-calf or even to the floor. Because black dresses were also worn by those who were not in mourning, it was necessary to distinguish mourning fashion from ordinary clothing by the fabric used. It had to be dull, with absolutely no highlights. During full mourning, garments were often made of crape.

89. Mrs. Howe in Mourning.
Courtesy of the Museum of the City of New York, Print Archives.
A widow dressed in what is, needless to say, full mourning. That Mrs. Howe chose to have a studio portrait made in a veil that obscures her identity suggests the importance of the outward expression of grief during the nineteenth century.

The second stage was called "ordinary" mourning. It could last for six months to a year for widows. The veil was shortened and made of a lighter, more comfortable fabric. Crape was used as trim, but the dress itself could be made of some other dull-finished fabric. White cuffs and collars were allowed, and towards the end of this period, silks and velvets might be worn. After ordinary mourning, bereaved women entered a six-month period known as "half-mourning." At last the widow was permitted to cast off her veil and wear colors of gray, mauve, purple, lilac, lavender, and white or a combination of these colors. The fabric could be a solid or a print. Women who had lost a child or a parent might also wear full mourning for one year.

For a grandparent or sibling, the period was typically six months; for aunts, uncles and cousins, one was permitted to adopt half-mourning from the beginning of a three-month mourning period.

Ordinary black dresses could sometimes be augmented with crape trim to accommodate the requirements of mourning, or the family seamstress could be called upon to create new mourning dresses when needed. Frequently women dyed their existing clothing or had the dyeing done by establishments that specialized in the service. There were also mourning stores, which dealt exclusively in mourning fashion. In 1854 Bartholomew & Weed distributed an advertising circular announcing the opening of their firm on Broadway. It advised that they were

> prepared to supply full and complete Mourning of any character at ten hours' notice ... ladies will find a large assortment of mantles, cloaks, bonnets, &c on show at all times, whilst they can have their dresses made up on the premises, in the most fashionable style, from any material they may select or prefer.

Accessories were also regulated. During full or ordinary mourning, black bonnets, gloves, and parasols were required. Handkerchiefs were edged in black, but the edging diminished in size as time wore on, just as the length of the veil was progressively shortened. Women in mourning frequently wore a locket containing a lock of the departed's hair or brooches or bracelets made from the hair of the deceased. Sometimes hair jewelry was made-to-order by professional jewelers, but women often made their own mourning jewelry, relying on instruction manuals. Hairwork was a highly skilled type of fancywork requiring enormous patience. Practitioners of the craft created not only mourning jewelry but wreaths, pictures to hang on the wall, and other ornamental objects.

While she was in mourning, a woman's social activities were limited. For the first month of full mourning, she could attend church, but that was all. Festive parties were off-limits for the entire mourning period, but she could attend lectures, quiet social gatherings and concerts once the period of full mourning had passed. Women could find themselves almost perpetually in mourning if, as often happened, a close relative died before they had finished mourning another. On May 22, 1855, Julia Lay wrote in her diary:

> I left off my mourning habiliments after having worn them nearly four years. It came back to me with freshness to my mind the death of my beloved mother for whom I put on deepest black and when about leaving off I had to put afresh those robes that denote bereavement. My sweet and only little daughter, I have mourned for thee and still my darling my feelings are unchanged.

She had worn black longer than custom dictated, but though her grief was undiminished, she decided to move on. Two days later, she purchased a bright colored dress and made a call.

On April 14, 1865, just six weeks after Seabury Tredwell's death, President Lincoln was assassinated, and the private grief of the Tredwell family was enveloped and intensified by an outpouring of national sorrow. On April 24 Lincoln's funeral cortege reached New York City, and over a million New Yorkers watched and wept as a team of six gray horses pulled the glass-sided hearse from the dock on the Hudson River to City Hall, now draped with a banner reading "The Nation Mourns." Here Lincoln's body was placed on a catafalque. From one o'clock that afternoon, all through the night, until noon of the next day, over 150,000 New Yorkers streamed past the casket to pay their final respects.

It was the end of an era. Wall Street financiers, railroad barons, and industrial tycoons were replacing the old merchants and mercantile interests, and the Federal Republic was giving way to a more centralized nation. Thirty-five thousand miles of railroad had been constructed, telegraph lines had crossed the continent, and the final effort to link the United States to Europe with the transatlantic cable was about to succeed.

Having established his hardware business in 1804, Seabury Tredwell was one of the last of the "old merchants," a fact noted by his obituary in *The New York Post*:

> Among the deaths noticed in our columns today is that of one of the oldest and most respected merchants, Seabury Tredwell. He was a gentleman of the old school, dignified and accomplished in his manners, and high-minded and honorable in all his transactions. He was born on Long Island in 1780—was the son of Doctor Benjamin Tredwell, of North Hempstead. His mother was a sister of Bishop Seabury. He came to this city in 1798, and after serving as a clerk for three years started the hardware business on his own account, which he continued with uninterrupted success till he retired, in 1835. He then purchased his city residence in Fourth Street, near Lafayette Place, between which place and his farm at Shrewsbury, New Jersey, he spent the remainder of his days. He now goes out from us, one of the last of his generation, honored, respected and beloved by all.[7]

90. SEABURY TREDWELL'S GRAVESTONE, CHRIST'S CHURCH, MANHASSET, LONG ISLAND.
Photograph by the author.
The beatitude inscribed on Seabury Tredwell's gravestone, "Blessed are the pure in heart for they shall see God," and the description of him from his obituary in the *New York Post* suggest a man of high moral standing.

---

7 *New York Post*, March 11, 1865.

Seabury's body was interred temporarily in the Kissam family vault in the nearby New York City Marble Cemetery on Second Street between First and Second Avenues. In August of 1866, it was moved to the Tredwell family burial plot in Christ Church graveyard in Manhasset, Long Island. There, Eliza and all of the couple's unmarried children would eventually be laid to rest beside the old merchant.

Epilogue

In 1865 during his last illness, Seabury made a new will. The bulk of his estate (his securities, the Fourth Street house and its contents, and the New Jersey real estate holding) was placed in a trust for Eliza. The will provided for a bequest of $10,000 for each of the children except for Samuel. At the time, Samuel was deeply in debt, having suffered severe business losses during the Civil War. Concerned that any funds left to his son would be used to pay off Samuel's creditors, Seabury directed that in lieu of a bequest to Samuel, $6000 be placed in a trust for Samuel's daughter, Lizzie, to be managed by her father. When Lizzie reached the age of twenty-one, the trust was to be turned over to her. At Eliza's death, the will directed that the remainder of the estate be divided equally among the children, except for Samuel's share, which was to be placed in a trust to be managed by the executor of the estate, with the income going to Samuel for the rest of his life and after his death to his children. By the time Eliza died in 1882, Samuel's debts had been paid and there no longer being a need to protect his money from creditors, he was made executor of the trust set up for his benefit.

At the time of his death in 1865, Seabury's estate was appraised at $126,386.55.[1] Effingham Nicholas, the husband of the oldest Tredwell child, Elizabeth, was the executor of Seabury's estate. Effingham and Seabury had a close relationship, for Elizabeth and Effingham lived in the Fourth Street house for fourteen years after their marriage in 1845. The two men were representative of different eras in the

---

1   Using the consumer price index, Seabury's estate would be worth approximately $1,750,000 in 2010 dollars. www.measuringworth.com/uscompare.

history of New York City. Seabury was one of the old merchants, who engaged in maritime commerce and laid the commercial foundations of the city after the Revolution. Effingham represented a new class of financiers whose interests were national in scope and who would come to dominate the city after the Civil War. He was a prominent figure in the westward expansion of the railroads. After he and Elizabeth left the Fourth Street house, they lived for a time in Brooklyn and then bought a house at Thirty-Fourth Street and Fifth Avenue, right across the street from William B. Astor, Jr. and John Jacob Astor III, whose houses were located on the present site of the Empire State Building. Effingham and Elizabeth's

91. EFFINGHAM NICHOLS (1821-1899). *Courtesy of the Merchant's House Museum.*

92. ELIZABETH TREDWELL NICHOLS (1821-1880). *Courtesy of the Merchant's House Museum.*

only child, Lillie Nichols, never married.

At the time of Seabury's death, most of the Rumson property was covered with thickets and rough fields with a few rutted roads. As executor of the estate, Effingham cleared out the thickets, drained some of the wetlands, and cut roads though the property in such a way as to give a front for villa sites. The piecemeal sale of the Rumson lots helped to sustain the unmarried Tredwell sisters in their later years. The last lot with the colonial farmhouse and the farmer's house was sold in 1928, just five years before Gertrude's death.

Neither of Seabury's sons served in the Civil War. Horace, as an unmarried man under the age of forty-five would have been subject to the draft but had the option of hiring a substitute, and that may be what he did. Or as family legend has it, he may have been excused from military service because of "delicate health." Horace never married and died in the house in 1885. Samuel, because he was married and over thirty-five years of age, was exempt from the draft. Samuel's wife died in 1870; their only child Lizzie, died unmarried in 1891 at the age of thirty-nine. Samuel remarried, and when he and his wife had a daughter, he paid tribute to his family's most distinguished ancestors by naming her Elizabeth Alden Seabury Tredwell.[2] She became a highly educated woman, receiving an A.B. degree from Barnard College and, in 1909, a master's degree in economics from Columbia University, an unusual accomplishment for a young woman at the time. She married Homer Stebbins, an attorney, and they had three children: Seabury, Ruth, and Roger. Only Roger had children.

Besides Elizabeth and Samuel, the only other Tredwell child to marry was Mary Adelaide. She had three children, John Tredwell Richards, known as "Tred," Effingham Pauline, known as "Effie," and Adele. Tred's marriage ended in divorce. There were no children. Adele never married. Effie married Mark Van Nostrand and had one child, Charles Van Nostrand, who never married. In 1874 at the age of forty-nine, Mary Adelaide was the first of Seabury and Eliza's children to die.

Sometime after Eliza's death in 1882, Sarah moved out of the house and lived a genteel life in a residential hotel where she was known for her card parties. The remaining three unmarried daughters, Phebe, Julia, and Gertrude continued to live in the house even as the neighborhood deteriorated.

Sarah died in 1906, and a *New York Times* reporter was dispatched to the neighborhood in search of material for a human-interest story about the Tredwell sisters. Rumors had been circulating for years about the old women who lived in the house on Fourth Street, but no one really knew much about them. Thus, the information the reporter gathered from his interviews with the neighbors was wildly inaccurate. In his story he claimed that Sarah was related to the Vanderbilt family and owned over $6,000,000 worth of real estate. He said her sisters, in spite of their great wealth, were seldom seen, led reclusive lives, and were eccentric.

Gertrude was indignant; she did not want the world to think she was extraordinarily wealthy, which she certainly wasn't. One could hardly blame her, con-

---

2   Samuel wanted to be sure that his daughter continued to carry the Tredwell name even if she married. Therefore he gave her the Christian name of Elizabeth Alden Seabury Tredwell.

sidering the shady characters she could see on the street outside her house. Nor did she want the world to think she and her sisters were eccentric. As far as she was concerned they were dignified and aristocratic in the only way that mattered, which was not necessarily the Vanderbilt way. So she wrote a letter to the *New York Times*. Mindful of the Victorian precept that a lady's name should appear in the newspaper only twice—when she was born and when she was married—she signed the letter with only her first initial and her middle name.

> To the Editor of *The New York Times*:
>
> As one of the oldest subscribers to your paper, I beg to insert this paragraph to contradict and absolutely deny the erroneous statements set forth in the columns of the daily TIMES of Saturday last respecting the surviving daughters of the late Seabury Tredwell. Suffice it to say, despite the assertions made to the contrary, they are only in comfortable circumstances and are practical, thoroughly good loyal citizens of the substantial old type of character handed down from generations back, among whom was the Rev. Samuel Seabury, first American Bishop, whose nephew and namesake was Seabury Tredwell.
>
> G. Ellsworth[3]

There is a nugget of truth that probably accounts for the false rumors of the Tredwell sisters' wealth as relatives of the Vanderbilts. Seabury Tredwell's oldest sister, Elizabeth, was the wife of Daniel Whitehead Kissam, who was the uncle of Maria Kissam, who married William Vanderbilt—hardly close enough to make the Tredwells members of the Vanderbilt clan, but on such slim evidence, rumors are often founded. Samuel was quick to set the record straight with a letter of his own to the editor of the *Times*.

> October 14, 1906
>
> The writer's attention has been called to the account of the death of Sarah Kissam Tredwell, a daughter of the late Seabury Tredwell in your issue of the 12th and to the statement ... that the family was related to the Vanderbilts. As the only direct male descendant of Seabury Tredwell and Eliza Earle Parker Tredwell, I ask you to correct the statement. This branch of the Tredwell family is not related to the Vander-

---

3   *New York Times*, October 24, 1906.

bilts except as joint descendants of Adam and Eve.

Samuel Lenox Tredwell[4]

In 1907 Phebe died in an accidental fall at home in which she broke her neck and femur. The death certificate was signed by the coroner at six a.m., suggesting that she might have died shortly after the fall, possibly descending the stair on her way to breakfast. It was a devastating blow to the surviving sisters, not only because of the traumatic circumstances of her death but because Phebe had long ago assumed the role of the mother of the family.

Noting Phebe's death, the *New York Times* got it wrong again. In the column, "Society At Home and Abroad," along with the news of Newport villa owners returning to the city and an expected influx of "well-known Anglo-Americans," including The Duchess of Marlborough, it was erroneously stated that Phebe was

> the last surviving daughter of the late Seabury Tredwell. With her sister, who died a year ago, she occupied an old-fashioned house on Fourth Street, just off the Bowery. In this most unfashionable neighborhood, the Misses Tredwells lived for many years. They were members of one of the oldest families in New York.[5]

Gertrude could not have been happy that the piece failed to note that she, not to mention Julia, was still alive, but this time there was no indignant letter to the editor. When Julia died of pneumonia three years later in 1909, Gertrude did become the "last surviving daughter" of the large Tredwell family that had moved into the Fourth Street house so long ago.

There was to be a final chapter in Gertrude Tredwell's life that would bring her a measure of happiness. It is not clear when, but sometime after Julia's death, her nephew, "Tred," moved into the Fourth Street house. Recently divorced, he was a gentleman of the old school who had practiced law in the city for many years. He had no children. He was dignified in appearance and accustomed to the finer things of life. He settled into the spacious front third-floor bedroom, which he furnished with an ebony bedroom suite, and for several years, he and Gertrude traveled together to exclusive watering holes like Saratoga Springs.

Tred died in 1930. There are four slips of paper in the Merchant's House col-

4 Ibid., October 15, 1906.
5 Ibid., October 13, 1907.

lection on which Gertrude has written in pencil the details of his death, probably drafting a death notice for the newspaper. They are identically worded:

> In New York City at Misericordia Hospital on Thursday May 1st 1930 after an illness of six weeks, John Tredwell Richards, son of the late Charles John Richards and Mary Adelaide Tredwell. He was born in New York City on August 28th 1851, died May 1st 1930. He was a graduate of Princeton University the class of 1871 and the law school of Columbia University.

It is as if writing the cold facts over and over helped her to accept the reality of Tred's death and the fact that she was now truly alone. She was then eighty-nine years old. As the years passed, she gradually became more frail and was eventually confined to her bedroom where the only source of heat was the coal grate. After she died, newspapers were discovered stuffed behind the shutters in an attempt to keep out the cold. The caretaker couple she had hired in 1917 and a woman who tended to her personal needs in exchange for room and board were her only companions. Her sister Elizabeth's unmarried daughter, Lillie Nichols, occasionally came to see her from her home in Connecticut and sometimes lent her money. Charles Van Nostrand, her sister Mary Adelaide's grandson, also visited her. But it was a sad and lonely finale to a life that had begun with so much promise.

In 1983 Elizabeth Ivory wrote a letter to the director of the Old Merchant's House describing a visit that her mother, an antique dealer, had made to Gertrude Tredwell in the 1920s in the company of Eleanor and Sarah Hewitt. The Hewitt sisters, granddaughters of Peter Cooper, were then collecting examples of antique furniture and textiles for what would become the Cooper Hewitt Museum.[6] It is likely that they visited Gertrude thinking that she might have something of interest that she would be willing to sell or donate to their project, though there are no records of any transaction ever having taken place. Elizabeth Ivory said that her mother remembered the parlor as being shabby but recalled that tea was served in a genteel performance characteristic of a bygone age.

Gertrude Tredwell died on August 22, 1933, in the house where she had been born almost ninety-three years earlier. Her casket was the last to be carried down the steps of the high marble stoop to a waiting hearse.

---

6 Now known as the Cooper Hewitt National Design Museum, housed in the old Andrew Carnegie mansion at Ninety-First Street and Fifth Avenue, New York City.

93. GERTRUDE TREDWELL (1840-1933).
Courtesy of the Merchant's House Museum.

The last person to have living memory of the Merchant's House when Gertrude Tredwell was still alive was Roger Stebbins, who died on May 22, 2009 at the age of ninety-one. Roger was the grandson of Samuel Tredwell and Samuel's second wife. He remembered visiting his great-aunt Gertrude as a child and sliding down the banister of the old house. At this writing, Roger's son and daughter, his three granddaughters, and a great-grandson are the only living descendants of Seabury and Eliza Tredwell.

Acknowledgments

I am deeply grateful to Pi Gardiner, Director of the Merchant's House Museum, for providing me with the opportunity to become immersed in the home and lives of nineteenth-century merchant Seabury Tredwell and his family. Because of her sensitive regard for the past as well as her practical management skills, the Merchant's House survives today as a unique historic document.

My thanks to the dedicated Museum volunteers, who over the years have shared their ideas and insights with me and have patiently listened to mine. I especially want to acknowledge Kate McCoy for her thoughtful reading of an early version of the manuscript.

During the time I have been at work on this book, many capable young interns have passed through the Museum doors, contributing in direct and indirect ways to my research. I am grateful to Cat Lukaszewski, my research assistant, not only for her meticulous work but for her sustained encouragement along the way.

I have been fortunate to have done much of my research at the New-York Historical Society Research Library, that serene depository of New Yorkers' personal memories. The cheerful willingness to be helpful on the part of the staff —Joseph Ditta, Eric Robinson, Ted O'Reilly and Tammy Kiter—made the experience an unfailing pleasure.

I am grateful to Otis Burger for sharing the unpublished records of her family history and providing me with the privately printed collection of letters of Henrietta Wilcox, and to Nicholas Bruen for allowing me to use his significant painting of the Fiedler family in their parlor.

Finally to the Furthermore Foundation, a division of the J.M. Kaplan fund, many thanks for their generous support of this project.

Mary Knapp
New York City, 2012

Selected Bibliography

Abell, L.G. *The Skillful Housewife's Book, or, Complete Guide to Domestic Cookery, Taste, Comfort and Economy.* 1852. Reprinted as *A Mother's Book of Traditional Household Skills.* New York: The Lyons Press, 2001.

_____. *Woman in Her Various Relations.* New York: J.M. Fairchild & Co., 1855.

Albion, Robert Greenhalgh. *The Rise of New York Port, [1815-1860].* 1939. Reprint. Boston: Northeastern University Press, 1984.

Alcott, William A. *Tight Lacing.* Boston: George W. Light, 1840.

Arthur, T.S. *Advice to Young Ladies on Their Duties and Conduct in Life.* New York: T.W. Strong, 1851.

Bader. Louis. "Gas Illumination in New York City, 1823-1864." PhD diss., New York University, 1970.

Bayles, James C. *House Drainage and Water Service in Cities, Villages and Rural Neighborhoods.* New York: David Williams, 1880.

Beecher, Catherine. *Treatise on Domestic Economy.* 1841. Reprint. New York: Source Book Press, 1970.

_____ and Harriet Beecher Stowe. *American Woman's Home.* 1869. Reprint. Hartford, Conn.: The Stowe Day Foundation, 1994.

Belden, Louise. *The Festive Tradition: Table Decorations and Desserts in America, 1650-1900.* New York: W.W. Norton & Company, 1993.

Berend, Zsuzsa. "'The Best or None!' Spinsterhood in Nineteenth-Century New England." *Journal of Social History* 33 (Summer 2000): 935-57.

Bode, Carl. *The Anatomy of American Popular Culture, 1840-1861.* Berkeley: University of California Press, 1959.

Bradley, Sarah. Diary, 1848-1850. Special Collections. Hanover, N.H.: Dartmouth College Library.

Bremer, Fredrika. *Homes of the New World: Impressions of America*. Vol. 1. Translated by Mary Howitt. New York: Harper & Brothers, 1858.

Brinton M.D., D.G. and G.H. Napheys. *Personal Beauty of the Laws of Health in Relation to the Human Form*. Springfield, Mo.: W.J. Holland, 1869.

Bristed, Charles Astor. *The Upper Ten Thousand: Sketches of American Society by a New Yorker*. London: John W. Parker and Son, 1852.

Bushman, Richard L. *The Refinement of America: Persons, Houses, Cities*. New York: Vintage Books, 1992.

_____ and Claudia L. Bushman. "The Early History of Cleanliness in America." *The Journal of American History* 74 (March 1988): 1213-38.

Casey, Marion R. "Friends in Need." *South Street Seaport Magazine* (Spring 1944): 1-6.

Catalogue of the Professors, Instructors and Students of St. Paul's College and Grammar School for the Season 1839-40. College Point, N.Y.: St. Paul's School, 1840.

Cayley, George. Diary, 1844. Manuscripts Division. New York: New-York Historical Society.

Chapman, Mary. "'Living Pictures'; Women and *Tableaux Vivants* in Nineteenth-Century American Fiction and Culture." Wide Angle 18 (July 1996): 22-52.

Child, Lydia Maria. *The Mother's Book*. 1831. Reprint. Bedford Mass.: Applewood Books, n.d.

Chorley, E. Clowes, D.D. L.H.D. *The Centennial History of Saint Bartholomew's Church in the City of New York*, 1835-1935. New York: The Rector, Church Wardens and Vestrymen of Saint Bartholomew's Church in the City of New York, 1935.

Citizens' and Strangers' Pictorial and Business Directory for the City of New York and Its Vicinity: 1853. Edited by Solyman Brown. New York: Charles Spalding & Co., 1853.

Henry Lunettes. *The American Gentleman's Guide to Politeness and Fashion*. New York: Derby & Jackson, 1857.

Cowan, Ruth Schwartz. *More Work For Mother: The Ironies of Household Technology from the Open Hearth to the Microwave*. New York: Basic Books, 1983.

Cremin, Lawrence A. *American Education: The National Experience, 1783-1876*. New York: Harper & Row, 1980.

Dayton, Abram. *Last Days of Knickerbocker Life*. New York: G.P. Putnam's Sons, 1897.

de Forest, Emily Johnston. *James Colles, 1798-1883: Life and Letters*. New York: Privately printed, 1926.

_____. *John Johnston of New York, Merchant*. New York: Privately printed, 1909.

DeVoe, Thomas T. *The Market Book: A History of the Public Markets of the City of New York*. 1852. Reprint. New York: Augustus M. Kelly, 1970.

Diner, Hasia R. *Erin's Daughters in America: Irish Immigrant Women in the Nineteenth Century*. Baltimore: The Johns Hopkins University Press, 1983.

Downing, A.J. *The Architecture of Country Houses*. 1850. Reprint. New York: Dover Publications, 1969.

Dressmaker's Account Book, 1854. Manuscripts Division. New York: New-York Historical Society.

Dudden, Faye E. *Serving Women: Household Service in Nineteenth-Century America*. Middleton, Conn.: Wesleyan University Press, 1983.

Ernst, Robert. *Immigrant Life in New York City, 1825-1863*. New York: King's Crown Press, 1949.

Farrar, Mrs. John. *The Young Lady's Friend*. Boston: American Stationers Company, 1838.

Finson, Jon W. *The Voices That Have Gone: Themes in 19th-Century American Popular Song*. New York: Oxford University Press, 1984.

Flaharty, David. "The Viewpoint of a Craftsman: The Old Merchant's House Ceiling Medallions." *Cultural Resources Management* 16, no. 8 (1993). Washington, D.C.: U.S. Department of Interior, National Park Service.

Foster, George. *New York By Gaslight and Other Urban Sketches*. 1850. Reprint edited and with an introduction by Stewart M. Blumin. Berkeley: University of California Press, 1990.

Foster, Vanda. *A Visual History of Costume: The Nineteenth Century*. 1984. Reprint. New York: Drama Book Publishers, 1986.

Francis, Dr. John Francis. *Old New York or Reminiscences of the Past 60 Years*. New York: W.J. Widdleton, 1865.

Garrett, Elisabeth Donaghy. *At Home: The American Family 1750-1870*. New York: Harry Abrams, 1990.

Gill, William F. *Parlor Tableaux and Amateur Theatricals*. Boston: J.E. Tilton and Company, 1867.

Gordon, Beverly. "Victorian Fancywork in the American Home: Fantasy and Accommodation." *In Making the American Home: Middle-Class Women & Domestic Material Culture 1840-1890*. Edited by Pat Browne. Bowling Green, Ohio: Bowling Green State University Popular Press, 1988, 48-68.

Gordon, Carol Emily. "The Skidmore House: An Aspect of Greek Revival in New York." Masters thesis, University of Delaware, 1978.

Grier, Katherine C. *Culture and Comfort: People, Parlors, and Upholstery, 1850-1930.* Rochester, N.Y.: Strong Museum, 1988.

Gurney, C. Gue. "The Speedways of New York Old and New." *The Horse Review,* December 12, 1889, 1262-65.

Habenstein, Robert W. and William M. Lammers. *The History of American* Funeral *Directing.* Milwaukee: Bulfin Printers, 1962.

The Habits of Good Society: A Handbook for Ladies and Gentlemen. New York: Rudd & Carleton, 1860.

Hale, Sarah Josepha. *The Good Housekeeper, or, The Way to Live Well, and to Be Well While We Live.* Reprinted as Early American Cookery. Mineola, N.Y.: Dover Publications, Inc., 1996.

_____. *Manners; or, Happy Homes and Good Society All the Year Round.* Boston: J.B. Tilton and Company, 1868.

Halttunen, Karen. *Confidence Men and Painted Women: A Study of Middle-Class Culture in America, 1830-1870.* New Haven, Conn.: Yale University Press, 1982.

Handlin, David P. *The American Home: Architecture and Society, 1815-1915.* Boston: Little, Brown and Company, 1979.

Harris, Luther S. *Around Washington Square: An Illustrated History of Greenwich Village.* Baltimore: Johns Hopkins University Press, 2003.

Hartley, Miss Florence. *The Ladies' Handbook of Fancy and Ornamental Work.* Philadelphia: J.W. Bradley, 1859.

Haswell, Charles H. *Reminiscences of an Octogenarian, 1816-1860.* New York: Harper & Brothers, 1896.

Havens, Catherine E. *Diary of a Little Girl in Old New York.* 1919. Reprint. Bedford, Mass.: Applewood Books, n.d.

Henrietta. Compiled by Arlene Norton. Sun City, Ariz.: Privately printed, 1986.

Hershkovitz, Leo. "Anatomy of a Riot: Astor Place Opera House, 1849." *New York History* 87 (Summer 2006): 277-310.

Hewitt, Edward. *Those Were the Days.* New York: Duell, Sloan and Pearce, 1943.

Hoffert, Sylvia D. *Private Matters: American Attitudes Toward Childbearing and Infant Nurture in the Urban North, 1800-1860.* Urbana, Ill.: University of Illinois Press, 1989.

Homberger, Eric. *Mrs. Astor's New York: Money and Social Power in a Gilded Age.* New Haven, Conn.: Yale University Press, 2002.

Hone, Philip. Diary, 1828-1851. Manuscripts Division. New York: New-York Historical Society.

Horlick, Alan Stanley. *Country Boys and Merchant Princes.* Louisburg, Pa.: Bucknell University Press, 1975.

"The Houses We Live In." *Harper's Monthly Magazine* 30 (May 1865): 735-41.

Howe, Julia Ward. *Reminiscences 1819-1899*. Boston: Houghton Mifflin, 1899.

Ierley, Merritt. *The Comforts of Home: The American House and the Evolution of Modern Convenience*. New York: Clarkson Potter, 1999.

————. *Open House: A Guided Tour of the American Home, 1637-Present*. New York: Henry Holt, 1999.

Ingerman, Elizabeth A. "Personal Experiences of an Old New York Cabinetmaker." *Antiques Magazine* 84 (November 1963): 576-80.

James, Henry. *A Small Boy and Others*. New York: Charles Scribner's Sons, 1913.

Kasson, John F. *Rudeness & Civility: Manners in Nineteenth-Century Urban America*. New York: Hill and Wang, 1990.

Kirkland, Mrs. C.M. "The Mystery of Visiting." *Sartain's Magazine* 6 (May 1850): 317-21.

Koeppel, Gerard T. *Water for Gotham*. Princeton, N.J.: Princeton University Press, 2000.

Koren, Elisabeth. *The Diary of Elisabeth Koren, 1835-55*. Translated and edited by David Nelson. Northfield, Minn.: Norwegian-American Historical Association, 1955.

Koza, Julia Ecklund. "Music and the Feminine Sphere: Images of Women as Musicians in *Godey's Lady's Book*." *The Musical Quarterly* 75 (Summer 1991): 103-29.

Lamb, Martha. "A Neglected Corner of the Metropolis: Historic Homes in Lafayette Place." *Magazine of American History* 16 (July 1886): 1-29.

Lawrence, Vera Brodsky. *Strong on Music: The New York Music Scene in the Days of George Templeton Strong*. Vol. 1, *Resonances 1836-1849*. Chicago: University of Chicago Press, 1998.

Lay, Julia Anna Hartness. Diaries, 1818-1879. Rare Books and Manuscripts Division. New York: New York Public Library.

Leavitt, Judith. *Brought to Bed: Childbearing in America, 1750-1950*. New York: Oxford University Press, 1986.

Leslie, Eliza. *The House Book: A Manual on Domestic Economy*. Philadelphia: A. Hart, 1850.

Leslie, Miss Eliza. "Mr. and Mrs. Woodbridge." In *Mr. and Mrs. Woodbridge, with Other Tales, Representing Life as It Is: And Intended to Show What It Should Be*. Providence, R.I.: Isaac H. Cady, 1846, 13-123.

Lester, Andrew. Diaries, 1836-1888. Manuscripts Division. New York: New-York Historical Society.

Lester, Mary Harris. Diary, 1847-1849. Manuscripts Division. New York: New-York Historical Society.

Lynch-Brennan, Margaret. *The Irish Bridget: Irish Immigrant Women in Domestic Service in America, 1840-1930*. Syracuse, N.Y.: Syracuse University Press, 2009.

Lockwood, Charles. *Bricks and Brownstone: The New York Row House 1783-1929*. New York: Rizzoli, 2nd ed., 2003.

_____. *Manhattan Moves Uptown*. New York. 1976. Reprint. New York: Barnes & Noble, 1995.

Lyman, Susan. *The Story of New York: An Informal History of the City*. New York: Crown, 1964.

Marcuse, Maxwell F. *This Was New York! A Nostalgic Picture of Gotham in the Gaslight Era*. New York: LIM Press, 1965.

Maril, Nadja. *American Lighting: 1840-1940*. West Chester, Pa.: Schiffer Publishing Ltd., 1997.

Matthews, Glenna. *"Just a Housewife": The Rise and Fall of Domesticity in America*. New York: Oxford University Press, 1987.

Matthiessen, F.O. *American Renaissance: Art and Expression in the Age of Emerson and Whitman*. New York: Oxford University Press, 1941.

McCabe, James Dabney [Edward Winslow Martin]. The *Secrets of the Great City: A Work Descriptive of the Virtues and Vices, the Mysteries, Miseries and Crimes of New York City*. Philadelphia: Jones Brothers & Co., 1868.

McCullough, Jack W. "Living Pictures and the New York Stage." PhD diss., City University of New York, 1981. Ann Arbor, Mich.: UMI Research Press, 1983.

Mescher, Virginia. *Powdered, Painted, and Perfumed: Cosmetics of the Civil War Period And Their Historic Context*. Burke, Va.: Vintage Volumes, 2003.

Mines, Jon Flavel. *A Tour Around New York and The Recreations of Mr. Felix Oldboy*. New York: Harper & Brothers, 1892.

Minnigerode, Meade. *The Fabulous Forties, 1840-1850*. Garden City, N.Y.: Garden City Publishing, 1924.

Montez, Lola. *The Arts of Beauty or Secrets of a Lady's Toilet*. 1858. Reprint. New York: Ecco Press, 1978.

Moody, Richard. *The Astor Place Riot*. Bloomington: Indiana University Press, 1958.

Morris, Lloyd. *Incredible New York*. New York: Random House, 1951.

Moss, Roger. *Lighting for Historic Buildings*. Washington, D.C.: The Preservation Press, 1988.

O'Neill, Rosetta. "The Dodworth Family and Ballroom Dancing in New York." *Dance Index* 2 (April 1943): 44-56.

Parkes, Mrs. William. *Domestic Duties; or Instructions to Young Married Ladies on the Management of Their Household, and the Regulation of Their Conduct on the Various Relations and Duties of Married Life*. New York: J.J. Harper, 1831.

"Parlor Amusements." *Godey's Lady's Book* 49 (December 1854): 561.

Patterson, Henry. Diaries, 1832-1849. Manuscripts Division. New York: New-York Historical Society.

Pierson, George Wilson. *Tocqueville in America*. Baltimore: The Johns Hopkins Press, 1996.

Plescia, Vincent P. "Successful Innovations in Domestic Oil Lighting, 1784-1859." *The Magazine Antiques* 168 (December 2005): 93-101.

Pomerantz, Sidney I. *New York: An American City, 1783-1803*. New York: Columbia University Press, 1928.

"The Prince in the Metropolis." *New York Times*, October 13, 1860.

Rainwater, Dorothy. "Victorian Dining Silver." In Kathryn Grover. *Dining in America, 1850-1900*. Amherst: University of Massachusetts, 1987, 173-204.

Resserguie, Harry E. "A.T. Stewart's Marble Palace—The Cradle of the Department Store." *New-York Historical Society Quarterly* 48 (1964): 131-62.

Richards, Caroline Cowles. *Diary of Caroline Cowles Richards, 1852-1872*. Canandaigua, N.Y.: Privately printed, 1908.

Ryan, Mary P. *Women in Public: Between Banners and Ballots, 1825-1880*. Baltimore: The Johns Hopkins Press, 1990.

Schrier, Arnold. *Ireland and the American Emigration, 1850-1900*. 1958. Reprint. Chester Springs, PA.: Dufour Editions, 1997.

Sedgwick, Catherine Maria. *Morals of Manners; or, Hints for Our Young People*. New York: G.P. Putnam & Co., 1854.

Sigourney, Lydia. *Letters to My Pupils*, 2nd ed. New York: Robert Carter & Brothers, 1852.

Skidmore, John. Diary, 1858. Manuscripts Division. New York: New-York Historical Society.

The Sociable or One Thousand and One Home Amusements. 1858. Reprint. Bedford, Mass.: Applewood Books, n.d.

Spann, Edward K. *The New Metropolis: New York City, 1840-1857*. New York: Columbia University Press, 1981.

Stansell, Christine. *City of Women: Sex and Class in New York, 1789-1860*. New York: Knopf, 1986.

Steele, Valerie. *The Corset: A Cultural History*. New Haven, Conn.: Yale University Press, 2001.

Still, Bayrd. *Mirror for Gotham: New York as Seen by Contemporaries from Dutch Days to the Present*. New York: New York University Press, 1956.

Storke, Elliot. *The Family and Householder's Guide*. Auburn, N.Y.: Auburn Publishing, 1859.

Strasser, Susan. *Never Done.* New York: Henry Holt, 1982.

Strong, George Templeton. *The Diary of George Templeton Strong.* Edited by Alan Nevins and Mlton Halsey Thomas, abridged by Thomas J. Pressly. Seattle: University of Washington Press, 1988.

Sutherland, Daniel E. *Americans and Their Servants: Domestic Service in the United States from 1800 to 1920.* Baton Rouge: Louisiana State University Press, 1981.

Tailer, Edward. Diaries, 1848-1917. Manuscripts Division. New York: New-York Historical Society.

Tawa, Nicholas. "The Performance of Parlor Songs in America:, 1790-1860." *Anuario Interamericano de Investigacion Musical* 11 (1975): 69-81.

_____. *Sweet Songs for Gentle Americans: The Parlor Song in America 1790-1860.* Bowling Green, Ohio: Bowling Green University Press, 1980.

Thornwell, Emily. *The Lady's Guide to Perfect Gentility, in Manners, Dress, and Conversation.* New York: Derby & Jackson, 1859.

Tillman, Maria. Diary, 1848-51. Collection Rensselaer County Historical Society, Troy, N.Y.

Todd, Maria. Diaries, 1837-1868. Manuscripts Division. New York:. New-York Historical Society.

Tracy, Berry. "The Decorative Arts." In *Classical America, 1815-1845, An Exhibition at the Newark Museum, April 26 through September 2, 1963.*

Tracy, Charles. Diaries, 1856-1857. Manuscripts Division. New York: New-York Historical Society.

Trollope, Fanny. *Domestic Manners of the Americans.* 1832. Reprintw edited and with an introduction by Pamela Neville-Sington. London: Penguin Books, 1997.

True Politeness: Etiquette for Young Ladies. New York: Leavitt and Allen, 1854.

True Politeness: A Handbook of Etiquette for Gentlemen. New York: Leavitt and Allen, 1848.

Van Slyck, Abigail A. "The Lady and the Library Loafer: Gender and Public Space in Victorian America." *Winterthur Portfolio* 31 (Winter 1996): 221-42.

Van Wyck, Frederick. *Recollections of An Old New Yorker.* New York: Liveright, Inc., Publishers, 1932.

Voorsanger, Catherine and John K. Howatt. eds. *Art and the Empire City: New York, 1825-1861.* Published in conjunction with the exhibit "Art and the Empire City" at the Metropolitan Museum of New York, September 9, 2000–January 7, 2000. New York: The Metropolitan Museum and New Haven, Conn.: Yale University Press, 2000.

Ward, John. Diaries, 1854-1867. Manuscripts Division. New York: New-York Historical Society.

_____. Medical notebook, 1863-64. Manuscripts Division. New York: New-York Historical Society,

Welling, William. *Photography in America: The Formative Years, 1839-1900*. New York: Thomas Y. Crowell Company, 1978.

Welter, Barbara. *Dimity Convictions: The American Woman in the Nineteenth Century*. Athens: Ohio University Press, 1976.

Wharton, Edith and Ogden Codman Jr. *The Decoration of Houses*. 1902. Reprint. New York: W.W. Norton, 1978.

Wilcox, William Henry. Memoirs. Private collection.

Williams, Susan. *Savory Suppers and Fashionable Feasts: Dining in Victorian America*. Knoxville: University of Tennessee Press, 1996.

Wilson, John L., M.D. "Medical Care and Public Health: 1800-1850." *Stanford University of Medicine and the Predecessor School: An Historical Perspective*, Part I, Ch. 5. Stanford University, http://elane.stanford.edu/wilson (February 7, 2009).

Wright, Mabel Osgood. *My New York*. New York: MacMillan, 1926.

Young Lady's Book. Boston: C.A. Wells, 1836.

"Young Lady Who Sings." *Godey's Lady's Book* 18 (June 1839): 279-80.

Zagarri, Rosemarie. "Morals, Manners, and the Republican Mother." *American Quarterly* 44 (June 1992): 192-215.

Zakim Micheal. *Ready-Made Democracy: A History of Men's Dress in the American Republic, 1760-1860*. Chicago: University of Chicago Press, 2003.

Index

CPSIA information can be obtained at www.ICGtesting.com
Printed in the USA
BVOW08s1613161214

379518BV00003B/8/P